SHED SIDE
IN SOUTH LANCASHIRE AND CHESHIRE

THE LAST DAYS OF STEAM

KENN PEARCE

The History Press

First published 2012

The History Press
The Mill, Brimscombe Port
Stroud, Gloucestershire, GL5 2QG
www.thehistorypress.co.uk

British Library Cataloguing in Publication Data.
A catalogue record for this book is available from the British Library.

ISBN 978 0 7524 6120 5

Typesetting and origination by The History Press
Printed in Great Britain

Contents

Acknowledgements

This book would not have been possible without the assistance of a great number of people who have ably helped me in compiling details about the steam sheds of South Lancashire and Cheshire and obtaining photographs taken during the post-war steam era. Contributors have been patient and generous in providing information, loaning material, checking draft sections and answering mailed and emailed enquiries. In particular I want to extend a special thanks to the former railwaymen – many of them in their seventies and eighties – who have diligently responded to my queries, surprising me with their recollections of fifty years ago or more. I do regret that a few of this group of men have unfortunately passed away and will not see their efforts in print. To everyone who has assisted, my sincere thanks for your help in realising this book.

In particular, thanks are extended to: Robin Bamber, Clarice Bedford, Eddie Bellass, Clive Boardman, Steve Boreham, Kathryn Boyd and her mother Mrs Bessie Darbyshire (for permission to use material from Fred Darbyshire's book about Lower Ince and Springs Branch), Adrian Bradshaw, Jennifer Broadbent of Wigan Heritage Service, Ian Casey, Alan Castle, Eric Clayton, Ron Clough and his daughter Beverley, Chris Coates, John Corkill, Michael Dawson, Roy Dixon, Brian Dobbs, Gerald Drought, Brian Elsey of Wiganworld website, Ian Dunbobbin, John Frisby, Roger Griffiths, Peter Hardy, Lynn Hart, Sherryl Healey at the Railway Studies Collection, Devon Library Services, Mrs L. Holmes, David Jackman from the RCTS, Bob Jolly, Stan Jones, Lyndon Knott, Raymond Knowles, Kevin Lane of the Industrial Railway Society, David and Michael Littler, Joan Livesey and Alex Miller of Wigan Archives Service, Alec Macdonald, Steve McNicol (a great enthusiast and true friend), Richard Mercer, Anne Moville of Newton-le-Willows Library, Keith Naylor, Arthur Nettleton, Thomas O'Neill, Sheila from the Ormskirk Library, William Pearson, Phil Prosser, Alan Ravenscroft, Mrs Cynthia Richards, Dave Richardson, William Roberts, Roger Scholes, Ted and Fay Slater, Keith Sloan, Andrew Smith of the Industrial Railway Society, Graeme Southern, Linden Stokes, Tom Sutch, Jeremy Suter, Sutton Historic Society, Brian Swinn, Ruth Taylor, Mel Thorley, Colin Turton, Stephen Wainwright of Sutton Beauty & Heritage, Bill Walker, Christine Watts of Wigan Leisure & Culture Trust, Lynn Wolfenden, Paul Wright of the 8D Association, and also the supportive staff at The History Press.

Finally, a warm thank you to my ever-patient wife, Michelle, who long ago resigned herself to the fact that my fascination with railways is more than a passing fad!

The Engine Shed Society

Special mention should be made of the Engine Shed Society and the support they give to members who are undertaking research (or simply seeking information) about engine sheds, both past and present. Archivist Stephen Wolstenholme and the society's editor of its *Link* publication, Paul Smith, have been especially helpful in my quest to get as much information about the sheds (and sub-sheds) of the region covered in this book, and to locate suitable photographs of a few of the trickier sheds that are covered.

I can highly recommend membership of the Engine Shed Society to anyone who has an interest in railways, locomotives and the facilities that maintained and stabled them. Whether your interest lies in the past or the current railway scene, joining the Engine Shed Society will be the best £12 investment you'll make all year.

Introduction

Two memories of a misspent youth typify the wonderful atmosphere that existed amid the steam railways and the locomotive depots of south Lancashire and Cheshire during the British Railways (BR) era. Scene one: A grimy Black 8 (we called them 'Consols') hauling a long freight blasts its way towards a lattice-framed overbridge in Widnes, flanked on either side by grim factory walls. Three young boys watch fascinated by the theatrics of the scene. Soon enveloped by the grey exhaust of the 'Consol', they watch the locomotive and its long line of loose-coupled, filled mineral wagons trundle below and clank off into the distance; the pipe-smoking guard of the freight gives the boys a cheerio wave from his van.

Scene two: A warm summer's day (in 1960 or 1961) and a posse of trainspotters gather on an embankment beside a road bridge which spans the lines adjacent to Warrington Dallam shed. The young spotters' attention is fixed on the shed's turntable not far away, where a commendably clean Jubilee 45582 *Central Provinces* is easing down to be turned. They watch the scene mesmerised and then discuss their chances of successfully 'bunking' the smoke-hazed engine shed. Unfortunately they see the dust-coated, hatted shedmaster doing his rounds in the shed yard and reluctantly decide that, on that day, Dallam with all its hidden delights was off limits.

In contrast, Widnes shed never held the same apprehension as did Dallam. As a smaller shed within the '8' district, it was comparatively easy to inspect the two dozen or so resident engines that would be found there. A courteous request in the office for permission to have a look around the shed usually received a nod, with a cautionary: 'Be careful not to fall into the pits'. It was at Widnes Motive Power Depot (to give it its official title) that I first enjoyed the thrill of a cab ride in a steam locomotive. One golden summer's evening, a friendly crew invited our small group of locospotters into the cab for a spin up the shed yard. For an impressionable schoolboy, the sound, smell and imagery of that short jaunt was enduring.

Shed Side in South Lancashire and Cheshire is intended as a complementary title to *Shed Side on Merseyside: The Last Days of Steam* released by The History Press in 2011. This book covers the other non-Liverpool/Birkenhead sheds that were in the '8' district of British Railways, from 1948 onwards. These were largely the smaller 'garage' sheds such as Widnes, Sutton Oak, Lower Ince and Northwich, plus larger depots such as Springs Branch, which once was an 'A' shed with its own district responsibilities. Although these sheds and the locomotives they maintained were far less glamorous than those found say at Edge Hill, Carlisle Kingmoor or Crewe North, the eight covered in this title (and several sub-sheds) played an important role in ensuring the railways of south Lancashire and Cheshire ran efficiently and effectively from the late nineteenth century, through two world wars, and almost to the end of steam on BR in 1968. Also briefly included is Ormskirk – a pre-war casualty.

Working-class towns such as Wigan, Warrington, Widnes, St Helens (all good northern rugby league towns, incidentally) and Northwich built their prosperity on what could be mined from beneath the earth in the region and turned into energy – or manufactured in cotton, chemicals, glass, cables or machinery – and the railways played an essential part in ensuring the expansion and profitability of such industries. The 'odd town out' in this grouping was Southport – considered the 'more refined seaside resort' facing the Irish Sea, which was a popular daytrip or summer holiday resort for tired factory workers or miners, as well as a residential address for businessmen who commuted to Liverpool or Manchester. This seaside town attracted its own particular mix of railway traffic.

The six towns featured in this review of the steam sheds of south Lancashire and Cheshire figured prominently in the Industrial Revolution and expansion of the railway network at a phenomenal pace, from 1830 through to the late nineteenth century and the early years of the twentieth century. The rivalry between railway companies to become the dominant transport provider in these towns, and to capitalise on the profits to be earned by moving huge volumes of passengers, coal, sand, chemicals, steel and engineering commodities that were produced in this part of north-west England, was fierce. In towns such as Wigan, the London & North Western Railway vied with the

A scene that would be very familiar to anyone visiting Warrington Dallam in the early to mid-1960s. A fine mix of engines is on view, including a Standard 9F, a Royal Scot (with yellow stripe through its cabside number), some Fowler 4Fs and the inevitable Stanier Black 5s. The smoke and steam perfectly evoke a large British Railways' running shed in the north-west of England in the '60s. (Eddie Bellass)

Sutton Oak's Standard 4MT, 76079, heads a Warrington to St Helens evening freight under Old Alder Lane bridge at Winwick, around summer 1964. These engines were a feature of the St Helens shed from their delivery in the late 1950s until Sutton Oak's closure in 1967. They handled anything thrown their way, from passenger through to freight and lesser dignified duties. Happily, this engine survives in preservation, having been rescued from Barry scrapyard in the 1970s. (Eddie Bellass)

Lancashire & Yorkshire Railway and the Great Central Railway for a share of the region's lucrative freight and passenger market. They also competed for bragging rights in providing the best, the fastest and most comprehensive services to shift those goods to larger cities or the nearest port for overseas shipment.

Following the Second World War and the Nationalisation of the 'Big Four' railways in 1948, the duplication and unprofitability of some of these railway routes necessitated services being rationalised or axed. Timetables were trimmed, lines and stations were shut and inevitably closure of steam engine sheds followed.

The British Railways' modernisation plan of 1955 proposed spending more than £1.24 billion (conservatively, £25.7 billion in 2012 money) in modernising the railways and replacing steam with diesel and electric locomotives, while in 1963 Dr Beeching's Report (*The Reshaping of British Railways*) resulted in more than 4,000 miles of railway and 3,000 stations being closed in the decade following release of his thesis. Both only hastened the process of rationalisation and closure. Wigan's Lower Ince and Southport Lord Street sheds were pre-modernisation casualties, succumbing in the early 1950s; sub-sheds at Tanhouse Lane at Widnes and Arpley at Warrington followed in subsequent years and then Widnes itself and Wigan 'C' closed in April 1964.

The diversity and 'colour' of immediate post-war British Railways would soon give way to standardisation and utilitarianism by the late 1950s and early 1960s. Diesel shunters began to infiltrate many of the sheds, where they replaced ageing steam relics from the nineteenth century and more modern locomotives. At sheds like Springs Branch work began in October 1966 on the construction of new diesel servicing facilities. This may have been progress that was long overdue, but nevertheless, during the 1950s and 1960s a wealth of railway heritage was lost: bulldozed, scrapped or unceremoniously dumped in a headlong attempt to modernise the railways to make it competitive with road transport.

There is an image in this book that poignantly illustrates the transition of British Railways during this epoch. Gerald Drought took his camera to St Helens station in early 1955, where an ageing ex-Lancashire & Yorkshire Railway steam locomotive, built in 1896, was simmering beside the station platform, when the 3,300-horsepower prototype Deltic main-line diesel thundered through on an inaugural test run to Carlisle.

It must have been a thrilling and somewhat bemusing experience for any bystanders on that platform when the blue Deltic roared through. Thrilling, certainly, to view that brand-new diesel, representing a new era of high-speed passenger travel promised by this powerful, new motive power. But also unsettling because it signalled that the old, established ways were about to disappear. The clanking 'dinosaur' wheezing its way through the station would soon become a fleeting memory

In this wintry scene, Standard 9F 2-10-0 No.92194 heads a train of coal empties (destined for return to Yorkshire) through Warrington Bank Quay low level. Outshopped from Swindon Works on 30 June 1958, 92194 spent most of its life on the Eastern Region of BR and was withdrawn, prematurely, in December 1965 after barely seven and a half years' service. (Eddie Bellass)

of an earlier time, when railway operations were less hurried, less efficient but nevertheless often profitable. With no ceremony, such relics (but happily not that particular loco) and thousands of other BR steam locomotives – some seeing barely five years of service – would be rounded up and scrapped by the end of the 1960s, as the rush to 'modernise' British Rail became frenetic.

By 1968, only Northwich of this region's group of eight steam sheds still remained operational and by early March, it too would banish steam. At Springs Branch (closed to steam in December 1967) twenty-seven steam locomotives awaited their fate. But tellingly, so too did six diesel shunters.

For many railway employees, their attitude to the transition to modern motive power reflected their age and length of service with the railways. For younger people like Keith Sloan, who was a fitter at Springs Branch in the 1960s, the change was perceived this way:

> There was more mateship on steam as the older blokes knew all about steam locomotives, but as diesels and electrics came in everything was new, and it seemed like the older era resented being shown by us young lads.

However, for men who had spent their entire working lives 'on the railway' and working only around steam, the changes were tinged with regret, coloured by nostalgia, and there was also a feeling that some great spirit had been 'lost' and would never be reclaimed, as explained by former Wigan signalman Charles Melling:

> All engines had a personality of their own. I've ridden on engines from the signal box to go home and ... one driver ... he would know that engine just like he would know a son or daughter. Once this personality of the engine was got rid of, by bringing in the diesels ... this feeling went; the diesel could never take the place of the steam engine, something great had been lost, this personal touch between the driver and his engine.

Kenn Pearce
Wynn Vale,
South Australia

Glossary

CLC The Cheshire Lines Committee was formed in 1863 by the amalgamation of four lines: the Stockport & Woodley Junction Railway, the West Cheshire Railway, the Cheshire Midland Railway and the Stockport, Timperley and Altrincham Junction Railway. In 1865 the Midland Railway Company also joined the committee, which was incorporated as a separate undertaking in 1867, under control of these three companies, as the Cheshire Lines Committee. A company was created with one-third shares owned by the Great Northern Railway, the Midland Railway and the Manchester Sheffield & Lincolnshire Railway (later Great Central Railway). In 1921 the management passed to the London & North Eastern Railway (LNER) in association with the London Midland and Scottish Railway (LMS). The CLC continued to operate as an independent railway with three London Midland Scottish directors and six London & North Eastern Railway directors. The CLC finally lost its independence under the Transport Act of 1947, becoming part of British Railways' London Midland Region.

Control The line control which oversaw movement of train traffic over respective routes.

DLS District Locomotive Superintendent.

EWS English, Welsh and Scottish Railway, a British rail freight company set up in the 1990s.

Fully fitted (wagons) Rolling stock or an entire train of vacuum-brake fitted stock.

The Grouping The term to describe the amalgamation in 1923 of a number of disparate railway companies into four major (but still private) railway companies: the London Midland Scottish Railway, the London & Northern Eastern Railway, the Great Western Railway and the Southern Railway. This 'Big Four' continued until the end of 1947 when the Nationalisation of the railways created British Railways from 1 January 1948.

IRF Inside Running Foreman.

LE Light engine (an engine that will travel on its own with crew to pick up a train or make its way on or off shed).

Lodging turn A roster in which engine crews would rest over at a railway barracks after completing their shift, before returning to their home shed.

ORF Outside Running Foreman.

The 'Premier Line' The term describing the London & North Western Railway which from 1923 became part of the London Midland Scottish Railway.

Spade Term sometimes used to describe a fireman's shovel – long-handled spade, etc.

One

8B WARRINGTON DALLAM AND ARPLEY (SUB-SHED)

Warrington Dallam shed was located on the west side of the west coast main line, about a mile north of Warrington Bank Quay station. It would take about half an hour to walk to this busy shed, although a bus service operated from Horsemarket Street to the end of Kerfoot Street, where nearby Folly Lane gave access to the shed site. It was a brick-built, ten-lane, dead-end shed dating from 1888 and was built using materials from the closed London & North Western Railway (LNWR) works in Jockey Lane.[1] Before this, there had been a small locomotive shed at Dallam Lane from 1831–36, and a larger facility near Bank Quay station existed from 1851 to 1888. The railway's locomotive superintendent, F.W. Webb, sought a new shed opposite the company's Jockey Lane works, capable of holding forty locomotives at an estimated cost of £13,140. However, this was not approved by the company until May 1887 and then conditional on 'using the materials from the Jockey Lane works now discontinued'. The shed was opened almost a year later.

Dallam shed was built originally with a northlight-pattern roof. Original facilities included a 42ft-diameter turntable and a coaling stage with a water tank above. Offices and storerooms were at the rear of the shed. In later years the turntable, situated in the north-western area of the shed site, was enlarged to a 65ft-diameter version. Dallam initially had the shed code of 23, later becoming 8B in the LMS reorganisation of shed codes in 1935.

In 1957 Dallam was reduced to nine tracks and was refurbished with a louvre-style roof. A brick screen was also installed, in the centre of which a construction stone bore the year of refurbishment. Dallam shed was closed to steam from 2 October 1967 and closed completely from 11 August 1968. The shed is still standing and is now in industrial use.

The late Ted Slater spent forty-two years on the footplate, retiring in 1993, and spent time working from both Warrington Dallam and Arpley sheds:

> In the 1960s we had passenger and freight work. The passenger work was between Liverpool Lime Street and Manchester London Road [now Piccadilly] but mainly Ditton Junction and Timperley.
>
> A lot of these trains were push and pull and were quite well [patronised] especially in the rush hour, but Dr Beeching decided they were not paying and closed the services. The freight was mainly from Arpley sidings or Ellesmere Port to Stockport Edgeley or Guide Bridge, returning with coal for Garston and then Ireland; so it was passenger [trains] in the day and freight in the evening.

Mr Slater was first employed as a number-taker at Warrington Central, on the CLC, when he was aged sixteen. But to get on to the footplate, he had to resign and start work as an engine cleaner at Dallam when he reached eighteen. However, he was able to keep his pension rights. He would sign on for duty at 8a.m., grab a bucket filled with 'oily cleaning fluid' and a pile of old cotton waste and spend his day cleaning various parts of the locos until the shift ended at 4p.m.

Eventually he became a 'passed cleaner', meaning he could begin to get some firing turns when opportunities arose through staff shortages or illness. At some point you were examined

The unique Stephenson link motion Stanier Black 5 No.44767 receives a final oil around from Dallam driver Bert Williams in this 1960s view taken at that shed. Fortunately, this engine was saved for posterity and today in preservation carries the name *Stephenson*. (Eddie Bellass)

to go on shunts only; later you were taken on to the main line and examined by an inspector who rode with you and saw whether you had the ability to fire a main line loco. If he was satisfied that you were capable, you then became a passed cleaner and could go on shifts around the clock covering sickness or a passed fireman (doing driving duties). Mr Slater said you got a variety of work and drivers. Some were good, some bad. But you were always looking for a firing turn as you got more money:

> If a fireman reported in sick, or was taken off for driving duties, you worked his train. Very often this involved overtime which was always welcome. Of course, the system worked on promotion and links; the lowest links being shunting turns, then trip turns (involving going into local factories) and then passenger links where there was no overtime. After [completing] all of those links you were getting on a bit.

Mr Slater said that the duration of time you had to complete firing turns was equivalent to one year's firing before qualifying for the top rate of the cleaner's pay.

Stan Jones joined Widnes shed in January 1953 but spent some of his time on the railways 'on loan' to Warrington Dallam:

When I was on loan ... I was working in the goods yard at the rear of Crossfield's Soap Works and my lasting memory of that place was when my Mam made me some salmon paste sandwiches for my baggin. When it came time to eat them and have a cup of tea, they tasted of soap, so now every time I have a salmon sandwich my memory tunes in on Warrington goods yard.

Another turn from Warrington was a night trip via Daresbury, Runcorn East, [and] Frodsham to Helsby. From Helsby we had to travel via a single track through to Stanlow complex and at Bromborough we had to call at the signal box and pick up a staff. This device was to stop another train entering the track at the same time for safety reasons. This was another first for me, seeing the lights at Stanlow because I hadn't seen anything like it close up before.

With a Class 2 rocker we used to shunt along the canal behind Fiddlers Ferry and the marshes down at Spike Island, also in and out of the chemical works through to West Bank docks and Fisons and Bush Boake Allen. I used to work a lot of early shifts because I swapped shifts with some of the married men because they got extra [wages] for working nights and it enabled me to go out at nights and have a drink and go dancing.

Dallam's two-track, brick sub-shed, Warrington Arpley, was visible from the southern end of Bank Quay station. The straight-through shed had a gable-style slate roof and facilities included a turntable, water columns and a coal stage with a water tank above. The shed opened on 1 May 1854 and was originally part of the Warrington and Altrincham Junction Railway.

Observed at Arpley shed on Sunday 27 April 1952 were: 40042, 40107, 41323, 43282, 43314, 43357 and 50703. A little over a decade later, in July 1962, the following engines were noted at this sub-shed: 41210, 41213, 41217, 43657, 44063 and 84000.

Railway enthusiast Robin Bamber visited Arpley shed on 19 June 1955 and recorded eight engines on shed from five different classes, including ex-L&YR 'Radial' tank No. 50644:

The big seed warehouse near the shed had the name 'Gartons' on its roof in large letters. This was visible from the west coast main line and had amused us for years, as spelt backwards it produced an interesting word! Also seen on the same trip were thirty-four engines on Dallam shed.

Ten days before Christmas in 1957, railway photographer Brian Swinn visited Arpley and noted eleven engines in residence:

40134	40156	41212	42606	43398	43657	43787	44232	48457	48715	52432

Arpley shed was roofless and fairly derelict by the time of its closure on 27 May 1963; however, it was not demolished until 1973. During this time, it continued in use as a steam and later diesel servicing point.

The author fondly remembers Arpley shed from trainspotting jaunts to Bank Quay in the early to mid-1960s, recalling it as being almost exclusively inhabited by grubby Fowler 0-6-0s or tank variants. On a few memorable occasions, a grubby B1 class would trundle by with a freight headed for Stockport. Often a fleet of mineral wagons would be parked in an intervening siding, annoyingly obscuring cabside numbers of engines on Arpley shed from the platform at Bank Quay, with only boilers and chimneys tantalisingly on view!

* * *

In May 1960, Warrington Dallam's turntable was closed for repairs and this meant that the Earlestown triangle was used for turning locomotives. This happened at the same time as Euston–

Ivatt 2MT 2-6-2 tank No.41213 rests at Warrington Arpley shed in the early 1960s, in company with a Stanier 8F. This engine had previously been allocated to Walsall in the Midlands. Generally, Arpley shed had a mix of ageing 0-6-0 tender freight engines with the odd Black 5 or Black 8 present. Even after official closure, you could usually find a few locos pottering about the shed site. (Courtesy of the Engine Shed Society)

Patriot class 4-6-0 No.45546 *Fleetwood* inside Warrington Dallam shed in the early 1960s. The car to the right of the loco is a Renault Dauphine and was the pride and joy of Dallam engine driver Kenneth Buckley Mellor. Mr Mellor also on occasions acted as either a train crew supervisor or shedmaster. Former Dallam engineman, William Pearson, said Mr Mellor always insisted on everything being immaculately clean and tidy. He said everything about Ken was the same: his garden with never a stone out of place, his house was always the envy of the neighbours, and of course his car was always spotlessly clean, inside and out. It was probably also the reason he liked it kept undercover. (Eddie Bellass)

Liverpool trains were routed via Earlestown for the first fortnight in May, while important work was done on the electrification of the main line from Liverpool to Crewe.

Warrington Bank Quay station was an excellent spot from which to observe west coast expresses in full flight, fast freights trundling through and 'on the bottom line', and even local passenger trains until the early 1960s. A local service from Bank Quay to nearby Earlestown was known affectionately as the 'Earlestown Jennie' and was usually a job for one of Dallam's Ivatt 2-6-2 tanks such as 41210 or 41213.

At Crewe Works on 31 October 1961 were two engines, Jubilee No.45630 *Swaziland* and Black 5 No.45401, that were damaged in a collision near Warrington Dallam shed on 28 August. Both engines were condemned in November 1961; the condemnation of the Black 5 was the first of the 842 engines of this class.

Former Speke Junction footplateman, Clive Boardman, remembers seeing *Swaziland* the day before the collision: 'On the Saturday morning I was at Crewe South shed and there, on the shed front, was Jubilee 45630 *Swaziland*, straight from the shops, gleaming from stem to stern and an absolute joy to behold.'

Busy day at Warrington Arpley on 2 March 1963 with Fowler 4F No.44494 and Johnson Midland 3Fs Nos 43657 and 43282. Although appearing largely intact in this image, the amount of light filtering through to the locos inside the shed clearly demonstrates the shed roof was in poor condition. (A.C. Gilbert, courtesy of the Engine Shed Society)

The following day, Roy Dixon (who joined Dallam shed early in 1962) recalls that Edge Hill's Black 5 No.45401 was hauling a freight train while *Swaziland* was leaving Dallam shed when the two collided. Jack Peacock of Dallam was the driver. Mr Dixon says the fireman of *Swaziland*, Keith Hewitt, also from 8B, died on 31 August from injuries suffered in the crash.

Clive Boardman remembers next seeing the two damaged engines 'roped off' in Dallam shed where they remained for several weeks, presumably for enquiry purposes and, although [the] damage was superficial, both engines were withdrawn. The Jubilee had covered perhaps 25 miles since overhaul.'

Roy Dixon joined Dallam shed as a sixteen-and-a-half-year-old engine cleaner. His reason for joining BR was to simply satisfy a longstanding interest in steam engines. Although employed at Dallam, after being passed to fire engines, he sometimes booked on at Arpley for freight turns. By the early 1960s Arpley was just a booking-on point with a very poor roof; it had no locos of its own, all were assigned from Dallam shed. 'There were two shedmen per shift at Arpley; their duties included coaling, cleaning fires, lighting up [engines], keeping the shed tidy and knocking up [crews],' he said.

Typically in the early 1960s there would be up to eight engines at Arpley. Mr Dixon said the shed's administration was run from Dallam, as too were any running repairs or engine cleaning. Watering and coaling facilities were available at the sub-shed, and the latter provided one amusing incident. Mr Dixon recalls:

We were coaling a Midland '3' tender engine at Arpley one day, the driver and I were coaling it from a wagon there and some coal flew off my shovel and brought down some light fittings. My driver couldn't stop laughing – he said they hadn't worked for some time anyway. I was a bit worried I'd get into trouble for the damage but he just said throw the fittings in the scrap bin.

Mr Dixon recalls spending only around five weeks as a cleaner before being made a passed cleaner and going out on his first firing turn. He remembers his first firing assignment was on an ex-Midland Railway Class 3 tender engine (43257) on a local pilot job. He enjoyed the experience even though it was only a local turn.

Pages from a Fireman's Notebook – Roy Dixon

Thursday 15 November 1962
11a.m. – Arpley sidings – Oakamoor to Macclesfield. Travel home passenger.
Loco No.48106 (8B).
Driver: Joe Walsh.

Saturday 19 January 1963
Relieve 10.30a.m. Guide Bridge-Birkenhead (goods) at Arpley Junction.

Black 5 No.44732 heads through Arpley Junction at Warrington, bound for Liverpool, with a Yorkshire to Garston coal train in 1964. Built in 1949 by British Railways, 44732 spent much of its life in the north-west and was a Speke Junction engine from September 1964. It was reallocated to Springs Branch from May 1966, from where it was withdrawn in July the following year. (Eddie Bellass)

Loco No.48422 (6C) [Birkenhead].
Detach/attach Ellesmere Port, Birkenhead Brook Street. L.E. to Birkenhead shed. Prepare Crab 42934 (6C) to work the 4.35p.m. Birkenhead-Healy Mills, to Arpley Junction.
Driver: Arthur Bell.

Initially, Mr Dixon did well, receiving many firing turns, but by the end of 1962 the shed lost quite a few regular jobs and he returned to cleaning. The year 1963 also witnessed the upheaval of the Beeching Plan to rationalise the railways and that further limited his ability to advance.

When he started work with BR, Mr Dixon said footplatemen were on a forty-two-hour week – they would work three forty-hour weeks and one forty-eight-hour week to make up the required hours over a month. The shifts included Saturday work while Sundays was overtime:

They were very unsociable shifts; any time around the clock you could be required to book on. We had a lot of freight work and they tended to run at night. It wasn't too bad if you were on the passenger links.

A lot of it was local freights to places such as Birkenhead, Mold Junction, Bolton, Chester, Stockport and the Manchester area in general, as well as Liverpool, Wigan, Preston, St Helens, Widnes, Macclesfield and even Stoke-on-Trent.

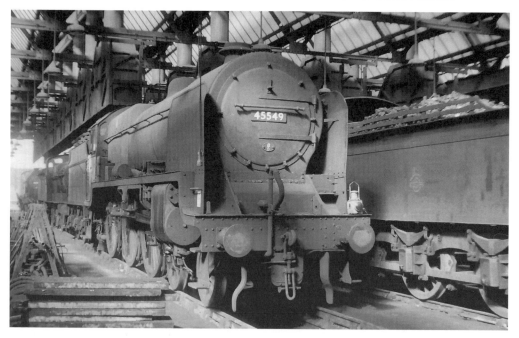

The well-lit interior of Warrington Dallam shed is the location for this fine portrait of Fowler Patriot No.45549, which was not accorded a name, unlike most of the class. This undated photograph would have been between late June 1959 and May 1962 (when it was withdrawn), during which time it was a Dallam engine, having previously been a Carlisle Upperby loco. (Eddie Bellass)

You were carrying all sorts of things on these freights: chemicals and oils, with Ellesmere Port being nearby, and Stanlow. [There was the] soap factory at Crossfield's and they made chemicals adjacent to Warrington Bank Quay [station].

Mr Dixon recalls there being some 'colourful characters' at Dallam and Arpley sheds with similarly interesting nicknames, among them: Mad Mick, Desperate Dan, Daddy Woodentop, Bugs Bunny and Mighty Mouse! He found most people 'fairly easy going on the railway'.

By 1962, Dallam shed had sixty-five engines allocated, the majority of them steam. Interestingly, its allocation included three of the surviving unrebuilt Patriot class 4-6-0s and four Jubilee 4-6-0s, the latter a type that would, by the end of 1965, be among the final survivors of this class on the London Midland Region.

WARRINGTON (DALLAM) allocations in 1962

D2864	D2865	D3796	D3797	D3834	D3835	D3851	12075	41210	41211	41213	41288
43240	43257	43282	43410	43615	43657	44061	44063	44232	44237	44356	44384
44494	44589	44827	44986	45035	45150	45256	45271	45321	45328	45343	45354
45380	45381	45414	45495	45546	45549	45550	45583	45638	45655	45671	47362
47406	47594	47603	47654	47657	47669	48094	48106	48129	48188	48268	48373
48715	48746	84000	84001	84024							

Warrington engines ranged far and wide and was evidenced in early 1962 when Dallam's Jubilee 45583 *Assam* was noted on March shed on 5 February, while at the end of that month another from 8B, 45671 *Prince Rupert*, spent a week at the Eastern Region shed.

On 22 January 1963 Duchess Pacific No.46220 *Coronation* was at Dallam shed ready to work the 08.20hrs fitted freight to Carlisle. This engine had only returned to traffic the previous month, after being in store, to head a royal train to Liverpool. Three days later another unusual visitor to Dallam was B1 class No.61269. Warrington Arpley meanwhile hosted recently withdrawn 3F 0-6-0s 43240, 43257, 43282, 43615 and 43657, awaiting their call to the scrapyard.

Warrington was the starting point on 27 April 1963 for the Railway Correspondence & Travel Society's 'Cheshire Rambler' tour, which was hauled by B1 class 4-6-0 No.61039 *Steinbok* of Gorton shed.

On Whit Saturday (1 June) 1963 B1 No.61094 from 41A shed (Sheffield) passed through Warrington Arpley heading a Sheffield Midland to Chester excursion via the Hope Valley, Chinley, Cheadle Heath, Cheadle, Skelton Junction, Arpley and Walton Old Junction route.

Page from a Fireman's Notebook – Roy Dixon

Saturday 31 August 1963 (special diagram)
Prepare Class 5MT 45187 (8A) [Edge Hill] to work 6a.m. Warrington–Carlisle passenger train to Preston. (Then) travel passenger to Carnforth. Prepare 8P No.46237 *City of Bristol* (12B) [Carlisle Upperby]. L.E. to Morecombe Promenade to work 9.05a.m. to Birmingham (New Street), as far as Crewe. Travel home passenger.
Driver: Percy Clough.

Dallam's locomotives could range far and wide in their travels, often turning up in the most unusual places during the 1960s. For example, Jubilee class No.45580 *Burma* was reported to have made its debut at Wrexham in early April 1964 hauling a freight train from Shrewsbury. *Burma* later worked a 4.30p.m. Birkenhead to Paddington express.[2]

Enthusiast and railway photographer Brian Swinn visited Dallam shed on Sunday 20 September 1964 and noted thirty-two engines resident that day, with one of them, Jubilee No.45730 *Ocean*, withdrawn from service the previous October (the author too noted this engine still at Dallam in 1965):

D2391	D2393	D3837	42849	44115	44181	44294	44349	44356	44384	44522
44730	44819	44930	44986	45017	45131	45238	45303	45590 *Travancore*	45604 *Ceylon*	45633 *Aden*
45655 *Keith*	45664 *Nelson*	45703 *Thunderer*	45730 *Ocean*	47395	47416	48108	48451	48515	90721	

Promotion for men at ex-LNWR sheds like Dallam was often 'painfully slow' according to Roy Dixon, so it took cleaners and passed cleaners quite some time to progress through the grades. In Mr Dixon's case it wasn't until March 1965 that he became a registered fireman: 'Being on the main line we did much better than other sheds that were on secondary lines.'

Of the engines based at Dallam, Mr Dixon recalls the shed having a number of 'Jinties' allocated there and also one ex-L&YR A class 0-6-0 which, despite its age, he rated as quite a good loco, except it was open to the elements in winter or on rainy days; crews tried to afford some protection by pulling down a tarpaulin from the cab roof.

By 1965 Warrington Dallam's locomotive allocations had been cut to thirty-eight and many of the locomotives from the 'Big Four' railway companies had been superseded by BR Standard types, including an influx of modern 9Fs. Still, the Jubilees continued to find gainful employment from the shed (*Australia* and *Travancore*, although No.45633 *Aden* was only nominally based there, being actually stored at Edge Hill for some time). The numerical class leader of the Black 5s No.44658 was also Dallam based, and was even observed by the author heading a local passenger train from Warrington Bank Quay to Manchester shortly after being outshopped from the works.

Jubilee No.45664 *Nelson* near the end of its career at Warrington Dallam shed, to where it was allocated from 18 July 1964, having previously been briefly at Speke Junction depot. It was withdrawn from Dallam shed in May the following year. Dallam, Bank Hall and Stockport Edgeley were the final London Midland sheds to find gainful employment for the Jubilees. (Bob Bartlett)

Warrington Dallam's last Jubilee to remain in service, No.45590 *Travancore*, is the Motorail pilot loco waiting in the sidings at Newton-le-Willows in this evocative night-time study by Eddie Bellass taken in 1965. Ex-Dallam man Roy Dixon rated this loco highly during its time at 8B. This engine also had some expensive boiler repairs carried out on it at Edge Hill shed earlier in the year, but sadly was withdrawn by the end of 1965. It was broken up at Cashmore's, Great Bridge in March 1966. (Eddie Bellass)

Roy Dixon got to work on the Jubilees a fair bit while at Dallam and said that in good condition they were fine engines: 'But a lot of the work we had was not suited to them. They were okay on express freight work or some of the remaining passenger turns we had.'

He rated *Cornwallis* and *Travancore* among the best of the bunch (*Travancore* in fact survived to be the last of its class in service at the shed and indeed underwent expensive repairs at Edge Hill shed early in 1965, only months before its withdrawal). Mr Dixon comments:

But some of the Jubilees were pretty run down and you had problems to get them to steam. I think the Black 5s were the best all-round loco but the Jubilees were a little more powerful – with their three cylinders as opposed to two – but the drivers didn't like getting underneath to oil them. From the preparation point of view, the Black 5s were preferred. The most popular locos of them all, really.

We also got an allocation of Standard 9Fs from 1965 and these were a good all-round loco when in good condition but even by 1965 a lot of them were badly run down. They were used on passenger turns in summer and I've had passenger jobs with them on the Llandudno specials in summertime.

Britannia Pacific No.70012 *John of Gaunt* presents a chilly scene on 21 January 1964 as it heads a Llandudno–Manchester train, passing Old Alder Lane bridge at Winwick, near Warrington. Summer North Wales excursion trains were fondly recalled by ex-Dallam loco man Roy Dixon, with those sourced from Yorkshire sometimes bringing B1 or K3 class engines to Warrington. (Eddie Bellass)

Speaking of the North Wales summer specials, Mr Dixon recalls that sometimes these trains, which were sourced from Yorkshire, were hauled by ex-LNER B1 4-6-0s or even K3 2-6-0s. At Warrington they changed crews – the trains often having begun at Sheffield, Leeds, Harrogate or Mexborough – with Dallam men then manning the trains to Bangor or Llandudno on the Welsh north coast. Often these specials were 'one behind the other' on a summer Saturday with up to twelve carriages on some trains:

> Sometimes you worked back on another train, sometimes you came home as passenger. They were nice jobs, you got a run out but it was summertime only. It meant drivers had to know the road to Bangor and Llandudno, and you had the Butlin's [holiday camp] specials to Penychain.

By 1965 the five Fowler 4F 0-6-0s allocated to Dallam shed were among the last survivors of a class that had once numbered 580 engines. They now sported the distinctive diagonal yellow stripe through their cabside numbers, signifying they were banned from working under wires south of Crewe; the only other examples of this class in service by this time were at Crewe Works as shunters.

By 1965, Dallam's five Fowler 0-6-0s were among the few survivors of a class that once numbered 580 engines. This loco, No.44115, came to Dallam in November 1963 and was withdrawn in July 1965, being among the last of its class in service. In the background can be seen one of Dallam's Jubilees, 45655 *Keith*. (Courtesy of the Coltas Trust)

WARRINGTON (DALLAM) allocations in 1965

44115	44181	44294	44349	44522	44658	44730	44731	44819	44930	44935	45041
45078	45109	45129	45238	45256	45303	45436	45563 *Australia*	45590 *Travancore*	45633 *Aden*	92048	92049
92053	92055	92058	92059	92070	92078	92086	92116	92119	92124	92126	92156
92160	92163										

In 1966 Dallam's locomotive allocations had only fallen marginally. Gone were the Fowler 4Fs and the Jubilees, and in their place were more modern machines, post-war-built Stanier Black 5s and a dozen Standard 9Fs, some of which (92218, for example, built in January 1960) were barely six years old. Yet these too would be consigned to the scrapyards within two years such was the pace of 'modernisation'.

Colin Turton was a passed cleaner who was made redundant when nearby Widnes shed (8D) closed its doors in April 1964. He left the railways but realised afterwards that he was missing the job, and steam, too much. So he secured a job at Dallam shed:

I was the only [ex] Widnes person at Dallam. It was very different ... there were main-line turns but passenger work had been lost by then. There was a lot of overtime at Dallam (there had not been at Widnes), as much as you wanted. I would work up as far as Carlisle and book off there (lodging for eight hours). We also worked the CLC route from Dallam. My favourites were [Stanier] Black 5s. We had 5s, [Standard] 9Fs and [Stanier] 8s. We got Britannias to work but they were not our engines. I was fine with the Standards but older hands were more critical of them.

Dallam 9F No.92160 rests at its home shed in 1965 in glorious sunshine. Already souvenir hunters have removed the loco's front number plate. Outshopped from Crewe Works at the end of November 1957, the loco went new to Wellingborough. It was transferred to Dallam shed in March 1965 and then was allocated to Birkenhead from February 1966. It stayed there until that shed's closure in November 1967, surviving to be transferred to Speke Junction, and again survived that shed's closure in May 1968 to be sent to Carnforth. It was among the last of its class in service when withdrawn in June 1968. (Gerald Drought)

Royal Scot No.46115 *Scots Guardsman* makes a fine study on Warrington Dallam shed in 1965 and provides a thrill for a young schoolboy. By the summer of 1965, only two of the seventy-one Royal Scots remained in service, this loco and No.46140. *Scots Guardsman* found much gainful employment in its final year in service, often working to Merseyside or Warrington on goods trains and returning on fast freights to its final home shed of Carlisle Kingmoor. It was withdrawn at the end of 1965 and was saved for preservation. It has now been returned to main-line operating condition. (Gerald Drought)

Page from a Fireman's Notebook – Roy Dixon

Thursday 7 July 1966 (Lodge Turn)
Booked on duty 6.47p.m.
Prepared Class 5MT No.44689 (of) 12A (Carlisle Kingmoor). L.E. to Froghall sidings, to work the 8.17p.m. Warrington to Carlisle via Hellifield.
Load 39 vehicles equal to 46.
Lostock Hall pilot driver from Lostock Hall to Carlisle Bog Junction. L.E. Kingmoor yard to Kingmoor shed. Booked off duty 3.30a.m., 8 July.
Driver: E. Cox. Fireman: R. Dixon. Guard: C. Bowden.
Remarks: Locomotive in good mechanical condition, and steaming free (sic).
First night to be routed via Hellifield.

An unusual visitor to Warrington on 23 July 1966 was B1 class 4-6-0 No.61238 *Leslie Runciman* that was observed on a freight train in the marshalling yard.

A little less than a month later, Brian Swinn visited Dallam shed on a Sunday and recorded the following thirty-three engines on shed. The unusual sight of a 'Brit' on shed was *William Wordsworth* that had been withdrawn from service in June and was no doubt en route to its final destination, Ward's Beighton scrapyard in Sheffield, where it was broken up later in the year:

12075	12078	12102	D2391	D2392	D2393	D2562	D8155	D8156	D8157	42782	43106
44819	44933	45061	45129	45140	45256	45288	45312	45323	45374	45436	48029
48623	70030	92080	92095	92112	92119	92124	92126	92224			

An excursion on Easter Monday (27 March 1967) was hauled from Warrington to Blackpool North by Black 5 No.44777.

By 9 September 1967, Dallam shed was less than a month away from closing as a steam depot. Just twenty-four engines were on shed when enthusiast and railway photographer Brian Swinn visited that Saturday, but three of the four 9Fs noted were withdrawn from service, while Black 5 No.45256 was in store. A glint of green livery was provided by visiting 'Brit' 70051 *Firth of Forth* of Carlisle Kingmoor shed.

Stanier Black 5 4-6-0 No.44672 is turned on Warrington Dallam's turntable in 1965. This engine, which was outshopped from Horwich Works in February 1950, spent a fair proportion of its career at Lancashire depots and was finally withdrawn from Lostock Hall (Preston) in March 1968. (Eddie Bellass)

Standard 9F No.92078 awaits its fate on the scrap line at Warrington Dallam shed on 2 August 1967. This loco had been withdrawn in May that year after barely eleven years' service. At this stage, Dallam itself had only weeks remaining until it closed to steam. For footplatemen like Colin Turton, steam's sad end also extinguished any desire they had to continue working for the railways. (Stephen Wolstenholme collection)

12032	12078	D2088	D2376	D2379	D5273	D7554	D7556	D7643	44934	45041	45055
45221	45256	45323	45375	48293	48551	48669	70051	92055	*92078*	*92156*	92224

Engines shown in *italics* were withdrawn from service.

For Colin Turton, the end of steam at Warrington Dallam shed ended his desire to work for the railways. He stuck it out until December 1967 but then left: 'I wish I had started in 1956 [as he'd wanted to] but I still would have left at the end of steam.'

Ironically, although Warrington was nominally now a dieselised area, Roy Dixon's last turn at firing steam in BR days came six months *after* Dallam's closure to steam and almost five years after Arpley had shut its doors for the last time.

Page from a Fireman's Notebook – Roy Dixon

Friday 26 April 1968
Remanned the 08.20(hrs) Rotherwood–Garston coal train at Arpley Junction, with loco No.48252 (9F) [Heaton Mersey], worked to Garston, L.E. to Speke Junction shed. Travelled home passenger. Driver: Bill Humberstone.
Comments: It was good to be back on steam, my previous steam turn having been on Friday 16 February 1968. I didn't really like diesel or electric locomotives.

Mr Dixon admits to feelings of 'sadness' at the passage of steam to more modern power. Although he eventually became passed to drive locomotives, 'unfortunately it was [in the] post-steam' era, but he had done quite a bit of unofficial driving with regular steam drivers as part of his learning process.

After Dallam's closure to steam, the depot continued to operate as a diesel servicing point for ten months until it closed completely on 11 August 1968 – coincidentally, the final day of main-line steam operation, when British Railways' infamous '15 Guinea' Farewell Special ran from Liverpool to Carlisle and return.

Mr Dixon continued with BR, working on both diesel and electrics on the west coast main line but decided to take early retirement in 1997 shortly after the railways were privatised:

They were the happiest days of my life working on steam. I remember them as a boy and I did work on a lot of the important locos like the Britannias, Jubilees, Royal Scots and the Duchesses before they were taken out of service in 1964. The Duchesses, they never, I think,

BR Clan Pacifics were rare but not unknown visitors to Lancashire, including Warrington Dallam. Carlisle Kingmoor's 72005 *Clan Macgregor* eases back while taking coal from Dallam's mechanical coaler before taking its next turn – probably back to its home town. *Clan Macgregor* was among the five survivors of this class after the first five members were withdrawn in 1962. It was withdrawn on 1 May 1965 and later scrapped at the West of Scotland Shipbreaking Company at Troon. (Eddie Bellass)

Dallam in decline with its grime, debris on the shed floor and grubby workmanlike steam locomotives. In this evocative inside-looking-out viewpoint, Black 5s Nos 45391 and 45303 raise steam alongside a Standard 9F. (Peter Ditchfield)

got the full potential out of them because it would be too much work for one fireman to achieve that. I know when they had them on test they had two firemen. If they'd fitted them with mechanical stokers, they'd have got so much more out of them.

In 1997 a new single-road diesel depot was built on the north-western edge of Warrington Arpley yard. This depot replaced Springs Branch which had closed in May 1997 and ended the longstanding but wasteful practice of engines at Warrington, when requiring fuel, having to go light on a 25-mile return trip to Wigan.

Warrington Central

This was the location of a small one-track, straight-through shed that was established by the Cheshire Lines Committee on the southern side of Warrington Central station. The shed was opened on 1 August 1873. The shed was reportedly demolished around 1905. However, an extra siding was added and the two sidings and original engine pit continued as a servicing point for locomotives until around 1966, when the 'depot' was closed.

The shed by May 1950 was a sub-shed of Liverpool Brunswick – with Central's engines on 22 May that year being J11 No.64376 and J10s Nos 65163, 65172 and 65182.

Although assigned the code 8F until Springs Branch (10A) was re-designated 8F in the late 1950s, Warrington CLC shed (sometimes referred to as Warrington Central) then became a sub-shed of Warrington Dallam. Despite briefly having its own shed code, it appears never to have had its own allocation, certainly in BR days.

The *British Railways Locomotive Shed Directory* referred to the sub-shed as being 'an office and a pit' on the south side of Warrington Central station and 'there is no shed building' so it is difficult to understand why it was accorded its own shed code of 8F in the 1955 *ABC Combined Volume*. Similarly, it was accorded a separate coding in the 1948–50 *Combined* reprint, listed as '8E [sic]' directly after Brunswick with the same code – clearly a misprint.

Robin Bamber remembers Warrington Central as a teenager when he visited it on 19 June 1955, noting J10s Nos 65182, 65185 and 65196 on shed. Robin highlighted the misnomer too: 'It was just an open stabling point at the side of the station. The tops of the three locos were visible from the main road below.'

Railway enthusiast and long-time Engine Shed Society member Alec Swain visited the sub-shed on Sunday 10 April 1960 and found three Fowler 4F engines resident: Nos 44232, 44489 and 44494.

A Fowler 4F stands on the site of Warrington Central 'shed' in this 14 August 1960 view. The central station building can be seen to the right, while in the right foreground a small outhouse is clearly the property of 'Loco'. Despite having no allocated engines, this stabling point would often have a couple of engines on shed right up to the mid-1960s. (R.S. Carpenter, courtesy of the Engine Shed Society)

On Friday 1 March 1963, Warrington Dallam fireman Roy Dixon was sent on loan to Warrington Central. Mr Dixon recalls:

> They had three 'Derby 4Fs' out-based from Trafford Park (9E) shed. It was all local work. I remanned loco No.44489 [to] service sidings at Whitecross Wire, Rylands Wire and Central Warehouse.
>   Later, during the shift, 44565 arrived from Trafford Park to change over. No.44489 was due for a boiler washout. Following some more shunting the loco returned to the shed. [My] driver was Roy Mairs.

Railway enthusiast Lyndon Knott visited Warrington Dallam and Warrington Central on 6 March 1966 and recorded three engines present at Central 'shed': 45269, 48344 and 48356.

After Warrington Central was no longer used as a steam servicing point in the late 1960s, the tracks were lifted and the site redeveloped as part of road improvements. By 1997, Warrington Central had joined Heaton Mersey and Rose Grove on a select list of former shed sites you are now able to drive through, as a relief road uses the arches immediately south of Warrington Central station as part of its route.

Over & Wharton

This single-lane, brick built, straight dead-ended shed was built by the London & North Western Railway and opened on 1 June 1882. It was located near Winsford, to the north of Over & Wharton station on the west side of the line. It was a sub-shed of Warrington Dallam.

The shed had a gable-style slate roof and facilities included a brick-based overhead water tank and ash pits. Some time before the shed's closure fire damaged part of the roof, which was evident in a photograph taken in June 1947.

An ex-LNWR 2-4-2 tank was retained for the branch passenger service, outstationed from Dallam shed, until this service was withdrawn in the same month. Despite cessation of the passenger services, the line remained in use for freight traffic (chiefly rock salt from Winsford's mines) for many years and did not finally close until March 1991. The salt (and some coal) traffic also required the allocation of freight engines from Dallam to this sub-shed.

The sub-shed was closed by the LMS on 30 August 1947; however, engines continued to be stabled on the shed road at least six years after its closure and possibly as late as 1964.[3]

The Over & Wharton branch of 1 mile 22 yards in length was built by the LNWR that connected to the 'Premier Line's' west coast route, just north of Winsford. The line was built to

Ex-LNWR 0-6-2 tank No.6906 at Over & Wharton shed, Cheshire, on 12 June 1947. Inside the shed can be seen ex-LNWR 2-4-2 tank No.6637 which was the branch engine. The shed roof was damaged by fire and has been partially removed. Both engines were from Warrington Dallam (8B). (W.A. Camwell, courtesy of the Engine Shed Society)

Ex-Great Central Railway C13 4-4-2 tank No.67436 rests at the site of Over & Wharton engine shed, Cheshire, on 17 October 1953. This was a Chester Northgate engine for much of the early 1950s. The engine shed here has been largely demolished (a fire had damaged part of the roof before its closure on 30 August 1947); however, part of the shed office appears to have survived. Engines continued to be stabled at the shed site for many years after its closure. (Brian Hilton, courtesy of the Engine Shed Society)

give access to the salt traffic for which Winsford was well known. Passenger services included a shuttle which ran to Hartford station and from there passengers could connect to local and long-distance services.[4]

The Over & Wharton branch was originally built as double track, but worked as a single-line operation following the First World War, the second line being effectively used as a long storage siding. On Saturday 5 September 1959 the following thirty-five condemned steam locos were being stored on the Over & Wharton branch, pending despatch to various scrapyards:

Ex-London, Tilbury and Southend Railway 3P 4-4-2Ts:

41928, 41939, 41941, 41945, 41946, 41948, 41950, 41977, 41978

Ex-London, Tilbury and Southend Railway 3F 0-6-2Ts:

41982, 41983, 41984, 41985, 41986, 41987, 41990, 41991, 41992, 41993

Ex-London & North Western Railway 7F 0-8-0s:

48905, 48945, 49010, 49109, 49113, 49117, 49157, 49180, 49181, 49226, 49228, 49229, 49308, 49330, 49368, 49409

Following the closure of the branch line, the track was lifted almost immediately. Wharton Park Road (A5018) now runs through the western side of the former station site.

The Engine Shed Society's *Link* journal reported that on 11 March 2008 the whole shed and station area was covered by a Morrisons supermarket and its large car park, with a new road following the line of the track bed. The actual shed site was near a bus stop on this road.

Earlestown Wagon Works

Although not on British Railways' official shed listings, Earlestown Wagon Works[5] had a single-track engine shed, adjacent to the Up main line at Earlestown. Until the early 1960s a Dallam shed 'Jinty' tank was allocated there on weekdays for shunting around wagons undergoing repairs or being broken up at the facility.

Former Dallam fireman Roy Dixon recalls Earlestown Wagon Works in 1962, after he had joined 8B as a cleaner:

This undated photograph of Earlestown Wagon Works' single-line engine shed shows it was quite a substantial structure, more than capable of accommodating the one or two 'Jinty' tanks that fussed around the works, moving wagons being repaired or scrapped. (Courtesy of the Engine Shed Society)

A Jinty was out-based there Monday to Friday, working mornings and afternoons. During 1962, locos 47362 and 47406 normally worked alternate weeks on this duty. They were best suited for this location, both being right-hand-drive locos. The Wagon Works was still very busy at this time; the two resident drivers were Tommy Warburton and Reg Turner, while the firemen travelled out from Dallam.

Mr Dixon's diary notes indicate he worked the morning turn at the Wagon Works on Thursday 6 September 1962 and his driver was Tommy Warburton; their engine was 47362, which had been a Warrington engine since November 1952.

The works was closed in 1964 when its work was transferred to Horwich Works.

The Earlestown locomotive shed was still in situ in October 2001, as outlined in an entry in 'Sights of Sites', in the Engine Shed Society's *Link* journal:

Most of the old works buildings have recently been demolished and have been replaced by modern industrial units. Amazingly, the works shed still stands isolated in one corner of the site, with a large concrete floor area in front of it waiting for more new units ... The loco shed is at present used to store some building materials, although the side door was wide open which defeats the object of security. Whether or not the shed itself will be demolished when its role for this purpose is over is not known.[6]

Demolition of the shed is believed to have occurred around 2007/2008.

Two

8D WIDNES AND WIDNES TANHOUSE LANE (CLC SUB-SHED)

Opened originally by the London & North Western Railway as a two-lane shed in 1874, Widnes shed only had an initial allocation of six engines. Within six years, however, up to twenty-six engines were daily in steam and complaints about the lack of space were rife. In 1881 the shed was enlarged to a six-lane facility, each of 200ft in length, capable of housing twenty-four engines. Nearby, Speke Junction shed opened in May 1886 and Widnes, coded 35W, became its sub-shed.

Widnes was a typical shed of its era, built to a standard design with a northlight-pattern roof; it also was provided with a 42ft-diameter turntable and a small tank over a coaling stage. However, Widnes was beset by its constrained site: bounded by a road at its rear and the Appleton and Carterhouse Junction lines to its north and south. Despite the turntable, several reversals were necessary for engines to be completely serviced before entering the shed.

A growth in local freight, minerals haulage and shunting duties led to the shed's allocation increasing to thirty-five engines by 1923. In fact, accommodation for engines may have been a further problem by the late 1920s had not a large proportion of engines been tanks. By 1929, however, tender engines began to make up nearly half of the shed's allocation. In that year engines based at the shed included: four 2-4-2Ts, four 0-6-2Ts, eight 0-6-0 saddle tanks and a single 0-4-0T; a dozen LNWR Cauliflowers and seven LNWR 0-8-0s made up the shed complement.

Little in the way of improvements was carried out by the LMS at Widnes, other than an extension of the offices at the shed's rear in 1937. By now it was recoded 8D, under Edge Hill the district shed, and kept that code until its closure. The roof was renewed in the louvre style by the LMS in 1946. Two years later, Widnes acquired a sub-shed – the single-lane, ex-Cheshire Lines Committee depot at Tanhouse Lane, half a mile away. In 1948 the main shed's allocation of twenty-five locos included eleven ex-LNWR types of 0-6-0 and 0-8-0 wheel formation. By then, too, Ivatt 2-6-0s had begun to arrive and this type along with its BR variant became a feature of the shed right up to its closure in 1964, taking over the work of the ageing Cauliflowers, such as shunting the works yard

Widnes shed on a sunny summer's day in June 1944 with a selection of pre-Grouping locos on show. Ex-London & North Western 2F, 28221, in the foreground, became nominally BR No.58342 upon Nationalisation when it was still allocated to Widnes shed. However, the engine was withdrawn from service from Stafford shed on 31 January 1949 and later that year cut up at Crewe Works, where it had been built sixty-eight years before. (Courtesy of the Engine Shed Society)

Widnes shed on a gloomy day on 27 October 1946, shortly after the new roof and front screen had been fitted to the shed building. The shed's collection of locomotives shows an interesting mix of late nineteenth-century survivors and more modern locos like the tank engines. (Stephen Wolstenholme collection)

Widnes Tanhouse Lane shed shown on 10 November 1951. Already the shed is showing signs of its age with broken shed windows and parts of the roof hip exposed to the elements. By this time, an ex-LNER J67 or J69 sent from Liverpool's Brunswick shed was usually the sole inhabitant. (Harry Townley, courtesy of the Industrial Railway Society)

adjacent to the shed. Eight Stanier 8Fs eventually supplanted the 0-8-0s and a single Ivatt 2-6-2T was employed on the remaining local passenger turns previously worked by the Webb 2-4-2Ts.

Although Tanhouse Lane became a sub-shed of Widnes shed, engines for the sub-shed (demolished in 1956) continued to be supplied by Liverpool Brunswick as the only connection with the ex-LNWR lines at Widnes was over a private industrial line and tolls were charged if BR engines had to travel over these. In January 1954, for example, J67 No.68547 was supplied by Brunswick shed for Tanhouse Lane; previously (in 1950) it had appeared as a direct allocation to the shed. The CLC connection also resulted in J10 class 0-6-0s appearing regularly at Widnes: Nos 65138 and 65198 were transferred there in 1955. In the same year all shunting and pick-up duties were handed over to 3F tanks and BR or ex-LMS 2MT Moguls.

Stan Jones, who joined Widnes shed as a cleaner in January 1953, remembers Tanhouse Lane during his first year at the main shed:

The first time I visited the place was in my first year at the sheds: we had to go to the BRS depot at Tanhouse to collect a couple of gallons of petrol to put in the engine of the conveyer belt for coaling the engines [at 8D]. This used to run out of petrol about twice a week; this belt was run in conjunction with the coaling stage that was next to the ash pit. Later, when I was a fireman and used to work out of Tanhouse, we used a tank engine, with a very small footplate ... when the new style cobble coal had come out. It was just a matter of opening the firebox door and of the bunker and the coal would [almost] just slide in.

Diesel shunters began to appear from 1960 and Austerity and Stanier 8Fs finally supplanted the old LNWR engines around the same time. Dieselisation and a loss of much of the local freight traffic eventually led to Widnes shed's redundancy and it closed on 13 April 1964. However, steam engines continued periodically to be serviced for a few years. The shed building was sold to a private concern and by 1974 the shed and yard was occupied by a scrap merchant.

* * *

The author recalls first visiting this small shed in around late 1959 or early 1960 with a group of like-minded railway enthusiasts from Warrington Road Primary School, Widnes.

Widnes shed usually presented no problems for the young enthusiast to negotiate; however, it was advisable to always check with the shedmaster or on-duty foreman in his bay-windowed office, which was accessed up a flight of steps from the street below, before venturing on to the depot. On one of these early forays I recall seeing at the shed's perimeter, near an iron overbridge, a group of redundant, rusting Fowler and Stanier 2-6-2 tanks which were awaiting their call to a scrapyard.

Another time, one mellow summer's evening, our group was mucking about in the sidings near the shed when we heard a voice bellow to us. The instruction was yelled again, but this time it was picked up clearly: an invite to 'get in' came from the crew in the cab of a Standard Class 4 tank which was trundling around the shed. Our small group needed no further enticement and we all happily climbed on to the footplate for an impromptu cab ride (a first experience for myself) down the shed yard.

Former Widnes engineman David Littler joined the railways as an engine cleaner at 8D in April 1952 and remained there until the shed's closure twelve years later. 'I did nearly twelve months as a cleaner and in January 1953 I went to Garston [Speke Junction] for two weeks' school,' he said. 'I passed out on 16 February as a passed cleaner, which is a junior fireman.'

Although Mr Littler was only sixteen at the time, he gained 'seniority' over five other young blokes who were older than him but had just joined the railways by attending the school classes at Garston. They got 'put back' behind him as he'd been with the railways since the previous April. 'It was a very good shed, a six-lane depot with a turntable, a coal escalator; it had its own staff for

A view of Widnes engine shed on 16 April 1962 with a pair of redundant Stanier 2-6-2 tanks in the foreground. Blowing off steam is one of the shed's Ivatt 2-6-2 tanks, while behind can be seen the old ex-LNWR coaling stage, by now superseded by a coal elevator just out of camera range on the right of the picture. (Stephen Wolstenholme collection)

cleaning the fires and coaling,' he said. 'We had eight sets, they had what they called link work. There were eight jobs in the link: you had the night Leeds, the day Leeds, the 7.50 Farnworth–Bold–St Helens, the 8.10 to Wigan; Crewe; and Buxton.'

Mr Littler said cleaning engines was a job that would sometimes leave the cleaners as grimy as the engines they were working on:

> They just made sure you were doing it right. They used to have a white cleaning oil, you'd mix it with water and wash off the grit and grime and you had paraffin to get the oil off the big ends and wheels. And if it was inside motion you'd have to get in there and clean it. And you'd come out like an oily rag! The weekly wage was for a forty-eight-hour week (you only got Sunday off) and was £2/10 [shillings] for a fifteen-year-old cleaner.

He recalls the shedmaster at Widnes, a Mr Gravelin, who was 'strict but very fair'. The shedmaster was assigned to permanent days; others he can recall from this era include Jack Witter and Gilbert Draper, who used to work afternoons and nights alternatively. One was a fitter who applied for, and got, the job and the other two were assistant shedmasters. Then there were drivers who used to go into the office when the others wanted relieving – or when they took holidays. In turn, passed drivers and firemen would step up a level to fill in for them. Mr Littler recalls a Mr Brooks as being the shedmaster when Widnes shed finally closed. He was a Yorkshireman who was a fitter by trade.

Mr Littler experienced his first firing turn when he was still only sixteen years of age:

> The first firing turn I had was on a Class 8 locomotive. I was on the 6a.m. to 2p.m. cleaning [turn] and the fireman failed on the 10.50 Farnworth and Bold. The driver's name was Jimmy Murray and Gravelin was the shedmaster. He said, you're going on the 10.50 Farnworth and Bold but you won't be doing the full job, you'll be getting relieved at St Helens. Which was a mistake – I was only sixteen and you weren't supposed to go out on the main line firing until you were seventeen.

Widnes shed's Black 8 No.48045 rests on shed, ready for its next turn on 20 September 1963. To the right of the loco can partly be seen the ex-LNWR coaling stage with overhead water tank. Ex-Widnes fireman Colin Turton records in his diary having worked on this engine to Bolton on Saturday 11 May 1963. Note the pairing with a Fowler tender, rather than the later Stanier tenders usually seen on these locos. (Brian Swinn)

I got to Sutton Oak and a St Helens fireman was there waiting for me. They gave me eight of these disks (that you used to get for milk) to give to the corporation bus driver (to get home). I said where do I get a bus from here? I'd never been in that area before.

Another man who joined the shed staff at 8D in January 1953 as a cleaner was Stan Jones. Mr Jones said his eventual employment with the railways came from a visit to the engine shed in Croft Street, Widnes, when he was fourteen years old:

I went with another lad who was about three or four years older than me; he worked on the railway and had to make a call to check on his shift time. It was a new experience for me; it was the smell of the oil smoke and steam all mixed together; this gave me the impression of 'burnt steam' during this visit, a few months before I left school at Christmas of 1952.

Mr Jones finished school at Christmas time and his birthday was on 28 December. He visited a small education office near Widnes Town Hall to register for employment and receive some guidance about what occupation he could take up:

As far as I can remember it was a waste of time. The railway sheds were about half a mile away, so I decided to walk down and see if there were any vacancies. I think the boss's name was Mr Gravelin. He took my details and arranged for me to have a medical.

When he left school Stan Jones says he was 'only around five feet tall and weighed about six stone'. The only time he had travelled on a train previously was when he was a member of the army cadets in Widnes. On that occasion the cadets had travelled from Farnworth station (now named Widnes North) to Liverpool Central, before marching across the city centre to catch a train to Southport for a weekend camp at Altcar Army Firing Range.

After having a chat with Mr Gravelin at Widnes shed, Mr Jones was given a return ticket to Manchester Central station to receive a full medical, so one can only imagine how strange and exciting this was to a fourteen-year-old lad – his first foray into the grown-up world, unaccompanied on a rare outing by train.

After passing his medical, Mr Jones was advised he should start work at Widnes shed on 3 January 1953, six days after turning fifteen years of age. He was the only new starter that day. No one was allowed to work on the footplate until they were sixteen years of age, recalls Mr Jones:

Promotion was slow and you only got paid for the time you worked on the footplate at the upper rate because a cleaner's rate of pay was low. When you had worked on an engine for approximately 260 days you were entitled to [the first scale of three in the] fireman's rate.

A sunny day at Widnes shed in the early 1950s with an interesting collection of locos on display, including a couple of Webb Cauliflowers, a pair of ex-LNWR Super Ds and more modern ex-LMS power including Ivatt Mogul 46424. (Stephen Wolstenholme collection)

A roster was posted (at the shed) every day to see who was needed to fire an engine or engines the next day or days. When you had completed two hours or more on each trip it was counted as a turn; so once you had completed 264 days you remained on that scale of pay. When I reached sixteen I went to the front of the queue for first selection for the next jobs on the footplate. Because I had started the day before the other lads I was classed as a 'senior hand' because I was first in, so I accumulated my 264 turns in my first year on board.

Despite being only allowed to work around the engine shed cleaning engines in his first year at Widnes, Mr Jones was amazed at the various other skills he picked up. Cleaners also helped with coaling the engines; they learnt how to fire the engine by shovelling coal into the firebox at the correct amounts; how to operate the water injectors to keep the correct water levels in the boiler and maintain the steam pressure at 175 to 225 per square inch (depending on the class of loco). Other tasks included knocking-up duties to the homes of drivers or firemen, for call-out cover on late-listed jobs.

After doing these various jobs around the sheds, Mr Jones also learnt how to raise steam from zero (by placing firelighters soaked in creosote in a nest of small pieces of coal, then lighting it and putting it on a bed of coal in the firebox and making sure it took hold); this was then monitored for the two hours it took to raise the steam, ready for the engine to make its way off the sheds to begin duties. He recalls two days never being alike, and he got to 'mix with different people every day and each had different personalities and techniques'.

The young recruits were issued with regular bib and brace overalls and jackets, a peaked cap and either a donkey jacket, a large coat called a reefer jacket or a waterproof mack, along with the railwayman's rule book. The latter was revered as the railwayman's 'bible'. The first few pages contained drawings of how a steam locomotive was assembled and how it worked. The new lads had to learn about the passage of steam and the most important rule (Rule 55) – protecting the train. They also had to answer questions such as what is steam (an invisible, elastic vapour generated from water by the application of heat). Another fundamental they needed to become conversant with was the workings of the vacuum brake.

Mr Jones recalls the pay being £2 11s 6d for a cleaner when he began in 1953 – that was for a forty-eight-hour week spread over weekdays and 8a.m. to noon on Saturdays. The night rate was paid at time and a quarter, while any overtime on Saturday was paid at time and a half, with Sundays being time and three-quarters. Double-time payments only 'kicked in' when crews were rostered on Saturdays and it ran into Sunday. 'Sunday work only used to come around about once in eight weeks: if you had to work on a bank holiday, you would get Sunday [rates] with a day off in lieu.'

Mr Jones said that when cleaners 'passed out' they had to put in at least two hours working on the footplate for it to be classed as a firing turn. This rule applied to every passed cleaner until they had completed 260–264 turns and then became a fireman. Then their hourly rate of pay would rise to 3s 9d and 3 farthings for days, plus a shift allowance on top. Shed staff would collect their weekly wages in a 'little round tin approximately 3in long by 2in in diameter – all in cash with a pay slip'. Mr Jones recalls:

After our twelve-month stint working in the sheds, about eight of the younger lads, including myself, who all had reached the age of sixteen, had to travel to Edge Hill sheds to take a verbal test on how to perform on the footplate and about safety procedures; we had to recite Rule 55. As I remember [the safety procedure, if] during fog or falling snow ... there is an accident or derailment, [then] the fireman has to retreat back along the line as far and as fast as possible carrying flags, detonators and a lamp at night, then place three detonators on the steel rail not less than 10 feet apart, then continue for approximately another 100 yards, place one detonator, continue for another 100 yards, place one detonator, continue for another 100 yards, place a last detonator, then return to [the] engine until everything is made safe.

Mr Jones went on to recall that when a fireman booked on for work, he would first sign on then go to the stores where he would pick up a sealed can containing eight safety detonators; two safety

A young Stan Jones fires one of Widnes shed's Super D 0-8-0s in the early 1950s. For many footplatemen there was nothing 'super' about the Super Ds and they were often hard work, even if capable of taking a good thrashing if necessary. By 1955, Widnes shed had seven of these locos on its roster, but by the end of the decade most had either been scrapped or transferred away. (Stan Jones collection)

flags (one red, one green); two oil lamps (one front, one tail lamp) used for identification of the type of journey (the lamp or lamps were fixed on the front of the engine for the correct identification sequence, the tail lamp had a red shade for the lens); a firing shovel and pick-axe for breaking up large pieces of coal; and a short-handled shovel needed for use on Super D engines due to there being less space on the footplate.

He recalls his first year employed on the footplate as a mixture of working around the shed (shed turning duties) and doing work in and around the local factories and the goods yard by Widnes Central station:

> The 'Lanky' engines ... were prone to lose brake power when low on steam. Well, on this particular day I went to move the engine towards the turntable when I realised that the table wasn't set for the ash pit line and that the steam had dropped low. When I slammed the brake on nothing happened, so I had to frantically keep turning the reverse and forward levers for a good ten minutes before it came to a stop; my heart was in my mouth.
>
> On another occasion, when a large-wheeled passenger engine was ready to be put in the shed after being watered and coaled etc. ... I moved the engine up past the points to put it in one of the spaces in the shed. I reversed the movement, pushed the steam regulator a fraction to start the engine on its way, jumped off and ran to the points, pulled the points lever to the correct line and when the engine had passed, released the lever, but I wasn't fast enough.
>
> By the time I had put the brake on it was travelling too fast and the wheels locked and the engine slid into the shed with an almighty bang, crashing into a couple of engines that were parked there. Of course, I disappeared and kept my head down for a while. Health and safety wasn't as strict in those days; the driver or I should have been on the footplate while the other held the points, but on this occasion the driver must have gone to the toilet, so I thought I was being clever by trying to do the job on my own to quicken things up.

Mr Jones recalls another time he was sat in the shed turner's hut (down the north side of the sheds), having a cup of tea while reading the paper, when he heard an 'intermittent swishing sound' outside the hut. He looked up in time to see an engine slowly going past the window with nobody on the footplate. The sight almost gave him a 'heart attack' but he had the presence of mind to dash out and stop the loco to prevent it crashing into the buffers at the end of the line.

He explained that he and a mate had prepared a Super D engine for its next job, but had to leave it on the coaling track, next to the ash pit, on a slight incline. However, when the taps were left closed on a Super D, condensation would often build up pressure in the cylinder, and this had caused the engine to move down the incline past the hut.

David Littler remembers some of the other pre-Grouping survivors that lingered on at sheds like Widnes into the 1950s, including the ex-LNWR 18in goods or Cauliflowers, three of which survived into 1955, with No. 58427 being at Widnes:

> Well we only had them on shunting turns when we had them, but they had used them on passenger turns ... they were built in 1887, or something like that. [Condition-wise] by the

The men of Widnes shed pose for the camera in front of one of the shed's Super D 0-8-0s. *From left to right*: Eddie Meade, Taffy Roberts, Jack McGuiness, Gerry Dobson, Eddie Davies, Peter Kilshaw, George Cowley (Cynthia's father), Bill Ramsdale and Joe Merser. Photograph believed to have been taken in the 1950s. (Courtesy of Cynthia Richards)

Widnes's ex-LNWR Webb 18in goods or Cauliflower No. 58413 at the back of the shed in the early 1950s, possibly awaiting some repairs. This engine was withdrawn to the period ending 31 January 1954 after fifty-three years' service. It was scrapped later that year at Crewe Works. (Stephen Wolstenholme collection)

1950s they were clapped out really, they were just used on shunts ... What amazed me was the driving wheels had steel brake blocks on but the tender had wooden ones. It didn't make any difference ... we never did fast work with them, they were always on shunts.

We had one on the Marsh, one in the goods yard and one at the bottom of Farnworth and Bold bank, as a bank engine. Because the gradient up the Bongs was 1 in 93 or 1 in 96.

The late 1950s was also a time of transition on British Railways and new power was beginning to be trialled as part of the modernisation plan of the system. Mr Jones got first-hand sight of this one day when working in the goods yard, when a message came through that a new diesel-electric locomotive called a Deltic was making its way from Garston hauling '100 wagons of timber' for Evans's timber yard at Ditton:

But when it arrived outside the goods yard the Deltic driver wouldn't cross the local points leading to the goods yard, so they had to send for a Class 8 engine to come out and prove that a large engine could negotiate the points into the goods yard. A Class 8 could pull forty-five loaded wagons, so the Deltic was to prove that diesel engines were for the future. I never got on the footplate of the Deltic but the memory stays with me; when I stood by it with its engine running, the ground trembled from its enormous power.

Mr Jones also recalled sometimes working the 5.15p.m. passenger train from Liverpool Lime Street to Acton Bridge (near Warrington) during summer. Another train was timetabled to leave for London around the same time. If the 'local' got a head start – hauling just three or four carriages – and got to Allerton station and left before the London train caught up, it would keep pace with the express up to the water troughs just outside Ditton Junction station. 'You can imagine the excitement for the passengers of both trains waving and cheering each other when the race was on,' he says.

Another turn he remembers included an afternoon run from Widnes to Bickershaw Colliery at Wigan. Crews would take forty-five empty loose-coupled wagons to the colliery and bring back forty-five loaded with coal:

On one trip to Bickershaw, my driver at the time … said, 'I heard that you get up singing in the local pubs.' I said, 'Yes, after a couple of pints.' So before we set out he called the guard over and told him that I sang in the pubs and, as it turned out, the guard used to practise his saxophone [Michael Meaney]. So, for that outward trip, [for a bit] I travelled in the guard's van where he was playing his sax and I was singing along with him.

Mr Jones also recalls an early passenger run from Liverpool to Chester, in which Widnes crews used to take a 7.30a.m. passenger train to Chester, stopping at all stations through Runcorn, Frodsham and Helsby:

Stanier 3MT 2-6-2T No.40201 near the turntable at Widnes shed on a sunny summer's day, 31 July 1956. This was one of three of the class based at Widnes shed in 1955 and a type that remained present in the area until the early 1960s. They were sometimes noted by some railwaymen for providing some anxious moments when their fusible plugs became exposed through sudden shortage of water. (RCTS - JAY1920)

One morning, when we were leaving Frodsham and passing the empty fields between there and Helsby, the driver shouted, 'Have a look at this.' He'd grab the whistle handle and give a long blast on the whistle for about three or four minutes and then you would see thousands of rabbits dashing about in the fields. This was before myxomatosis had set in in the rabbit population and long before they built the M56 motorway.

Over the years, Widnes shed had always retained a modest allocation of mainly mixed traffic or freight engines; 'namers' were not regularly seen there, except in the case of the odd Jubilee. The interesting mix of engines of pre-Grouping and post-war construction that could usually be found together at the shed by the mid-1950s included a pair of Pollitt J10 class 0-6-0s dating from the late nineteenth century. Until the early 1960s, these engines could be found in a number of ex-Great Central sheds around Lancashire and Cheshire, the two examples listed here having come from Northwich and Heaton Mersey respectively, but both had moved away to Wigan Springs Branch by the end of the 1950s.

Enthusiast Robin Bamber visited Widnes shed on 19 June 1955 in a ninety-mile cycling trip from Preston. He was rewarded for his efforts by observing seventeen engines on shed, ranging across Fowler 2-6-2 tanks, a single Stanier 2-6-4 tank, several Ivatt 2MT moguls, a few ex-LNWR Super Ds and three ex-LNER J10s.

Cycling on further, Robin called in at Widnes CLC shed at Tanhouse Lane where he noted ex-Great Eastern J69 No.68598 from Brunswick shed, Liverpool.

David Littler said there was a variety of freight work coming out of Widnes sheds in the 1950s and early 1960s, including two trains a day to Leeds, and much work in relation to the chemical facilities in the town and neighbouring centres. The ageing ex-LNWR 0-8-0s or Super Ds played an important role in some of the local freight work:

> We had one job that ran twenty-four hours a day, Target 92. It went off in the morning, usually a Super D, a Class 7; you went from Widnes to Ditton [Junction] to Runcorn and backed down to Folly Lane. Then Folly Lane–Runcorn–Ditton and back to Widnes.
>
> Two trips, coal to the power house and also mixed goods and you would clear them out from ICI – chemicals and wagons that the ICI [Works] had produced and then back.
>
> You did two trips in the morning, you got relieved and the engine did two trips in the afternoon, then it went back on the shed and the night man took an engine off to do the same two trips at night. That was usually a Class 7 [Super D].

Some other Widnes shed turns that were recalled by Colin Turton, who joined the shed in 1961 as a cleaner, included Targets:

Widnes Tanhouse Lane shed, most likely captured in the early 1950s, with a small tank engine stabled inside. This was probably one of the ex-LNER J69s which were sent from Liverpool Brunswick shed to work from this ex-Cheshire Lines Committee loco shed. (Courtesy of the Engine Shed Society)

81 – Bank engine (Vine Yard to Farnworth and Bold)
84 – West Bank Dock (for the power station)
85 – Marsh sidings (Widnes Dock)
86 – Afternoon Farnworth & Bold
88 – Hutchinson Street yard shunting
90 – Trip work from Hutchinson Street to Marsh sidings (Widnes Dock)
93 – Farnworth & Bold; and
96 – Ditton sleeper yard.

Many of the author's jaunts to Widnes 'motive power depot' often seemed to align with grey, rainy days (frequently in summer) that seemed forever to mark this location in a pall of drabness. Occasionally we would see one of the larger, modern Standard 9F types being serviced on shed, but increasingly the fewer locomotives being seen at Widnes hinted at its imminent closure in the early 1960s, for much of the motive power needed for its declining number of workings could be sourced from neighbouring sheds.

Mr Littler recalls Widnes shed having three or four Sunday rosters which crews would work on a rotational basis. In theory everyone worked these Sunday rosters at some time; however, 'elderly drivers' didn't want to work them because some by then were in their sixties. Therefore, the rosters came around more quickly. Mr Littler personally looked forward to working Sundays, which were paid at double time. For Saturday work, crews were paid time and a half, while night shifts attracted time and a quarter payments.

When he married in 1958, Mr Littler was on a wage of £9 a week; however, if he got some shifts such as the 'night Leeds' he could earn nearly double that amount. The night Leeds was a freight which departed Widnes at 9p.m., while a daytime version of it departed at 9.50a.m. Widnes crews worked the train as far as Stockport Edgeley and worked home from there, or often to Garston. On the outward trip, the train stopped at Warrington, where wagons were dropped off and picked up, and then the train went straight through to Edgeley. Mr Littler said that before the war, crews would often do a double trip from Widnes to Leeds, staying in Yorkshire for eight hours before working back the return train the following day. Customary power for the Leeds trains was either a Stanier 8F or a War Department Austerity 2-8-0 hauling 'between thirty and forty-five wagons'.

Mr Littler rated the Austerities highly:

> They were quite powerful but when they were free-wheeling they had a long drawbar between the tender and the engine and the tender used to jump and bump, bump, bump behind you. But for pulling they were quite a strong engine. They were a rough ride but a good strong locomotive. Occasionally you'd get a Crab on it – a '5' with a sloping running plate. They were a good engine too.

In this scene in the early 1960s an Austerity lurks near Widnes shed's old coaling stage, while another class member pokes its smokebox out of the shed building. (Ken Fairey)

One of the 'Breadvan' Fowler 3P 2-6-2 tanks inside Widnes shed in the early 1960s, No.40007. Built at Derby Works and entering service on 8 April 1930, this engine was reallocated to Widnes shed from 27 August 1960, having previously been based at Willesden. It was withdrawn from Widnes shed less than a year later on 22 July 1961. The loco was cut up at Central Wagon Works, Wigan, by late October that year. (Chris Coates collection)

You'd have stuff coming from all over England to Warrington and shunted and then made up for a train to go to Manchester onwards. The main freight coming out of Widnes would be chemicals and asbestos from the Everite Works.

Everite was at the top of the Bongs bank, 2 miles from the shed that was in production up to the 1970s before they closed that factory down. They produced asbestos pipes that headed all over the country.

Another job was you used to go [as a] passenger to Bolton and work back from Bolton to Widnes. Then there was a job that used to work from Widnes to Warrington, to Northwich; Northwich back to Widnes, to St Helens and then light engine back on to Widnes shed.

Yet another job, you travelled passenger from Widnes to Garston, picked up a Class 8 or an Austerity; then went light engine to Folly Lane at Runcorn and then worked from Runcorn to Crewe. Then travel home as a passenger.

Mr Littler also recalled another turn – the five o'clock Cheadle – which involved departing at 5a.m. 'off the Marsh', usually manning a Stanier Black 5 or Black 8 with forty wagons behind it headed for Cheadle Junction where the crew was relieved; then returning home as passengers on a train. He said crews were usually back on shed by 11a.m.

One type of engine that was unpopular with Mr Littler was the 'Derby 4s' or Fowler 4F 0-6-0 tender engines. By contrast, a few years ago Mr Littler met a fellow in Victoria, Australia, who worked at Heaton Norris and who used to love the 'Derby 4s' but, in contrast, disliked the Super Ds, mainly because of unfamiliarity. In fact, a Northwich driver's unfamiliarity with the Super Ds resulted in his putting a loco through the stop blocks at Widnes shed and into nearby Alforde Street around 1957. The same driver later put another engine into the turntable pit at the shed

Fowler 4F aka 'Derby 4' No.44588 on shed at Widnes on 20 September 1963. These were engines not well liked by some enginemen like David Littler; however, it was what you were most familiar with. Note the enclosed cab fitted to the front of the tender which would provide much-needed shelter for crews in inclement weather, especially when working in reverse. Built at Derby Works in September 1939, this loco was withdrawn from its final shed, Derby, in May 1964 and scrapped at Cashmore's Great Bridge in January 1965. (Brian Swinn)

after not realising the table was set for another track. In Mr Littler's opinion, the Super Ds weren't as powerful as a Class 8 but they seemed to last longer and were not as much trouble. The older engines did, however, go in more frequently for maintenance but that was due more to their age than anything else.

Occasionally, Widnes would get a Jubilee class engine on shed; one that was frequently recalled as visiting was No.45600 *Bermuda*, for some unknown reason. For remaining passenger turns, by the 1950s Widnes had a few Stanier or Fowler 2-6-2 tank engines, as remembered by Mr Littler:

I think we only had two passenger jobs actually, but one of them, I think it was something like Ditton, Wigan, somewhere else, then Lime Street, and then you went on to Edge Hill shed to coal up.

You'd have an empty bunker when you got there and you used to fill it up and fill the bloody footplate as well. Then you'd bring it light engine back to Widnes. And you had to make sure you had enough coal to do the job the next day.

Widnes wasn't too bad but if you went to Edge Hill they always had good coal because they had a lot of passenger work. At Garston they had two coal chutes – one had good coal, the other had briquettes. But we didn't do too bad, we didn't get brilliant coal but it was quite good. Of course, if you filled up at Edge Hill you were laughing because you got the best.

Coal was dispensed at Widnes from the old LNWR brick-built coaling tower with an overhead tank, but in declining years this gave way to an old petrol-driven belt escalator (as it did at places like Warrington Dallam and Sutton Oak); men on this duty simply dropped the door on the coal wagon

This view of Widnes shed after official closure, taken on 7 August 1964, depicts the original LNWR coaling stage and in the foreground the lean-to that provided some shelter to the coalmen using the petrol-driven coal elevator that superseded the coaling stage. (Chris Hollins)

and shovelled it out. Three coalmen were employed on the 2p.m. to 10p.m. and 6a.m. shifts. The men, however, were largely open to the elements, although a rudimentary lean-to 'shelter' was provided for staff on this duty.

On promotion, Mr Littler said some men were quite happy to remain drivers. Similarly, there were some fireman who, when told they were to go for a driving exam, handed in their notice. Mr Littler ended up going for his driver's exam six months earlier than he would have ordinarily. He thought it was 'bloody great' when he finally passed to drive in 1962 (he eventually did 142 driving turns before Widnes closed in 1964) but reflected, 'you were just the driver; the guard was in charge of the train. He was responsible for the couplings and all the rest of the train, you were just responsible for the running time.'

Keeping trains to time was always an imperative, whether it was a passenger train or freight, but sometimes schedules were trashed because of matters beyond the control of crews. It required a sense of humour when drivers received 'please explains' from the authorities, as Mr Littler recalls:

> I was firing with Jacky Knight and we were on the night Leeds and they had control areas – like the Liverpool control went as far as Northenden on the way to Manchester, and then you come on to Manchester control.
>
> We were seven minutes late at Northenden but we got to Edgeley on time. And when we got relieved the driver there said: 'Driver, control want a word with you.' So he went into the shed and made a brew and then went into the office. They said to Jacky: 'Driver, you lost seven minutes at Northenden.' Jacky said: 'I'll look for it on the way back!'

On another occasion, Mr Littler was firing on the night Leeds with engine driver Arthur Ford. The pair was due off shed at 9.15p.m. but at the last minute Arthur rang in sick. Mr Littler was a passed fireman, meaning he could step in to drive, but the shed had no spare fireman handy, nor a passed cleaner. So he had to wait until 10p.m. when the night 'shed turner' – a man who disposed of engines when they came on shed – came on duty. This fireman turned out to be Mr Littler's cousin, Billy Delaney. By the time they left the shed the pair were already an hour behind schedule.

The crew got their train out past Warrington until they got to Lym station where they were called up into the signal box and told they were going to be backed into the siding.

A mishap at Northenden Junction, where an engine had come off the road, had blocked the line. The pair was backed into the siding at Lym at 11.30p.m. and was still there at 6a.m. when they went to the signal box to make a brew. They were informed their train would be allowed to leave at 7a.m. after the first passenger train went through. They finally got to Stockport Edgeley at 10a.m.

To make matters worse, the tired crew were told by control that their return train was waiting for them! Mr Littler had had enough:

> I said I'm not doing the return working, I've had fourteen hours on now, I'm going home as passenger. That was on a Friday, so when I got back to the shed it was 2.30p.m. that afternoon. So I couldn't go in on Friday night because I had to have ten hours' rest. So they had to pay me for a day off. I managed it three times in fourteen years.

Mr Jones recalls having a mixture of different jobs on the footplate while at Widnes, varying from shunting in the goods yard, and down on the marshes, to short trips on the main line with both goods and passenger trains. On several occasions while on shunting duties around the factories he cooked his breakfast on a shovel. This was done by placing an enamel dish on the shovel, placing a knob of lard in the dish along with a couple of rashers of bacon and an egg and a couple of sausages. He would adjust the steam jet control slightly to take the smoke away from the shovel, and place the shovel just inside the door over the flames from the fire. Within two minutes breakfast was cooked!

He recalls every day spent on the footplate being different to the previous one. In spring, it was good to get up early and go to work. But he also used to swap his late shifts with some of the married men who had kids. This enabled him to continue to go out dancing at night, and have a pint or two, while the married men benefited from the shift allowance. He recalls:

> Sometimes in the summer it used to get quite hot and we used to take cold tea (without milk) in a bottle – it was a really good way of quenching your thirst.
>
> One trip in winter that I didn't like too much was the trip from Ditton Junction to the ICI plant at Weston Point, Runcorn, via the Old Bridge and Folly Lane. We travelled from Ditton (using a Super D engine) and these engines didn't have a covered cab, so we had to put a tarpaulin sheet over the gap between the cab and tender. It was okay when we were pulling the wagons from Ditton to Runcorn because we were travelling forward, but on the way back we travelled tender first.
>
> The icy cold wind and snow used to blow through the gaps that couldn't be covered; I used to push my back into the boiler face and pull my collar up around my face as much as possible; this meant that I had a scorched backside but was freezing at the front. This is another of the enduring memories I have of being a fireman.

Mr Littler recalls another freight working known as Target 86, where the crew would have a guard and a brakevan and worked from Widnes goods yard to the Marsh, to Tanhouse on the Widnes to Warrington low-level line. And the train went to the Everite Asbestos Works to take up wagons or clean it out:

> It was a mixed goods train and empties. But we always took out a full load of wagons and vans of asbestos material; pipes, tanks, whatever. It was a Class 2 that worked that. Well, it was never a full train and they always had the bank engine behind to take it up there. The rest of the way it was downhill or on the level.
>
> They had the old 18 inch (as a bank engine). A Class 8 up there would be, say, forty mineral – but minerals like a 7-ton vehicle with 20 ton in it. Now your load would be thirty-eight or thirty-nine with a brakevan. But if your engine wasn't in bloody good nick, it wouldn't take it. If a couple of glands were blowing or [the engine] was a bit weak, or whatever, you'd automatically whistle for a banker. And you'd go clear of the signal box and they'd let the banker out behind you, not that they pushed very much. It would take three or four wagons off you because they were old blokes; it was the old men's shunting link. And these 18-inchers didn't pull much anyway.

The cramped interior of Widnes shed is shown to good effect in this scene of Standard 2MT No.78035. This was the type of engine often used on the Everite Asbestos Works job recalled by David Littler. A sister engine to this, 78039, was transferred away to Willesden in 1963 and Colin Turton took the engine as far as Crewe. (Roger Scholes)

Their mate would whistle and they'd push about six or seven wagons and then you'd start off and drag them off them ... and as you got to Farnworth and Bold, at the top on the level, they just eased off you and you carried on going.

Another person who worked at Widnes shed was Colin Turton, who began work there as a cleaner in October 1960. Holding an interest since childhood, he had wanted to join the railways straight from school at fifteen years of age but his father insisted he complete his education to seventeen:

I did so but the desire to go on the railway remained. I joined the railway at nineteen and was taken on as a cleaner but my first job was actually shovelling coal from the floor back into wagons. I went to a school at Garston for training for two weeks and passed out as a passed cleaner in January 1961. From that point on I carried out footplate duties.

Mr Turton recalls there being a mixture of older, middle-aged and younger staff at Widnes shed. The older blokes were fine with the younger staff and mostly the older men were considered to be 'like father figures', Mr Turton said.

Widnes's engines were chiefly freight types or shunting engines. Mr Turton recalls the facilities and the shed itself being kept in good order. 'We kept our engines in good order even though they were mostly old.' One interesting thing he recalls from the period was the transfer of two Riddles Standard 3 2-6-2 tanks Nos 84023 and 84024 which Widnes received from Folkestone: 'They did not stay long,' he recalls.

Pages from a Fireman's Diary – Colin Turton

Sunday 14 May 1961
Special with No.48338.
Start: 5a.m., finish 1.15p.m.

Monday 15 May 1961
Target 85 (Marsh sidings, Widnes Dock) with No.47616 and engine preparation.
Start 10p.m., finish 6a.m.

Tuesday 16 May 1961
Target 85 with No.47616 and engine preparation.
Start 6.30p.m., finish 2.30a.m.

Wednesday 17 May 1961
Shed turner's mate & engine preparation.
Start 6.30p.m., finish 2.30a.m.

Thursday 18 May 1961
Target 85 with No.78035.
Start 9p.m., finish 5a.m.

Friday 19 May 1961
Target 85 with No.78035.
Start 6.30p.m., finish 2.30a.m.

Saturday 20 May 1961
Special with Nos 48017 & 48296.
Start 3.30p.m., finish 11.30p.m.

Sunday 21 May 1961
Day off.

Monday 22 May 1961 (Whit Monday, bank holiday)
Passenger train with 42078 from Widnes (South) to Warrington Bank Quay then Timperley.
Start 12.13p.m., finish 7.50p.m.

Tuesday 23 May 1961
Engine cleaning.
Start 7.50a.m. to 3.50p.m. (Was to have been a rest day.)

Wednesday 24 May 1961
Shed turner's mate.
Start 6a.m., finish 2p.m.

Thursday 25 May 1961
Target 88 (Hutchinson St Yard shunting) with No.47616.

Friday 26 May 1961
Engine preparation.
Start 2.30a.m., finish 10.30a.m.

Saturday 27 May 1961
Special with No.44384.
Start 6a.m., finish 2p.m.

By 1963, Widnes shed's allocation had been nearly halved from that of 1955 and four diesels were beginning to share the stalls with steam.

Colin Turton remembers some of the ruses certain footplatemen would use to get in some overtime:

There was a steam banana run [Garston docks to the north] and we were supposed to be relieved at Preston. A young Garston driver was in control of the train. He deliberately did not stop at Preston, passing the relief crew. He did this purely to get overtime. When challenged he simply said he'd forgotten!

Widnes on a grey 10 September 1961 with Standard 2MT No.78035 and Ivatt 2-6-2 tank No.41244 prominent. The latter engine was transferred to Llandudno Junction from 1 December 1962 and then to Bank Hall shed, Liverpool, from July 1964. After that shed's closure in October 1966, it was briefly transferred to Aintree before being condemned in November 1966. (W.T. Stubbs, courtesy of the Engine Shed Society)

Pages from a Fireman's Diary – Colin Turton

Monday 6 May 1963
Shed turner's mate.
Start 8.30a.m., finish 4.30p.m.

Tuesday 7 May 1963
Special with No.78039 to Crewe (engine being transferred to Willesden). Handed over to relief crew who took engine on to London. Colin and his driver travelled home as passengers.
Start 6.15a.m., finish 2.15p.m.

Wednesday 8 May 1963
Rest day.

Thursday 9 May 1963
No record of specific duty.
Start 8.30a.m., finish 4.30p.m.

Friday 10 May 1963
Morning Leeds with No.42972.
Start 7.35a.m., finish 3.45p.m.

Saturday 11 May 1963
Bolton with No.48045.
Start 10a.m., finish 7.25p.m.

Enthusiast and railway photographer Brian Swinn visited Widnes shed on Sunday 22 September 1963 and noted the following sixteen engines on shed. The sole Austerity 2-8-0 No.90532 had already been withdrawn from service:

Widnes shed after closure; a posse of railway enthusiasts investigate an engine running by on the top line behind the coaling stage. Royal Scot 7P 4-6-0 No.46128 *The Lovat Scouts* runs by providing a bit of excitement for the visitors who would otherwise have found very little else around, 21 November 1964. (Stephen Wolstenholme collection)

D2372	D2394	D3794	44588	46423	46424	47616	47656	48045	48129	48139	48296
48536	48709	48758	90532								

Freight developments in the Widnes area were rapidly changing, as evidenced by this article which appeared in the railway press during 1964. It illustrated some of the problems being experienced in not having adequately trained diesel crews during the transition period to modern power:

> The former Great Central and Midland goods yard at Tanhouse Lane, Widnes, is now [mid-1964] handling probably its heavy [sic] freight tonnage, despite the fact that the Widnes Loop, upon which it is situated, is due for complete closure and is only awaiting the Minister's decision.
>
> Very little tonnage is received from the CLC route; the bulk now arrives over the chord line from Widnes LNW Vine Yard, a spur opened some three years ago to allow the Tanhouse yard engine to be serviced at Widnes MPD. In addition to the twice daily trains of anhydrite hoppers from Long Meg (between Settle and Carlisle) to the United Sulphuric Acid Corporation's Tanhouse plant, an increasing amount of cement traffic is being handled.
>
> Adjacent to the acid plant is the Cement Manufacturing Co. factory, which is also the main depot for an extensive road distribution fleet. To supplement the factory output a new bulk cement receiving bay has been built and is fed from a spur track on the USAC line. Since April 1964 a 1,000-ton train of bottom-discharge cement wagons from Snodland in Kent has been running three times a week, hauled by English Electric Type 4 diesels from Crewe, which reverses at Ditton Junction and Widnes Vine Yard, then propels its train over the chord line into Tanhouse yard. The empties return next day, hauled by a Warrington Class 5, which runs to Sutton Oak (St Helens) and then reverses to St Helens Junction, reaching Crewe via Earlestown. The loaded train was originally routed this way but the Type 4 diesel spread the track at Sutton Oak and is now temporarily banned from there.
>
> Under the freight rationalisation plans for the north west, Tanhouse Lane yard is due to close as the sidings are only accessible by setting back over a level crossing from the passenger station; the intention is to abandon these and lift the track if consent is obtained to withdraw passenger trains ... Elsewhere in the area, the closed yard at Widnes North, on the CLC direct line, has been reopened and leased to Motor Vehicle Collection Ltd, who have made it their distribution depot for the north-west home market and exports via Liverpool docks.
>
> Block trains of carflats are received from both Luton and Oxford on alternate days, and the Oxford train has been seen to depart loaded with Halewood-built Ford vans for the GPO. Crewe North Britannia Pacifics have been hauling the BMC trains, running via Manchester

With safety valves lifting, ex-LMS Ivatt 2MT or 'Mickey Mouse' No.46422 runs past the coaling stage at Widnes shed on 27 August 1949. When photographed, the engine was barely nine months old having been completed at Crewe Works late in 1948. The tender bears the original BR legend that preceded the large lion on wheel motif which was introduced in the early 1950s and superseded by the smaller lion on wheel emblem. (Ken Fairey)

Piccadilly and Cornbrook Junction to gain the CLC route. The Vauxhalls from Luton were scheduled to have BR/Sulzer Type 4 diesel haulage, but not until the very first run on 26 May was it discovered that the relief crew in the Manchester area were not diesel-trained.[7]

Colin Turton said crews used to like an 8a.m. start which involved a job where they travelled to Bolton as passengers and brought a freight back to Widnes yard. He recalls the train having originated 'out from Wakefield':

> We travelled to Bolton from Widnes North to Manchester Central and then walked over to Victoria to get to Bolton. We liked day jobs really. I liked turns that went a bit further ... Crewe runs and Carnforth. I also liked passenger turns but I never got many as we lost them in 1962. I did get to go to Helsby on a Ditton to Birkenhead Woodside and also got to work a Ditton to Warrington Bank Quay and on to Timperley service.
>
> Men at 8D did not like the 4.00p.m. to Bickershaw Colliery. You never stopped for a moment – lots of shunting back and forward. The main change I remember was losing passenger work.

Mr Turton said that there were no lodging turns from Widnes shed by the time he joined. Older shed staff had told him they were common in the war years. In the years he was there, Mr Turton said they worked out to Heaton Mersey (Stockport), Wigan, Warrington, Edge Hill, Crewe (from Runcorn Folly Lane) and along the North Wales coast.

Soon, news began to circulate of Widnes shed's imminent demise. Its allocation of engines had considerably declined during the early 1960s, passenger turns were removed from its rosters and generally there was an impression of decline in local train traffic.

Colin Turton said indications of the shed's impending closure 'started as gossip'. He was offered a transfer to work at Speke Junction but did not want to go, so was made redundant in early 1964.

Four years after Widnes shed had closed it was still possible to see steam working through the local yards less than four months away from the total elimination of steam from BR's standard-gauge lines. In this view Speke Junction's 8F 2-8-0 No.48206 heads a freight through Hutchinson Street yard, Widnes. The loco was barely a week away from withdrawal following Speke's closure to steam in May 1968. (Les Fifoot)

But it did not take him long to realise he was missing the railways and steam locos, so he eventually secured a job at Dallam in 1966, where he stayed until that shed closed its doors to steam later the following year.

David Littler recalls that Widnes men learnt about three months beforehand of the shed's impending closure. Some men decided to take, at the time, quite lucrative offers to retire, while others decided on transfers to other sheds, including Speke Junction, which was referred to by many men as Garston:

> When they started closing sheds they got rid of all the young men and kept all the old drivers and the old firemen. The youngest ones were let go. Seniority counted and the union rep [told] the railways, what you're doing is cutting your own throat.
>
> The top eighteen drivers at Widnes shed were sixty-three years or older, and then you dropped down to a load who were in their late fifties; and then ... down to the senior firemen thirty-five or thirty and the likes of ourselves who were twenty-eight or twenty-nine who had passed out for driving.
>
> And the union rep put it to them that they should call for volunteers because the older drivers, apart from getting, I think it was, three weeks' pay for every year of service ... also got a lump sum. I got £94 for my service, but I was only on £9 10 shillings a week then. So it was ten weeks' pay. But a driver [aged] sixty-three could then go on the dole.
>
> The railway came up with a scheme where they would pay them half-pay if they had turned sixty, until they became eligible for the pension, with most of the balance picked up by the dole. So every driver over sixty volunteered to be retrenched and it enabled the younger men to stay on.

When it became clear that Widnes was really going to close, Mr Littler also decided it was time to leave the railways:

A view of the turntable area at Widnes shed following closure. Years of ash and old coal clinker cover the ground and old factory buildings skirt the shed site. The viaduct on the left carries the double track Liverpool–Manchester line, with milepost 17 almost directly in line with the centre of the turntable. (Les Fifoot)

What put me off going to Garston was I was married with three kids and a mortgage. Now, I went on loan to Garston ... we'd been informed Widnes shed was closing and it was when the banana boats came in; they used to collect firemen and drivers [from other sheds] for two weeks.

I was with the same driver and we were just taking bad bananas to Wigan. But I used to sign on at Widnes, get an hour's walking time to Ditton station, get on a train there and get off at Allerton, twenty-five minutes walking to Garston, do a seven- or eight-hour day and then back. I was getting twelve hours' pay for a seven-hour day.

Now if I transferred and signed on at Garston [when Widnes closed] I was going to do a twelve-hour day for seven hours' pay ... That put me off and I ended up going in the ICI ... I ran a sodium bisulphite plant.

After Widnes shed's closure on 13 April 1964, its modest allocation of locomotives was transferred to Speke Junction or Sutton Oak sheds. But for a few years afterwards, Widnes would on occasions have an engine or two on shed being serviced with coal or water before taking out a local train working (in particular the return Long Meg anhydrite trains). However, my last visit there in 1965 presented a truly sad site – an entirely empty depot with the effects of abandonment plainly obvious.

By the early 1990s, one wall of the shed building was still standing but the general scene around the former shed precinct was one of industrial decay. In early October 1996, the Engine Shed Society's *Link* journal reported that the south-facing wall of the former shed had been incorporated into a new line of fencing forming the boundary of the new Widnes central bypass road, and the west wall remained partially intact. Access could be gained via the original shed entrance in Croft Street. In autumn 2000, *Link* reported that the derelict remains of the shed still stood but the site appeared to have been abandoned. The shed floor and remaining part of the yard were heavily covered in vegetation.

On 1 March 2002, a site visit report published again in *Link* said the western and southerly walls of 8D still remained up to a height of about 8ft. Access to the site proper was not possible. Over at the former CLC shed site at Tanhouse Lane, Dave McGuire informed *Link*'s readers:

The site is covered by a small industrial estate and car scrapyard. A single line of rusty railway runs past the site, across a level crossing and under a [disused] footbridge – a lot of steps were missing but that did not deter me from taking a couple of shots from a higher vantage point, and past the site of Tanhouse Lane station.[8]

Three

8E NORTHWICH

Northwich shed was situated on the south side of the town's station and the shed yard was visible from there. After leaving the station it was just a short five-minute walk along Middlewich
Road and across the railway bridge, with the shed entrance accessed on the left. Northwich was the
last Cheshire Lines Committee shed to remain open and the last CLC shed building to survive when
it was demolished in February 1991.

A shed was first established in Northwich by the West Cheshire Railway in the latter half of the
nineteenth century (possibly 1869) when a two-track straight shed was built. Facilities were basic
but included a turntable. In December 1876 the shed was enlarged into a brick-built, four-track,
straight dead-ended facility and a larger, 50ft diameter turntable was installed. The work was
undertaken by William Leicester, after his tender for £3,445 had been accepted. A plan from 1892
depicts a four-road shed with a 'saw tooth' roof on the same site as the building which survived
until 1991. The Midland Railway sub-shedded three of its engines at Northwich from the early
1870s, in all probability 1873, when construction of Brunner, Mond & Co.'s Winnington Works
was started, and a contract with the Tideswell and Millers Dale Coal & General Merchant Co. was
signed on 25 October for the supply of limestone.

Midland Class 2 0-6-0s were regularly used on limestone traffic trains until 4F 0-6-0s began to
assume responsibility for these workings in 1928. Purpose-built hopper wagons replaced the long
trains of dumb-buffered wooden wagons from 1936 onwards.

By 1935, the turntable at Northwich shed had been replaced by a 70ft-diameter unit. Other shed
improvements included its reroofing in 1948 in a louvre style and the building of a brick screen.

Northwich was one of the final sheds on British Railways to see regular steam activity, not closing to steam until 4 March 1968 – just five months before the end of regular main-line steam on
BR. Steam, however, triumphantly returned to the depot in 1980 when some of the engines taking
part in the 150th anniversary of the Rainhill locomotive trials were serviced and refuelled at the
shed en route to the Lancashire celebrations.

Steam returned to Northwich shed on many occasions in the 1980s following its initial use for servicing engines taking part in the 150th celebrations of the opening of the Liverpool–Manchester Railway. On 18 July 1981 Coronation Pacific No.46229 *Duchess of Hamilton* is prepared for another railway enthusiast special. This engine, formerly an Edge Hill loco, is now preserved and has been re-streamlined to the outline as it first appeared in the late 1930s. The *Duchess* is in the National Collection on display at York's National Railway Museum. (Allan Sommerfield, courtesy of the Engine Shed Society)

After its closure to steam in 1968, Northwich shed saw continued use as a servicing point for diesels (and was coded NW) until 1984, after which it was abandoned.

* * *

The CLC, which was formed in 1863, incorporated the Cheshire Midland and West Cheshire Railways and was worked by Manchester, Sheffield and Lincolnshire Railway engines from the start. A survey of that railway's engine workings in 1886 showed that fourteen double-framed Sacre locos were based at Northwich in February that year. The allocation was made up of four 2-4-0s for working the passenger rosters, ten 0-6-0s (one of them a comparatively new Class 6C, No.459, later designated J12 by the LNER) and nine of the much older Class 23s. Five of Northwich's allocation was outstationed at the shed's three sub-sheds: Helsby and Alvanley, Winsford (both closed in 1929) and Chester (closed in 1960).[9]

Being surrounded by various salt and chemical works, Northwich was by far the busiest place on the Manchester Central to Chester line. At Grouping, in 1923, the shed's allocation had grown to thirty-five locos: six D7 4-4-0s, twenty-seven J9s (the class only totalled thirty-one engines) and two J10s. A mass transfer of J9s to the North British section in Scotland during 1924/25 left just six examples of this class at Northwich (Nos 5738–43) and these stayed at the shed until their withdrawal in the 1930s. The last to go was No.5743 in December 1936.

On 16 July 1929 a brand-new Sentinel steam railcar CLC No.602 arrived at Northwich to work the Winsford branch passenger service, and the sub-shed at Winsford was closed as a result. The railcar's diagram began at 6.45a.m. with a Northwich–Winsford service, and for the rest of the day it worked a shuttle service between Winsford and Cuddington, apart from a 12.20p.m. (SO) Winsford–Northwich train, and return working at 1.10p.m. When the Winsford passenger service ended on 31 December 1930, the steam railcar was transferred to Brunswick shed.

In 1930 also, the D7s were transferred away and they were replaced with a batch of C13 class 4-4-2 tanks. These engines were responsible for the shed's passenger workings for the next decade. At the start of 1934, Northwich's shed allocation of twenty-nine engines consisted of:

C13s – 5002, 5009, 5020, 5050 and 6055
J9s – 5738, 5739, 5741, 5742 and 5743
J10s – 5081, 5116, 5640, 5641, 5678, 5787, 5790, 5793, 5794, 5795, 5799, 5802, 5803, 5829 and 5851
N5s – 5518, 5914, 5915 and 5935

Following the demise of the J9s, more J10s were drafted to the shed and these long-lived engines were a familiar sight at Northwich well into BR days, being responsible for most of the local freight work and even being noted on an occasional passenger roster. Two J10s were still at work at Northwich in 1959, but in December that year 65134 was withdrawn, leaving stablemate 65169 with the honour of being the last ex-LNER engine to be shedded there.

After some Stanier 8F 2-8-0s were trialled on the limestone trains in November 1938, some of these engines were drafted to the trains; the 8Fs would take seventeen loaded hoppers. For the first few years Nos 8026, 8044, 8074, 8087 and 8089 from Heaton Mersey shed were regularly used on these workings, and three were sub-shedded at Northwich. However, 0-6-0s continued to be used on these trains intermittently, including Midland 2Fs and 3Fs.

During the 1940s a variety of former Great Central loco classes broke new ground at Northwich, including the three varieties of 4-4-0s (D6, D9 and D10s), J11 0-6-0s and L1 2-6-4 tanks. The first D6 No.5865 arrived in November 1941, staying four years before being transferred to Brunswick, only to be transferred back to Northwich in mid-1946 renumbered as 2104, ending its days at the shed that December. Three other D6s were transferred to Northwich and were each withdrawn from that shed: 5859 (June 1942, withdrawn September 1945); 2101 (ex-5855 arrived August 1946, withdrawn 16 December 1947); and 2106 (previously 5874) which also arrived in August 1946 and became the last member of the class to be withdrawn on New Year's Eve 1947, just

Northwich's ex-LNER D10 class 4-4-0 No.62658 *Prince George*, with safety valves hissing, awaits the green light at the town's station with a five-coach stopping train, probably to Manchester, on 14 September 1954. The surviving D10s were chiefly based at Northwich in their final years of service and this loco remained at this shed until 31 August 1955 when it was withdrawn. Soon after it was cut up at Gorton Works, where it had been built in November 1913. (RCTS - PHW0864)

missing out on becoming a BR engine. Two D9s (2305 and 2322) were at Northwich for a year from August 1946 and then were replaced by D10s No.2655 *The Earl of Kerry* and 2657 *Sir Berkeley Sheffield*. Classmate No.2652 *Edwin A. Beazley* replaced 2657 in September 1947, and two months later 2650 *Prince Henry* arrived to supplement the other two D10s.

Fred Darbyshire who spent several years at Trafford Park shed in the 1940s was on a shed job one morning having just prepared a tank engine for a passenger job, when shed foreman, Percy Cook, with the usual pipe in mouth, came to inform him he had 'a nice job' for him.

Mr Darbyshire was instructed to go with Sam Webb on ex-GN tank No.4517, which had been specially cleaned for the job to haul a Directors' special and work it from Manchester Central to Chester and return. The train was a Directors' coach and a luggage coach; the train had a guard and waiter-cum-chef aboard:

The Directors' coach was a special coach design for directors to use and had a connecting door to the luggage coach so their waiter could serve drinks etc.

We backed on to [the] luggage coach, leaving the Directors' coach with a clear view behind. We hooked on, and with a toot on the whistle, off we went. First stop was Northwich station where the directors got out; we pulled into a side road and waited. After a while we got the nod and pulled into the station and picked up our passengers.

Next we took them down a branch line to Bidston; not much time spent there, we pushed the train back to the main line, then drove towards Chester; we stopped en route for lunch ... Once the directors had been made comfortable, the waiter came into the luggage/guard's coach, where we'd made ourselves comfortable, with a large plate of sandwiches and a couple of bottles of beer each. Before we left the waiter came again, this time with the 'leav-ings': sponge pudding and custard. I did not need asking twice. After that little lot, we got the okay to carry on to Chester; it's not nice firing on a full stomach of sponge pudding. The directors got out of the train in the station and we pulled into a side road, where we hooked off and drove to the engine shed to water and turn, ready for the return trip.

The directors took a little longer than they thought and one came to Sam and apologised and asked would he try his best to get the train back to Manchester in a hurry as they had appointments to keep. We got a clear run and didn't get slowed anywhere, I'm sure Sam broke all the records ... I'm not sure [of the timing] but it was fast. On arrival at Manchester Central the same director came to Sam to thank him and give him a couple of pounds, one for each of us. It was standard practice for them to tip the engine crew. We then travelled back to Trafford Park to park the engine in the back road and then sign off. I then had to get home; this time it was via Manchester Victoria, I didn't want to wait for the 7.45p.m. to Wigan Central.[10]

Northwich became part of the Eastern Region of British Railways upon Nationalisation on 1 January 1948, having an allocation of twenty-nine engines, and was still 100 per cent ex-Great Central in allocated locos with a mix of D10, J10, J11, L1 and N5s. On 28 November 1948 logic got the better of historic allegiances and Northwich was transferred to the London Midland Region (LMR). It was expected that eventually the loco types based there would only be from LMS parentage; however, it took a little longer than was expected.

Once Northwich came under LMR control it was little more than a year before the shed received some Stanier 8Fs in its own right – five being drafted to the shed in January 1950: 48045, 48046, 48555, 48706 and 48756. The following month, Northwich was assigned the shed code 13D but it is doubtful that many locos carried the shedplate because the code was changed again to 9G from 22 May 1950. On that day, the shed's allocation was thirty-nine engines, eleven of which were former LMS engines. By the end of the year, eight of Northwich's J10s were in store at Trafford Park shed – they had been replaced with further Stanier 8Fs.

From the late 1940s, the ex-Great Central 'Directors' became a common sight in charge of Manchester Central–Chester Northgate stopping trains during the next six years or so and, by January 1954, 62650, 62652, 62656 and 62659 were working from Northwich shed. In May 1952 an 'Improved Director' (D11) No.62669 Ypres was also drafted to Northwich to assist the D10s. Five other D11s were eventually transferred to Northwich, until all were removed to the Eastern Region in April 1958. Eight of the D10s, however, were withdrawn from Northwich shed, the two exceptions being 62654 and 62657 which ended their days at Trafford Park, Manchester.

The large L1 (later reclassified L3) 2-6-4 tanks were new arrivals too in the 1940s to Northwich; two engines, 5274 and 5343, arrived in 1943 to work at Hartford Exchange sidings, carrying out banking duties on the Winnington branch. This had, at the end of its length, the CLC's steepest gradient, a short stretch of 1 in 53. A North Eastern A7 4-6-2 tank, No.1129, had briefly been tried on this exacting line but had stayed for less than a month. When the L1s were withdrawn in the early 1950s they were replaced with ex-LNWR Super Ds with 49435 replacing the withdrawn 69062 (previously 5343) in May 1951, while 49304 superseded 69052 (ex-5274) in August 1954.

Robin Bamber ventured on to Northwich shed in June 1955 after cycling all the way from Preston and was rewarded for his marathon efforts by seeing thirty-one engines, all bar one of them (ex-LMS diesel shunter 12032) being steam. Interestingly, there were six ex-Great Central Railway 4-4-0 'Directors' or 'Improved Directors' on shed: 62653 Sir Edward Fraser; 62658 Prince George; 62661 Gerard Powys Dewhurst; 62664 Princess Mary; 62665 Mons and 62669 Ypres. There were six other ex-LNER engines present on that day.

A new freight working appeared on the 1956 Working Timetable linking Wigan with Northwich, with the front portion of the freight being hopper wagons for the ICI plant in the Cheshire town. The 10.40hrs train started as a light engine movement from Springs Branch shed to Bamfurlong North End yard. From the grid iron sidings in that yard the train would work through Bamfurlong Junction to Warrington and on to Northwich. This train had a balancing turn which departed Northwich at 14.45hrs. In the early years this train was usually a roster for a Super D or an Austerity 2-8-0, but by the mid-1960s it was a regular booking for a Stanier Black 5.[11]

Another enthusiast and railway photographer, Brian Swinn, visited Northwich shed on Sunday 15 December 1957 and noted the following thirty-two engines on shed, all but two of them steam:

12030	13175	42440	42449	43538	43651	44155	44392	44341	44456	48045	48135
48155	48254	48257	48340	48368	48426	48521	48555	48626	48693	48697	48711
48717	48742	63681	63766	65134	65158	65169	65202				

As the 1950s progressed, the LMR influence began to gain the upper hand at Northwich shed and former GCR engines were either withdrawn or transferred to other sheds, with ex-LMS or BR Standards replacing them. On 20 April 1958 Northwich's code was changed again, this time to 8E. To illustrate the change in motive power lineage, by October that year, of the thirty-two engines allocated to the shed, only two were ex-LNER engines: J10s Nos 65134 and 65169. Following the withdrawal of the latter engine in February 1960, the Great Central's connection with Northwich shed was finally extinguished.

Ian Casey commuted to and from Northwich from 1959 while he was studying for his Eleven Plus. As he wasn't permitted to leave school five minutes early in order to catch the 3.45p.m. train home, he had to spend an hour each afternoon on Northwich station waiting for the next train. He recalls:

Fortunately, Northwich had its shed and turntable right alongside the bay platform. To pass the time away I watched all the usual shed activity which eventually led to my interest in railways.

Northwich shed on a cold, wintry 15 December 1957 with a couple of the depot's J10 0-6-0s present, No.65202 leading, by the shear legs. This was previously one of fifteen locos in store at Trafford Park shed in August 1954. This loco was condemned at Northwich in March 1958. (Brian Swinn)

During the next two years I saw a transition in locomotives from the mainly Robinson 2-8-0s to a mixture of Stanier 8Fs, Crabs and Fowler 4Fs, which were affectionately known locally as 'Coffee Pots'. I still can remember stalwarts being 48039 and 44155.

Mr Casey said that in all his time observing at Northwich, he could never recall any named ex-LMS engines being on shed. But it was a different matter with Thompson B1s:

Northwich shed provided me with the distinction of seeing the loco with the shortest name on British Railways, 61018 *Gnu*, and one of the longest, 61215 *William Henton Carver*. Another frequent visitor at the time was 61249 *FitzHerbert Wright* or 'Fizzy Right' as we came to know it.

Station activities also provided some entertainment, as I recall a Chester local which entered the station too fast, possibly with a trainee driver or one that was asleep. The brakes were slammed on half-way down the platform and I stood dumbfounded as, with all wheels locked, the ex-LMS Fowler tank flew past me showering the station in sparks! There must have been some relieved passengers that day.

Coming from a railway town I had a number of uncles and cousins who were either guards or firemen at Northwich. They worked mainly the heavy freight trains with the ICI limestone hoppers from Buxton. These would thunder through the station at full pelt, especially if they had no banker in order to make it over Weaver Viaduct north of the station.

Mr Casey recalls that around six months before his commuting finished, events taking shape elsewhere had the effect of turning him into a 'true enthusiast' and motivated him to travel nationwide to see all classes of steam:

With pre-Christmas snow resting on nearby roofs, a wintry scene is evident at Northwich shed where Gorton-based ex-LNER O4 2-8-0 No.63681 is in light steam near the shed's turntable. The date was 15 December 1957. This loco survived in service until withdrawn in February 1962. (Brian Swinn)

The rebuilding of Manchester London Road into Piccadilly was the event and I can clearly see even now the large locomotive sweeping off the Crewe branch with corridor coaches and headboards saying the *Pines Express*. That loco was 70045 *Lord Rowallan* and in that same month I was to see the poets: 70030 *William Wordsworth*, 70031 *Byron* and 70032 *Tennyson*, along with 70033 *Charles Dickens* and all the Firths, 70049 to 70054.

There would be Scots and Patriots *Sir Frank Ree* and *Sir Frederick Harrison*, and Jubilees with wonderful names such as *Bihar and Orissa* and *Bellerophon*, so a whole new world opened up to me and, with like-minded friends from the grammar school, I travelled far and wide to see as much as I could.

In February 1962 the Manchester–Crewe electrified lines suffered from gale damage to the catenary. Although a fair amount of diesel multiple units were procured to replace temporarily immobilised electric sets, on 12 and 16 February steam had to take over many long-distance workings due to insufficient diesel locomotives. On 16 February northbound trains were diverted via Northwich and Jubilee class engines appeared to be in charge of most of the expresses.[12]

Among the ex-LMS types to be based at Northwich from the period 1950 to 1968 were Fowler and Stanier 2-6-4 tanks, 4Fs and Ivatt Class 2 2-6-0s. Midland 3Fs came and went, while memories of the shed in earlier times were revived when 2Fs Nos 58120 and 58123 were briefly transferred to the shed in November 1959. The pair's holiday at Northwich was short as they were transferred to Springs Branch later in the same month.

Brian Swinn returned to Northwich on Sunday 29 July 1962, by which time the shed hosted twenty-eight locos on shed – diesel shunters again were evident, as too a decidedly LMS flavour to the steam engine mix:

D3583	D3763	42761	44155	44341	44456	48017	48039	48118	48135	48166	48295
48340	48462	48511	48521	48631	48683	48693	48717	48764	63767	76089	78019
78055	78057	90179	90323								

In *Modern Railways'* July 1963 issue, it was reported that Royal Scot 4-6-0 No.46115 *Scots Guardsman* on 21 and 22 May was seen working the 4.40p.m. Manchester Central to Northwich stopping train, normally a 2-6-0 or 2-6-4T duty, and the following morning's 7.25a.m. train back to Manchester. This was challenged in the following month's issue by another correspondent who claimed 46115 was in charge of a 'special' routed this way to Chester, out on 21 May and back on 22 May. Another special was noted on this route on 7 June with Royal Scot 46129 *The Scottish Horse* in charge.

Three passenger excursions from the West Midlands to New Brighton passed through Northwich on 7 August 1963. Two from Brownhills and Pelsall were unexpectedly hauled throughout by Ivatt Class 4 2-6-0s Nos 43003 and 43022, while the third train, which came from Birmingham, had Standard Class 4 No.75034 in charge.[13]

An interesting visitor to Northwich shed three months later was Standard 9F No.92220 *Evening Star* on 9 November; this engine, of course, was famous for being the last steam locomotive built for British Railways, in March 1960, and the only one of its class to wear green livery in BR service.

Other Standards to see service at Northwich included a pair of Moguls 77011 and 77014, which were regular visitors around the Liverpool area in the mid-1960s, until the latter engine was surprisingly transferred to the Southern Region where it survived in service until the end of steam on that part of BR in July 1967. A trio of Standard 2s were also based at Northwich: 78038, 78055 and 78057.

Block freight workings also provided work into the Northwich area by 1964. The ICI limestone working between quarries in the High Peak area of Derbyshire and the ICI Alkali Division Works near Northwich brought, on average, six trains a day moving over 1.5 million tons of traffic annually and giving a turnaround time of 1.25 days for the entire wagon fleet. This traffic was carried in 46-ton, fully fitted steel bogie wagons, with sixteen wagons to a train.[14]

A busy scene at a sunny Northwich shed in May 1962, with some evidence of the ex-LNER locos that used to dominate this shed's roster board. From left to right is ex-LNER O4/8 Nos 63895 and 63805, Black 8 No.48403, another two unidentified members of that class and a WD 2-8-0. (David Dyson)

Former Crosti-boilered 9F 2-10-0 No.92022 is about to take the turntable at Northwich shed on 20 August 1966. Already souvenir hunters have removed the big loco's smokebox number and its unkempt condition was typical of these experimental locos that were later converted back to a conventional boiler set-up. When the photograph was taken, this loco was based at Speke Junction shed. Later transferred to Birkenhead shed in February 1967, it was condemned when that shed closed in November that year. (Brian Swinn)

Patricroft shed's very grimy Caprotti valve-geared Standard 5MT No.73127 simmers beside the coal elevator at Northwich shed on 11 April 1965. In the foreground is the turntable pit and piles of ash and clinker from cleaned-out smokeboxes or fireboxes. This engine was sent new to Shrewsbury shed when it entered service with British Railways in August 1956. Transferred to Patricroft, Manchester, in early September 1958, it remained based at that shed until its withdrawal in November 1967. It was scrapped at Cashmore's at Newport in February 1968. (RCTS - CHO4693)

Ivatt 2MT 2-6-0 No.46405 depicted at Northwich shed on a hazy 20 August 1966. This engine had been transferred to Northwich in March that year, after previously being based at Liverpool's Bank Hall shed. It was withdrawn in December 1966 and subsequently scrapped at Cashmore's Great Bridge the following April. (Brian Swinn)

Stanier 8F 2-8-0 No.48754 shifts a sister class member at Northwich shed on 20 August 1966. There was always a good collection of Stanier 8Fs present at this shed right until the end. This loco was completed at Doncaster Works in October 1945 and spent time variously allocated to depots in the Midlands, London, North Wales and Cheshire. By the time of this photograph, No.48754 was a Chester Midland engine; it was withdrawn from service in June 1967 and scrapped at Cashmore's Great Bridge three months later. (Brian Swinn)

By far the most numerous class to be based at Northwich were the Stanier 8Fs which were working from there right up to the shed's closure. In all, thirty-one of this class ended their days at the shed; among them the now-preserved 48151. The longest resident of this class was 48717 which arrived in April 1950 and was not withdrawn from service until April 1967. By contrast, 48493 arrived in mid-February 1968 and then moved to Speke Junction when Northwich closed to steam on 2 March.

Steam locomotives did return to Northwich in later years: an open day on 18 May 1980 saw Merchant Navy Pacific No.35029 *Clan Line* in company with ex-LNER A4 Pacific 4498 *Sir Nigel Gresley*, BR tank No.80079 and Stanier Black 5, No.5000. Memories were revived of the good old days on the limestone trains when the last of that day's hopper trains arrived at Lostock Gralam with a Class 25 diesel hauling eighteen loaded hoppers. The Black 5 was coupled to the front of the 25 and then stormed through Northwich station up to the ICI Works at Winnington – the first steam-hauled hopper train for twelve years. No.5000 was based at Northwich so it could work a 'Rocket 150' special train on 22 June 1980. At least three other steam locomotives were briefly 'shedded' at Northwich in the early 1980s in preparation for working various railtour trains, including ex-Southern 4-6-0 No.850 *Lord Nelson*, ex-LMS Jubilee No.5690 *Leander* and Duchess Pacific No.46229 *Duchess of Hamilton*.

Final closure of Northwich shed occurred on 26 November 1984 and, by 1989, rails in the shed yard and inside the shed building had been lifted. In early 2008 it was reported that the whole of the shed site was occupied by a housing development. The access road to the housing is evocatively called Pullman Way, with the road approximately in the position of the former shed entrance.

W.A. Stanier's first of 842 Black 5s, a class built between 1934 and the early 1950s, No.5000 was photographed inside Northwich engine shed on Saturday 23 October 1982 after working light engine from Chester. This engine, shown here in its LMS livery, was selected to represent its class in the National Collection and was withdrawn from Lostock Hall shed in October 1967 as BR No.45000. (David Ingham/ Wikimedia Commons)

Northwich shed played host to a wide range of preserved locomotives after its closure to steam in March 1968. Here, ex-Southern Railway 4-6-0 No.850 *Lord Nelson* is seen coaled and ready for its next railtour, in company with British Rail diesel-electric 25160, 12 June 1981. (Allan Sommerfield, courtesy of the Engine Shed Society)

Four

8F SPRINGS BRANCH (WIGAN)

Springs Branch shed was established by the London & North Western Railway in around 1847, possibly even earlier, and initially contained a two-track, straight-through shed with turntable. In 1864 a timber-built, temporary single-track shed was added at the southern end of the shed yard but five years later both sheds were demolished to allow for track realignment. A new brick-built, eight-track, straight dead-ended shed with a twin-hipped slate roof was built and located to the south of the original shed site, on the eastern side of the main line, about a mile south of Wigan North Western railway station. Facilities at the new shed included a coal stage with overhead water tank. The shed entrance was at the end of a cul-de-sac in Morris Street.

The shed was extended by the addition of a brick-built, eight-track, straight dead-ended shed with a northlight-pattern roof along the eastern wall. The new shed became known as No.2, with the former shed referred to as No.1. In the mid-1930s facilities at Springs Branch were improved by the addition of a mechanical coaling plant and a larger water tank. The modernisation of Springs Branch was authorised in 1934 and took place the following year. Its final cost of £17,707 was recorded in January 1939.[15]

In 1946 the No.1 shed was reduced to a six-track shed by the removal of the two western tracks. It was re-roofed with a louvre-style roof and a brick screen was installed and, in 1955, the No.2 shed was re-roofed with a steel frame clad with corrugated iron sheeting.

Springs Branch was coded 10A until the late 1950s when it was re-designated as 8F, coming under the control of Edge Hill (Liverpool) shed. Until the mid-1950s the 8F code had been assigned to Warrington (CLC) 'shed'.

Springs Branch shed was closed to steam on 4 December 1967. Demolition of No.2 shed occurred in 1968 to make way for the diesel depot (subsequently coded SP). The No.1 shed continued in use for stabling, and later as a store, until it too was demolished in 1984. Springs Branch finally closed in May 1997 but was used by EWS to recover components from withdrawn locomotives. The sidings are still used for storage.

* * *

Eric Clayton joined the London Midland Scottish Railway (LMS) at Springs Branch in February 1943 when he was fifteen years of age. His father had wanted him to join the railway straight from school at fourteen, but when he went along to see if he could get a job he was told he was too young. Eric began work as a cleaner and did that until he became a passed cleaner (able to fire on any spare turns that came his way).

The key people at Springs Branch in 1944 according to Mr Clayton included the superintendent, a Mr Whitehead, the shedmaster, Mr Blake, and the shed foreman or running shift foremen: Mr A. Ramsdale, Mr J.R. Gaskell and Mr J. Green.

With the passage of time, Mr Clayton understandably can't remember his first firing turn but can recall one of his earliest:

We were on loan to Blackpool [shed] and worked from Blackpool North to Bradford on a passenger train and then the return journey. It was quite exciting seeing as I was only sixteen at the time – every young boy's dream.

In those days you had to get 313 firing turns to get on the first firing rate. When I went [on loan] to Willesden in 1944 I was firing all the time so I got my rate up quickly.

At Springs Branch there were about 100 cleaners in 1944 and 1945. When you got passed you knew there wasn't much chance of getting firing turns.

It was quite an experience at Willesden. I got matched with a driver who had come from Bangor in North Wales and he was in the top link. I worked mainly on freights but we had quite a few passenger jobs out of Euston. One of the jobs was to go to Camden and then to Carlisle. We'd book off at Crewe. Then work a fish train to Fleetwood. On Saturdays we'd work the Irish Mail.

We'd work trains with fifteen coaches on from Crewe to Euston ... we'd work on Royal Scots, 6112 [*Sherwood Forester*], a taper boiler version [and] some with parallel boilers too.

The rebuilt Scots used to ride better, they didn't roll about as much and they would steam much better than the parallel boiler engines.

Mr Clayton enjoyed his eighteen months spent at Willesden. The men brought in to assist with crews at that shed were put up at the railway barracks which were pretty basic:

All you had was a little single room and all that was in it was a bed and maybe a chair. There were places for a bath or to have a shave, a bathroom, and also a kitchen where you could buy a meal.

Most of the men were friendly, helpful and accepted us. On a few occasions we worked a train carrying [ex] POWs from Italy to Tilbury docks for repatriation. Also, trains from Kensington to Kirkham Lane with RAF personnel for demobilisation.

In 1946, after he had accrued the necessary firing turns, Mr Clayton decided to return to Springs Branch: 'While at Willesden rationing was on and I was looking after myself – doing my own shopping and washing – I just got fed up with it.'

The longest journey he covered during his Willesden stay was working Willesden to Blackpool and then returning the following day – both passenger trains – then back on duty after twelve hours, no consideration, it was part of the job:

I was doing twelve to fourteen hours' work a day. There were three little cafes [near the shed] that we used to use [for meals] but there was nothing open at 2a.m. if you finished then, so you had to buy some food in the barracks. We'd make sandwiches; we managed.

Upon returning, Springs Branch had to pay him the lowest rate for a fireman, as he had completed the required number of firing turns, so Mr Clayton knew they would make sure he was rostered on firing jobs instead of cleaning engines. Back at Springs Branch, the range of rosters he would get included goods and passenger jobs – trip jobs to the nearby collieries, some jobs to Carlisle on goods trains, some to Crewe or Manchester or the docks in Liverpool:

But when I got further up the links I got a really good driver – Percy Wilson – he was a proper good engineman, no doubt about it. But you had to know him. He would deliberately lose time; but he was saving the fireman work. But when he got to the top of a bank he would regain all the time he had lost.

Percy was in the Battle of the Somme in the First World War but he never mentioned it [during his working life]. I fired for him for over two years and he never hammered me once.

The late Fred Darbyshire was transferred to Springs Branch from Lower Ince shed when that facility closed in March 1952. He became a very good friend of Eric Clayton. At first, he was assigned to the Control link and after he had been at Springs Branch for a while he was sent to Plodder Lane for a week:

I remember being asked to travel passenger to Bolton Plodder Lane shed [ex-LNWR]. This job was all week working in the passenger link on the local push-and-pull train between Bolton Great Moor Street and Manchester Exchange ... and Bolton and Wigan North Western.

The train consisted of a 2-6-2 Class 2 tank engine No.84010 converted for push-and-pull, hauling one or two coaches to a destination then pushing them on the return journey; the rear coach had the facility for the guard on the trip out, and the driver on the return trip, which meant the poor fireman had to fire and drive the engine on the return trip; the fireman got his signals from the driver, all the fireman did was open/close the regulator and 'notch up' as we said on the LNER.

The driver controlled the braking of the train. I also remember working light engine to Horwich Loco Works, I'm not too sure what engine we took but it was due for breaking up as scrap.

Plodder Lane's passenger service was on its way out when I went there for the week.

My mate Bob Fox also worked at Plodder Lane; his only trip there was working a local goods. When they returned to the shed, the driver told Bob there was enough time left for them to dispose of the engine, [but] to the driver's amazement Bob said, 'Sorry, I've a train home to catch', and off he went. Bob never heard anything else about the incident. But remember, Bob had to first get to Bolton Trinity Street station, then walk to Springs Branch from Wigan L&Y station to book off duty; he finished up on overtime.[16]

Upon Lower Ince's closure, all of that shed's J10 class engines were transferred to Springs Branch, which took over responsibility for workings over the Wigan Central to Manchester Central route. In practical terms, however, the J10s quickly succumbed to more modern ex-LMS power on these trains. At the same time, passenger services were withdrawn over the St Helens branch from Lowton St Mary's, however the line continued to be used for trip freights.

Fred Darbyshire's term at Springs Branch lasted almost five years. Clearly he had mixed feelings about this 'progress' but apart from missing some of the camaraderie that existed at the small ex-Great Central shed, and not being paired with many of the men he'd previously worked with at Lower Ince, there were advantages:

Pollitt J10 class 0-6-0 No.65157 in store at Springs Branch shed on 12 August 1961. This loco was formerly at Widnes shed and before that based at Trafford Park. Fred Darbyshire found that Springs Branch crews preferred ex-LMS locos over ex-LNER locos. (RCTS - CH04052)

The good thing about Springs Branch was its canteen. [Also] no more cleaning fires [at the end of duty] – they had workmen who disposed and coaled the engines as they came on the shed.

The biggest shock was all the engines were left-hand drive, this meant left-hand firing. This wasn't bad for the likes of Jack Green, who was a natural left-hander, but the rest of us had to learn pretty quickly and that was not easy. Some of the drivers didn't like you firing from their side and told you so. I reckoned the Super D was the worst example of the lot to get used to; I did eventually master it but not before losing the skin off my thumbs. It was also difficult to accept the way all the [Branch] drivers used full regulator.

A problem for Springs Branch drivers was the J10s and they did not seem to be able to cope with them when working on the main line, [so] in the main the J10s were kept on shunting jobs and as time went by they were sent to Trafford Park shed.[17]

Fred Darbyshire also recalled his mate Bob Fox telling him about working a local goods job with a J10 when the driver, Jack Jones, persisted in trying to use full regulator. The engine started to prime and, when they reached Coppull, Jack asked Bob why this was happening. Jack had had enough and asked Bob to take over as driver. This he did and they finished their shift without further problems.

In the time he spent at Springs Branch, Mr Darbyshire was booked to work with a variety of drivers, including Billy Williams, Bob Francis, Albert Whittaker and Harry Tolman. Initially starting in the Control link, Mr Darbyshire and others were used as replacements for staff that for one reason or another were unavailable for duty,

The link covered twenty-four hours with two sets of engine crews booking on duty at 12.05a.m., then one set every hour afterwards, making twenty-five sets throughout the day. These crews sat in the control mess room waiting for instructions and covered any job that came up in their eight-hour shift. The area control centre provided the work for these engine crew members, for example when a train was running late and the crew needed to be relieved because their time was up, or if a driver or fireman had not turned up for duty, or if there were any special trains. Mr Darbyshire recalled this waiting game:

Stanier and Fairburn tank engines were synonymous with the Wigan area in the 1950s and 1960s for working local passenger services. In this view, Stanier 4MT 2-6-4 tank No.42465 is shown soon after Bickershaw while heading a Manchester Central to Wigan Central stopping train in September 1964. (Tom Sutch)

Donald Hodgson and shunter Cliff Halliwell find time for a break at Wigan Canal sidings in the late 1950s, with Jinty 47392 as the backdrop. (Cliff Halliwell collection)

You could sit in the mess room four or five hours doing nothing, then get sent out on a job and finish up working overtime. In this link you never knew what time you would finish. After a couple of weeks my mate Bill was revelling in making overtime, but this did not always suit me.

One of the first jobs I remember working with Billy Williams was on the bank engines between Bamfurlong Junction and Round House Junction on the Whelley line (the old Lancashire Union line). This helped me master the most uncomfortable engine I ever worked on, the Super D. They had a very open cab, no anti-glare sheets to hang between tender and engine cab, so if you were running tender first in winter or in rain it was tough. Also, if you didn't hang on to the cab, you would fall off the half-moon-shaped seat that was attached to the cabside; you could get your right cheek on with the left foot on the quarter-shaped 12-inch-high platform.

Another hazard was the soft spring between engine and tender: this caused the tender and engine to bounce back and forth, keeping you on a fine balance; the other thing it did was shake coal down for you.[18]

Mr Darbyshire said the only good thing to be said for the Super Ds was they were a free-running engine. But after a week of 'knocking the skin off both my thumbs', trying both a long-handled and short-handled spade, firing left- and right-handed, he reckoned he had mastered the locos. From then on he treated it as he would a Great Northern tank engine: spread the coal thinly all over the box and keep the fire bouncing on the bars; so no big fires, which didn't make the fireman's life any easier.

At the front of the tender of the Super Ds, Mr Darbyshire recalled there being two U-shaped pipes, and if by chance the water scoop wheel got stuck when picking up water from troughs at speed, the tender would fill with water pretty quick with the surplus water escaping through these two pipes, washing the coal down on to the small footplate and making life even more uncomfortable for those on the footplate: 'I suppose a lot of the Springs Branch drivers thought we couldn't handle the Super Ds; however, as I'd said before on many occasions, if you can fire a J10 with a tender full of Bickershaw coal, you can fire anything.'

The ex-LNWR G2s or Super Ds were a regular part of the landscape in this part of Lancashire until their demise in the early 1960s. Here the Belpaire firebox rebuild (from the mid-1930s) of the 1899-built loco No.49002 has its tender piled high with coal ready for its next turn of duty at Springs Branch shed on 17 June 1962. This loco was withdrawn in September 1962 after more than sixty-three years' service. (RCTS - CH01775)

Eric Clayton said the Super Ds were a workhorse for pulling weight and if there was one available at Carlisle shed they'd always save it for crews from Wigan: 'A lot of people didn't like them – they were used to putting a big fire on – but with the Super Ds they wouldn't steam if you did that. You'd have to keep the fire really hot with a light fire.'

Soon it was time to move up to the bottom goods link at Springs Branch and Fred Darbyshire was paired with a good mate, Albert Whittaker. The first job he recalled of note was to relieve and work an express goods to Crewe, where they were relieved at Crewe North. The men proceeded to Crewe South shed where they took a break in the mess room before preparing an ex-Midland 2P 4-4-0, nicknamed 'Beetles' by Lancashire & Yorkshire railwaymen, according to Mr Darbyshire, to haul an eight-coach, all-stations passenger train to Wigan, where another crew would work the train forward:

> Albert ran the train to time quite easy, however he did give it some stick to keep on time. I found that I could put a good fire on which allowed me some time on the small seat. The 2P was similar to an LNER 10 hundred but of course not as good.
>
> My old schoolmate and former Springs Branch driver, Eric Clayton, tells me there were two of these [ex-Midland] engines based at Springs Branch, numbers 447 and 561, and they were used specifically for double heading duties between Wigan and Carlisle. One such train was the 02.01a.m. from Wigan to Glasgow; this train was made up of the 01.10a.m. from Manchester Exchange and the 12.45a.m. from Liverpool Lime Street. A portion of the Manchester train would be shunted on to the Liverpool train on platform 10 and that's when the Class 2P was attached to the front of the train to double head as far as Carlisle.[19]

At Carlisle the Class 2P was detached and stood down. The Wigan crew would be relieved, their shift over, and they would either travel home as passengers or take the engine to the shed,

The final Patriot built, No.45551, rests on shed at Springs Branch in 1961. By now it was an Edge Hill engine and is pictured here paired with a high-sided Fowler tender, in contrast to the customary lower tenders. This engine was condemned in June 1962 and scrapped later that year. However, with the current project to build a new Patriot from scratch, who knows whether this scene might be replicated in future at a preserved railway? (Eddie Bellass)

lodge overnight and double head a train back to Wigan the following day, or even run back home light engine.

Eric Clayton, too, recalls trips to Carlisle – particularly a Sunday working taking newspapers from Manchester Exchange to Glasgow, as far as Carlisle. Other workings he would do included the banana trains from Garston to Carlisle and stone trains from Wales to places such as Northwich or Liverpool; heading south there were meat trains from Carlisle to Crewe, as well as football or rugby specials to Euston for cup final matches.

On his second trip with Albert Whittaker, Fred Darbyshire received his first and only formal warning for his zeal in ensuring he had a good fire on for a tight schedule from Preston to Lancaster. The pair had caught a train to Preston then walked to Preston shed to get two engines ready for the road, one of which was a Black 5 for their passenger train:

> Time to go, our coaches are inside the station and the passengers are beginning to arrive, we back on to the train ... Albert tells me to put a good fire on, as we have to do 21 miles in twenty-one minutes to our first stop at Lancaster. I'm busy using the short time left before we leave, putting a tidy-sized fire on, the blower is blasting the black smoke up in the air, the engine is blowing off steam, I've got a full boiler. I'm ready for the twenty-minute sprint to Lancaster [when] an inspector appeared on the scene and complained to Albert about the smoke and noise. It didn't bother me, it was a scene I had repeated many a time at Manchester Central before setting off on a trip. [But] a few days later I got a Form 1 delivered to me at Springs Branch, telling me to be a good boy and not to create black smoke in a main-line station again![20]

Several weeks later, a Saturday Carlisle job came up which meant Mr Darbyshire rising at 4a.m., having breakfast and an early morning walk to the shed, only to learn that the job was cancelled. Later, Albert came into the mess room with the news that they would still be going to Carlisle, but instead had to relieve a London crew and work a milk train to the border city. Some five hours after booking on, they finally received the call to relieve the Londoners. Mr Darbyshire recounted what then happened:

> We walked across to the signal box where the train was waiting alongside: a 'Scot' with six milk tanks and a parcels coach ... We got the okay from the guard, a quick blast on the whistle, the signal went to go and off we went. Before I could get the spade down we were approaching

Preston, I never saw Wigan or Coppull stations, a nice run through Preston station and then Albert opened up again.

A 'Scot' in full flight (remember we only had a coach and six milk tanks as a load), well we might as well have been light engine. The only thing I did before picking up the spade again was to get water at Brock water troughs, through Carnforth station and on up and over Shap summit, having a good look at the spectacular scenery en route. The London fireman had taken the trouble to find a nice large lump of coal that fitted at the front of my seat; this allowed me to put my feet up when I sat down.

I think we [may have] touched the 'ton' going down Shap on the Carlisle side. We got relieved at Carlisle after a great trip and Albert looked at his watch and revised his plans for the afternoon. 'Right Fred,' he said, 'we'll go to the barracks, clean up, then go and watch the local derby, Carlisle versus Workington at Workington, a third division football match.'

After cleaning up, I met Albert and he said if we walk to the station up the line we can sneak onto the football special train without paying. This we duly did, and sneaked off the train at Workington and watched a good match.[21]

During summer there were plenty of excursion jobs for crews to work and being based at Wigan it was natural that specials to nearby Blackpool were very popular. Mr Darbyshire recalled the excursion jobs providing many options: book on duty, work to Blackpool and travel home as a passenger; a second crew might travel to Blackpool as passengers and work a train back to Wigan; another option was to work a train to Blackpool, bed the engine down on shed, book off duty, have several hours' rest, then book on duty again and work the return train to Wigan. On some of these short 'rest trips' the engine crew would have their wife or girlfriend on the train and meet up with them after bedding down the engine on the shed. They'd spend their off-duty time with them in the seaside resort before working the excursion back to Wigan. Sometimes crews would travel as passengers to Crewe and then work an excursion from there to Blackpool.

The replenishing of tender engines with water at speed from water troughs provided many amusing tales of passengers receiving impromptu showers when tanks overflowed and carriage windows had been left open immediately behind the tender. Mr Darbyshire recalled:

My mate Eric Clayton and Driver [Jack] Rigby were working a troop train of sailors from Carlisle to Stockport and Eric tried to fill the [tender water] tank at Tebay troughs. No luck. He tried again at Hest Bank troughs and no luck; they [were] moving at a fair speed now. Eric dropped the [tender] scoop at Brock troughs, they are full. [But] now there is a problem; the pressure is too much for Eric and he can't get the scoop up and the tank overflows. There is water everywhere, including the corridors of the first couple of coaches (after water had obviously flown in through open windows). The first time the train [stopped], a sailor said to Eric, 'What went wrong, mate? I've never been shipwrecked on dry land.'[22]

Fred Darbyshire's final months at Springs Branch were notable for quite a bit of moving up and down the links: 'I seemed to be changing mates every two or three weeks,' he recalled. His final two months were spent working with driver Harry Toleman:

I was getting fed up working at Springs Branch, nothing to do with the actual job; I loved working on the footplate ... it must have been the system and the workmates that didn't suit me.

Harry and I were on an early morning goods from Bamfurlong to Birkenhead and the first job was to prepare two engines. It was common practice that if you had two engines to get ready, the driver did one and the fireman the other. I had always worked that way with a driver, so why should Harry be any different.

The engines we were preparing are inside the shed ... I decide to work strictly to the book, one engine at a time, which was not to my mate's liking. He asked me to oil the front bogies on the Black 5 he was working on. I told him I would do so if I had time; later he asked me to oil the front bogies on our engine, a Class 8 goods engine – again, the same answer. Harry is now fuming and goes to the shed engineman and reports me for refusing to do as asked. The shed engineman reads me the Riot Act in private, all to no avail. I just made my job spread out and crack every piece of coal, stack the coal on the tender etc.

We eventually leave the shed ... and we set off from Bamfurlong with a heavy load. I had not fired over the road to Birkenhead, so it was all new to me once we passed Warrington. Leaving Warrington, we pass over the River Mersey and Manchester Ship Canal viaduct, climbing all the time. As we approach Frodsham tunnel we get put inside [a siding] to allow a passenger train to pass. Harry sends me to the box to carry out Rule 55. Whilst there I had a chat with the signalman; after a while he tells me it's now clear for you to go [and] off I went back to the engine.

The signal now goes to green, I spring into action; just one round on the fire and sit down; at this point Harry should have warned me about Frodsham tunnel. But he didn't and paid the price.

After a short while the need arose for more steam, so I got stuck into the fire and put a large one on. Harry complained to me but to no avail, all I said to him was we need the steam and I didn't fancy stopping in the tunnel. He started to cough and got down low on the footplate. I didn't know how long the tunnel was, however we did get out of it before I needed to fire up again.

Outside the tunnel I'm hard at work with the spade; Harry was now very quiet and did not say much. But by the time we reached our destination, Harry had started chatting and we became good workmates with lots in common to chat about.[23]

Preston teenager Robin Bamber visited Springs Branch shed in mid-June 1955 during a quest to 'shed bash' depots in south Lancashire and Cheshire. A total of sixty-seven engines were observed on what was still at this time the 10A coded depot. Robin saw a wide range of engines from Stanier 2-6-4 tanks, to Crabs, Black 5s, a single example of both the Patriot and Jubilee classes, which in

The Fowler Patriots gravitated to the north in their final years, being seen at places like Warrington, Carnforth, Preston and Springs Branch. In 1961, work-weary No.45503 *The Royal Leicestershire Regiment* from Carlisle Upperby rests on Springs Branch. It was withdrawn from service in the period ending 12 August 1961 and cut up soon after. (Eddie Bellass)

both cases were the numerical final members, Nos 45551 and 45742 *Connaught*, and a solitary Britannia Pacific No.70047, the latter's only claim to fame being that it was the sole member of the fifty-five-strong class never to be named.

'There were no less than twenty-three good old Super D 0-8-0s [on shed] and ... because Lower Ince had closed by then, there were seven J10 class 0-6-0s on shed,' Mr Bamber recalled.

Former Edge Hill driver Charles Ebsworth recalled the ex-LNWR Cauliflowers, which in earlier times were sometimes used on a roster from Ince Moss to neighbouring towns:

> They were a dead loss compared to the modern types which were available. They would do the work but with usual LNWR conditions: no comfort or weather protection for the crew.
>
> We used to get one in the early days off Wigan Springs Branch shed on the 6.15a.m. tranships to Ince Moss, Wigan, pick up odd wagons at Huyton, Huyton Quarry, Rainhill, St Helens Junction, Earlestown, Newton-le-Willows and Golborne yards and warehouses, running with five to twelve wagons between sites.
>
> Then it would be on shed at Springs Branch and then home on a passenger – stand up all day.

Raymond Knowles joined British Railways on 12 May 1958 as an apprentice fitter at Springs Branch shed: 'I was part of a team of a fitter and fitter's labourer and we carried out overhauls and repairs to steam locos. The weekly wage was £2.50 for an apprentice, and a fitter £12.75.'

As an apprentice fitter, Mr Knowles worked 8a.m. to 4.30p.m. on weekdays and 8a.m. to noon on Saturdays. Mr Knowles said his apprenticeship (until he turned twenty-one) was 'first class and I enjoyed it immensely'.

The range of engines he would have to work on in the late 1950s and early '60s included Stanier Black 5s, Class 4 'Tankies', 'Middies' and Super Ds:

Cleaner John Daniels beside 'Jinty' tank No.47395 at Springs Branch in May 1964. This shed always had a reasonable roster of these small, sturdy tank locos – at this time their allocation was about six. (J. Daniels collection)

The Middies and Super Ds were awful to work on; they originated from the late 1800s and the motion was situated under the boiler [between the frames] and dirty and hard to get at.

Although I worked mainly at Wigan, for a short time I was at Sutton Oak, St Helens. This shed was much older than Springs Branch and the pits were shallower, making work harder by you having to crouch.

The Wigan Bank shunt job was one of Springs Branch's rosters and had always been part of the passenger link at the shed, even though it was a turn for the older drivers or those deemed unfit for main-line duty. The loco rostered for this turn was required to shunt the sidings adjacent to Wigan North Western station (on the Wallgate side) and assist any freight trains requiring banking up the steep incline to Boar's Head and Coppull. Passenger trains were rarely banked but if required, a push was provided to Standish Junction. The vast majority of slower freights were routed away from North Western station over the Whelley line, so demands on the bank engine were relatively infrequent.

In early BR days the Wigan Bank shunt duty was usually a roster for an ex-LNWR Cauliflower, but after Lower Ince shed closed the J10 locos formerly from that shed were favoured for this job. These in turn gave way to the 'Jinty' tanks by the 1960s.[24]

Keith Sloan joined British Railways in January 1959 also as an apprentice fitter at Springs Branch. Among the first tasks he got assigned were changing boiler gauge glasses in the cabs of locos and cleaning vacuum pipe drip valves. He was paid £2 7s 6d (£2.75) for a forty-four-hour working week:

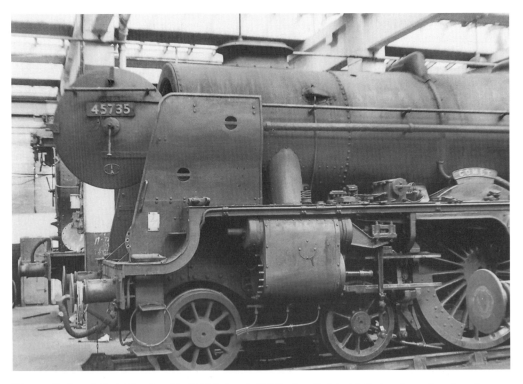

Three-cylinder rebuilt Jubilee class No.45735 *Comet* of Willesden shed, inside Springs Branch undergoing a piston and valve examination. Fitting staff such as Keith Sloan preferred working on such three-cylinder engines inside the back of the shed, 'where it was a bit warmer in winter'. This photograph dates from around 1961–62; *Comet* was later transferred to Annesley shed from where it was withdrawn in October 1964. (Eddie Bellass)

Royal Scot 7P 4-6-0 No.46155 *The Lancer* of Crewe North shed poses for the camera at Springs Branch probably around 1963 or early 1964. Scots, rebuilt Patriots and rebuilt Jubilees were often found around Wigan in the early to mid-1960s. For a brief period of time, Springs Branch even had its own allocation of three Scots. This loco was one of the last of its class in service, not being condemned until December 1964, by then based at Carlisle Kingmoor shed. It was cut up at Arnott Young scrap merchants at Troon in February 1965. (Chris Coates collection)

As an apprentice fitter at Springs Branch, I worked under men who had served in the First and Second World Wars; they were great blokes and proud men.

The shed was freezing in winter due to its being open fronted.

As apprentices we all disliked inside motion locos as these were very dirty and difficult to work on. The ones we liked working on were the three-cylindered 'Scots' doing mileages at the back of the shed where it was a bit warmer in winter.

The best ones were the 'Lizzies' and Duchesses – four-cylinder Pacifics – these locos came on our shed due to [occasional] hot axles or hot big ends.

In his book *The Wigan Sheds – volume 1, Springs Branch*, Chris Coates records that at least three Princess class Pacifics were at the depot in the mid-1950s at various times for certain mechanical faults: Nos 46203 *Princess Margaret Rose* and 46206 *Princess Marie Louise* on 27 August 1956, and No.46207 *Princess Arthur of Connaught* for tyre turning after an accident in the same year. This engine returned to the shed between 28 January and 20 March 1962, before departing for Crewe Works for scrapping the following day.

The 'Lizzies' successors – the Coronation Pacifics – also were notable (if infrequent) visitors to Springs Branch at various times during the post-war to 1964 period. Engines noted included 46222 *Queen Mary*, 46225 *Duchess of Gloucester*, 46226 *Duchess of Norfolk*, 46232 *Duchess of Montrose*, 46235 *City of Birmingham*, 46236 *City of Bradford*, 46237 *City of Bristol*, 46238 *City of Carlisle*, 46239 *City of Chester*, 46250 *City of Lichfield*, 46251 *City of Nottingham*, 46256 *Sir William A. Stanier F.R.S.* and 46257 *City of Salford*. However, the last engine of this class to appear at the shed was ex-Edge Hill's No.46243 *City of Lancaster*, very late in 1964 en route to Central Wagon Works at Ince for scrapping during 1965.[25]

Raymond Knowles remembered some other unusual visitors on shed during his time at 8F: 'The Royal Train stayed overnight in the sidings [near Springs Branch] sometimes, and we also

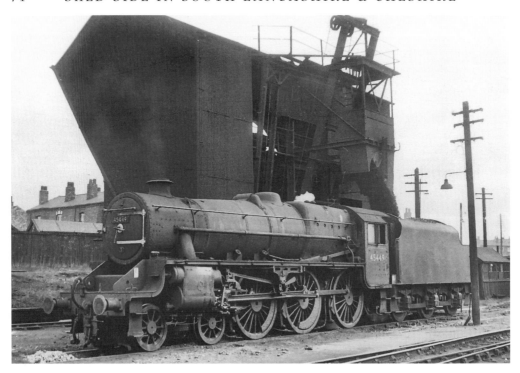

Black 5s were a regular part of the scene at Springs Branch in the 1950s and 1960s. In 1963, for example, there were twenty-five engines of this class based at 8F, among them No.45449 which is pictured receiving coal from the shed's coaling plant. This loco had a long association with Springs Branch, being based there from at least 1 January 1948 until November 1967 when it was withdrawn from service. (Eddie Bellass)

got engines that had failed close to our shed. Posh engines, the three- or four-cylinder engines that normally flashed by on the main line.'

Similarly, special excursion trains saw extra trains working out of Wigan. Football excursions to Hull on 19 March 1960 saw Jubilees Nos 45717 *Dauntless* and 45719 *Glorious* of Bank Hall shed, and Crabs 42721 and 42745 of Aintree, work trains from Wigan, while another train from Rainford Junction was hauled by Patriot 45517.

For brief periods, Mr Sloan also worked at nearby Sutton Oak shed but the contrast between the facilities at the two sheds was quite stark:

> Springs Branch was a running and maintenance depot with wheel drop and machine shop facilities, wheel lathe and metalling facility; it also had a breakdown and steam crane for re-railing engines. Sutton Oak, however, was just a running shed with a breakdown unit but no crane and no engineering facility, very basic.
>
> I worked at both these sheds, as apprentice at Springs Branch and as a fitter at Sutton Oak.

Apprentice fitters at sheds like Springs Branch took turns going out on the crane and breakdown unit. The apprentices would get extra money for such duties. All of the loco breakdown units were serviced by the running staff, usually a fitter and a fitter's mate.

In February 1959 a most unusual visitor was at Springs Branch when Edinburgh St Margaret's shed V2 2-6-2 No.60960 sought refuge after failing in the Wigan area while working an Oxley (Wolverhampton) to Law Junction class C freight. It was on shed from 18 February 1959 until 'at least mid-March after suffering a collapsed brick arch'. After repair the engine returned north, light engine.[26]

In September 1961 the former LNWR shed at Preston (Croft Street) was officially closed having succumbed to a major fire on 28 June 1960 and its allocation of engines and duties was transferred

Edge Hill Black 5 No.44772 reverses through the southern end of Wigan North Western station on 1 August 1964. After entering service in May 1947 upon completion at Crewe Works, this loco spent the early part of its career at Inverness in Scotland. By 1961, however, it had become an Edge Hill engine from where it was withdrawn in November 1967. It was scrapped at Cashmore's in Newport six months later. (John Corkill)

Springs Branch shed retained a couple of Fowler 4Fs which were fitted with snow ploughs in case of need each winter; however, some 8F fitting staff found it hard to recall them ever being used in the 1960s. Here Springs Branch's No.44500 stands ready for work that is unlikely to arrive even in these parts on 11 April 1965. (RCTS - CHO2889)

to Springs Branch, Lostock Hall and Carnforth sheds. As a result, Springs Branch acquired four Royal Scot locomotives for the first time (Nos 46161 *King's Own*, 46165 *The Ranger (12th London Regiment)*, 46167 *The Hertfordshire Regiment* and 46168 *The Girl Guide*).

Early in 1963, reconstruction work on the Lune Viaduct at Lancaster resulted in freight traffic being diverted from the ex-LNWR main line at Boars Head to Chorley, ex-LYR and LNWR joint line to Blackburn and onwards to Carlisle via Hellifield – with the banking engine being taken off at Brinscall. The banking engines used on these trains were Austerity 2-8-0s from Springs Branch.[27]

The closure of Wigan 'C' shed in April 1964 led to an increase in the use of tender engines from Springs Branch shed on Rochdale–Bolton line passenger trains; Class 5 4-6-0s, Standard Class 4 4-6-0s and Standard Class 2 2-6-0s were recorded on trains later in 1964 that were previously the preserve of Class 4 2-6-4 tanks. The Class 2 2-6-0s which were new to Springs Branch in 1964 were employed on passenger workings, including a train which arrived at Rochdale at 18.15hrs, with the 20.35hrs return to Wigan.[28]

A notable event occurred at Springs Branch on 18 July 1964 when Black 5 No.45094 of Edge Hill shed ran away from the shed yard and ended up running through a sand drag at Platt Bridge Junction. The engine, which finished up on its side, provided the breakdown gang with a very challenging assignment. Notwithstanding its exploits, this engine continued in service until withdrawn from Edge Hill shed at the end of February 1967.

The author made several visits to Springs Branch during the mid-1960s and among one of the images to linger in the memory was snowploughs fitted on the front of some Fowler 4Fs in late autumn. These engines were parked at the rear of bays in the demolished section of No.2 shed. However, according to Keith Sloan, in all his years as an apprentice at the shed (from 1959–64) he never saw the snowploughs go out on jobs. Another abiding memory was the stirring sight of Britannia Pacific No.70037 *Hereward the Wake* in full cry roaring past Springs Branch with a southbound passenger train in the mid-1960s.

Like any shed, Springs Branch had its characters among the many employees who worked there. Mr Sloan remembers Alan Mason (known as 'Splosh') being one character: 'I came into the machine shop at brew time one day and Alan was playing Christmas carols on his trombone; he was a bandmaster for the Wigan Brass Band.' There were also many pranks that shed staff would play on unsuspecting workmates:

> As an apprentice at Springs Branch, one of my tasks was to renew the garlic tubes in the big ends. One day I opened a garlic tube and threw it into the brew room where all the blokes were and wedged the door shut! Later, they caught me, tied me up and doused me with the rest of the garlic. Nobody came near me that day!

In late February 1965, Black 5 No.45378 became derailed at Crow Nest sidings near Wigan after running through the buffer stops and coming to rest near a bridge abutment. It lay there for several days before being removed early on 28 February.

In the same month, two Black 5s sustained damage in a smokebox to smokebox collision at Bickershaw Junction which resulted in both locos being condemned. Springs Branch's No.45313 had travelled light engine up the incline from Hindley South, after having worked Wigan Central's goods yard. Upon arrival at Bickershaw Junction, it was planned for the engine to reverse and take the main Manchester Exchange–Springs Branch line back to its home shed. However, it appears the engine was held at the box so its driver, Jimmy Lincoln, went off to see the signalman as required by the safe working rules.

Driver Lincoln found the delay was to allow a Manchester to Liverpool parcels train to come through, which it did, and so he returned to his engine. A short while later the signal was cleared and the loco proceeded off. What the crew of 45313 didn't realise was that the signalman had forgotten their presence and had actually pulled off the signal for another parcels train (believed to be a Manchester to Wigan) which was being hauled by 45414.[29]

Visibility was poor at the time and the first inkling the crew of the parcels train had that there was a loco in front of them was a somewhat hazy sighting of the engine a short distance ahead of them. The light engine would have been travelling around 20mph compared to the parcel train bearing down on it at 60mph – impact was inevitable, irrespective of any action that could have been taken by the parcel train's crew. No.45414 (not long out of Crewe Works after a major over-haul) hit the slow-moving light engine head on, resulting in major front-end damage to both locos. The train from the parcels train was derailed as were several of the parcels vans. Both engines were taken to Springs Branch shed where they were assessed as uneconomic to repair and were con-demned on 28 February. Both were cut up at Central Wagon Works, Ince; however, 45414 had to be cut up on the spot when the weighbridge underneath it collapsed at the scrap merchant.

Railway enthusiast Bob Bartlett set out in late April to try and see his last 500 locomotives needed to complete the listings in his *ABC Combined Volume*, a popular reference 'bible' for trains-potters in the 1950s and 1960s. First he had visited Merseyside in his quest, before setting off for a brief sojourn at Wigan:

> My next objective was Wigan and I was glad to have another Black 5 (45329) as my train engine. En route, two Jubilees were noted: 45627 *Sierra Leone* and 45698 *Mars*. I had done quite well so far in my quest for the wanted engines but at Springs Branch I was to draw a blank. However, a healthy total of forty-eight locos were on shed made up of five 'Jinties', four Stanier 2-6-4Ts, two 4Fs, five Stanier Moguls, eleven Black 5s, nine Stanier 8Fs, two 9Fs, seven WDs and three Ivatt Class 2 Moguls. By now it was evening so I decided to catch a train to Hest Bank (between Lancaster and Carnforth) where I knew of a very pleasant hos-telry where I could spend the night. Once more I was hauled by steam, this time in the form of 70004 *William Shakespeare*. The Britannia came off at Preston and a ride behind 45326 completed my day's travels.[30]

A reported visit to Springs Branch shed on 20 February 1966 revealed seventy-five steam locomo-tives on shed, of which sixty-nine were either in steam or under repair. Engines on shed represented eleven different classes, including Ivatt 4 2-6-0 No.43126 visiting from York (50A) shed.

Those rarest of BR Standard engines – the Clan Pacifics – were always a pleasure to see when making occasional forays into Lancashire or Cheshire. Springs Branch was not excluded from these border incursions which, by the end of 1962, were made by just five survivors. Clans recorded on Springs Branch during the 1950s and 1960s included: 72004 *Clan Macdonald* (on shed 28/3/52, waiting to be towed to Crewe Works); 72002 *Clan Campbell* (6/7/52, ready to work the 01.56hrs Carlisle freight); 72008 *Clan Macleod* (during 1954/55); 72001 *Clan Cameron* (29/4/62); 72007 *Clan Mackintosh* (29/10/63); 72005 *Clan Macgregor* (8/2/64); and 72006 *Clan Mackenzie* (10/5/66).[31] The visit of No.72006 to Wigan on 10 May, and its observation (with the diagonal yellow sash through its cabside number) in the Liverpool area the following day, was especially poi-gnant. The loco was by then the last of its class in service and condemned later in the month after only fourteen years' service.

The 1960s was also a time when it was quite possible to see B1 locos visiting Springs Branch from the North Eastern Region, besides the occasional K1 Mogul and, on one occasion, even a J39 0-6-0. The latter engine (64745) from Gorton shed was noted in 1960, leaving the shed light engine after servicing. The B1s became notable, if not regular visitors, especially during the mid-1960s, including these recorded visits: 61270 (27/1/63); 61031 *Reedbuck* (8/9/63); 61122; 61189 *Sir William Gray* (17/9/63); 61224 (4/7/64); 61017 *Bushbuck* (5–6/3/66); and 61329 (3/4/66). On 29 January 1967, K1 No.62065 was seen inside No.1 shed at Springs Branch, pos-sibly undergoing minor repairs.

On 9 May 1966 steam passenger services briefly returned to the Wigan North Western to Liverpool Lime Street line because of an industrial dispute at Allerton depot, with a resultant shortage of diesel multiple units (DMUs). Among those pressed into service included Sutton Oak's Ivatt 2-6-2 tank No.41286, which was photographed hauling the 6.45p.m. Wigan North Western–Lime Street train.

From 5 September 1966 local stopping services between Preston and Wigan, which had pre-viously been steam hauled, became entirely operated by diesel multiple units. The author, a year earlier, had experienced one of these surviving steam services travelling from Preston to Liverpool

Stanier Crab 2-6-0 No.42968 with a coal train for Springs Branch at Bickershaw Junction in the 1960s. The final examples of this class tended to aggregate at Springs Branch, with this example being the last in service. It was withdrawn on the last day of 1966 and fortunately despatched to Woodham's at Barry, South Wales, from where it was later rescued and restored to full working order. (Tom Sutch)

Exchange in non-corridor stock hauled by Stanier 2-6-4 tank No.42546. The introduction of DMUs to these services removed some of the last passenger turns for LMR-based Stanier and Fairburn tank engines in the north-west.

The Railway Magazine reported, in its October 1966 edition, that work had begun on a new diesel depot at Wigan which would cater for all types of repairs to main-line and shunting engines. The new depot was being built on the site of part of the existing Springs Branch steam shed, 1¼ miles south of Wigan North Western station.

By the summer of 1967 the 1a.m. Manchester Exchange to Glasgow/Edinburgh train was still being regularly steam-hauled as far as Wigan North Western, where it was combined with a portion from Liverpool Lime Street. On 18 July, for example, this train was hauled by Standard 5 No.73025. By early November this train was one of only a handful of regular steam-hauled passenger trains still remaining on BR. The service involved a returning 5.45a.m. Wigan–Manchester Exchange service, which was usually in charge of a Patricroft-based Class 5 engine.

Despite being officially closed to steam from 4 December 1967, Springs Branch still had four engines in steam on 21 December, all of them once named: Nos 45156 Ayrshire Yeomanry; 70004 William Shakespeare; 70023 Venus; and 70035 Rudyard Kipling. On Sunday 7 January 1968, a total of seventy-eight locos were on shed at Springs Branch and despite officially not being a steam depot, eleven of these twelve visiting engines were in steam: 44804, 45013, 48201, 48206, 48410, 48424, 48646, 48683, 92077, 92165, 92233 and 92249. These locos were based at sheds as disparate as Carlisle Kingmoor, Buxton, Speke Junction, Heaton Mersey, Lostock Hall and Trafford Park.

By 24 February 1968, there were twenty-seven steam engines in store at Springs Branch, together with six ex-LMS diesel shunters: Nos 12003, 12004, 12013, 12020, 12023 and 12031. The final removal of locos from the shed was a protracted affair: there were still four condemned locos on shed in June 1968 and the final example, Black 8 No.48752, was still present on 8 November 1968, eleven months after the shed had dispensed with steam.

Eric Clayton remembers that his last job on steam was to haul a train of empty coaches that had come from Carlisle, and heading for Holyhead, between Springs Branch and Llandudno:

Britannia 4-6-2 No.70029 *Shooting Star* at Springs Branch on a wet summer's day, 27 August 1967. This loco was less than two months away from withdrawal, which occurred on 21 October. A Carlisle Kingmoor engine, it was disposed of in February 1968 to McWilliams, Shettleston, where twenty-one other Britannias were cut up and two Clans. (Danny Preston – Chris Coates collection)

I can't remember the type of engine this was but I do recall the sadness at the end of the steam era. I felt very sad to see these old giants standing in line at Springs Branch, waiting to be scrapped and broken down, especially ones that I had fired and driven during my working days on steam.

I did not enjoy the diesels at first but later came to enjoy the more easy working conditions. However, not having a second man on the footplate made one feel lonely and isolated.

The transition to modern power was something that men like Keith Sloan had mixed feelings about. As an apprentice at Springs Branch in the early 1960s, he and other apprentices were sent on training courses for electric and diesel maintenance to Crewe station (classroom training) and Allerton and Edge Hill sheds. As well, all apprentices in the early '60s had to go to a works for nine months to obtain further experience and Mr Sloan spent part of 1962–63 at Horwich, obtaining a month's experience in each section. He recalls:

I would not have missed it for the world. There was more mateship on steam as the older blokes knew all about steam locomotives, but as diesels and electrics came in everything was new, and it seemed like the older era resented being shown by us young lads.

Another person who had strong feelings about the passing of steam was someone who was more removed than shed staff – former signalman Charles Henry Melling, who worked for BR from 1949 to 1960 at various 'boxes' in the Wigan district:

We all felt this, not only the engine drivers, every one of us because to us the steam engines were something you'd been brought up with from a child.

They were a friendly monster to us ... they had their own peculiar smell of oil, coal and smoke; they were giants but in other ways they were like a friend ... it was terrible to see these things go.

Patricroft-based Caprotti valve-geared Standard 5MT, No.73128, hauls a failed, named Class 40 diesel-electric loco on to Springs Branch shed on 7 March 1968. Note the improvised shed code painted on to the smokebox door and the crude home-made number plate replacing the original which had probably been stolen by a 'trophy hunter'. (John Corkill)

WD 2-8-0 No.90173 has just banked a train over the Whelley line and is ambling back to Bamfurlong sidings to await its next banking task. The CWS Glass Works at Platt Bridge are in the background. This scene was taken from bridge 28 on the main line, between Bamfurlong Junction and Springs Branch. This engine had an interesting story. Chris Coates, in his book *Springs Branch Motive Power Depot*, recounts how the real 90173 was mistakenly cut up at Central Wagon Works in lieu of 90147, which had been withdrawn in May 1964. Realising their mistake, Springs Branch salvaged 90173's smokebox plate which was affixed to 90147 still on shed at 8F. The cabsides of that engine were repainted and renumbered with the 90173 number. However, the smokebox plate had to have an additional hole drilled into it to secure it to the smokebox. This 'second' 90173 was eventually also cut up at Central Wagon Works after it was withdrawn in July 1964. (Tom Sutch – Eric Clayton collection)

All engines had a personality of their own. I've ridden on engines from the signal box to go home and I know personally ... one certain driver, I'd be sat on the engine with him and he would know that engine just like he would know a son or daughter at home. If there was just a clinking noise, a little ticking somewhere, he would know immediately what it was.

You used to see them [crews] on banks and they would persuade their engine to do that little bit extra. They seemed to be living things, not a thing made of metal, and the drivers and the engine had something between them, it was wonderful to watch this.

Once this personality of the engine was got rid of, by bringing in the diesels ... this feeling went; the diesel could never take the place of the steam engine, something great had been lost, this personal touch between the driver and his engine.

Working in a signal box at all hours of the day, Mr Melling recalled the familiarity that would be developed with certain types of engines and the eerie but evocative sounds and sights that only steam power could convey at night:

I used to know certain engines as they were approaching the signal box, even on night duty and they would be half a mile away; I could tell the distinct sound between various engines and various classes of engines and I don't think there was any nicer sound than the old steam engine whistle in the night.

Sometimes it could seem very ghostly but to me it was a friendly sound and as a signalman it was more than friendly because it told me he was on his way, or he was leaving me, one or the other ... a whistle meant something.[32]

The demise of steam and British Railways' extensive passenger services went back much earlier and according to Mr Melling a microcosm of the malaise besetting the railways was evident in certain local services which failed to take account of passengers' needs:

It started in the mid-1950s by the closing down of small stations ... such as the line from Wigan, the Wigan to Chorley, Blackburn line.[33]

There was a type of engine called the push and pull, which would be an engine with two carriages and if they had run a service from Wigan to Chorley with this little push and pull ... backwards and forwards [with a] half hourly service, it would have paid for itself and those coaches would have always been full, but no one seemed to listen.

They would prefer to run up to eight trains a day at the times when no one could use them. One at 6a.m. from Blackburn to Wigan – no one travelled from Blackburn to Wigan at 6a.m. – and then 9.30a.m. They were either too late for women or too near meal times, so these trains were never used but no one higher up wanted to listen ... they wanted to make this the death wish of the railways.

End of the Line

Springs Branch and the nearby Central Wagon Co. at Ince, Wigan, were noteworthy in the 1960s for being the collection point and final dismantling location for 305 steam locomotives from all over British Railways.

On 24 July 1962, for example, G3 0-8-0s Nos 49618 and 49640 formerly of Agecroft shed, together with ex-LYR tank No.51408, were moved to the scrapyard for breaking up. During December 1963 the following engines were noted waiting for dismantling at the scrapyard: 90425, 90508, 90526, 90608, 61182, 61254 and 61363.

Over the years Springs Branch would host unusual accumulations of engines, some of types never before seen in the north-west let alone the district, including twenty-two ex-GWR engines comprising pannier tanks, Halls and even a Castle class engine awaiting movement to the Ince

Jubilee class 4-6-0 No.45601 *British Guiana* is in the process of being scrapped at Central Wagon Works, Wigan, 11 April 1965. Built at the North British Locomotive Company in Glasgow in April 1935, this loco was latterly at Newton Heath, Manchester shed, from where it was withdrawn in late September 1964. (RCTS - CHO2887)

Springs Branch after the closure to steam. A couple of railwaymen have a chat amid a backdrop of redundant steam locomotives awaiting their fate at the shed, early in 1968. The last of these engines was not removed until November of that year. (John Corkill)

scrapyard. As well, there was the more intermittently seen Eastern Region B1s, fourteen of which were dismantled locally.

The October 1964 issue of *The Railway Magazine* reported that several more engines had arrived at Springs Branch shed ready for breaking up at the Ince Wagon Works (Central Wagon). They included Nos 42378 and 42569, 90595 and 90667, 41205, 47228, 44119 and 42820, and 42888. On 28 July 1964 they were joined by 4950 *Patsull Hall* and 4976 *Warfield Hall*.

By 27 March 1965 the following engines were also recorded as awaiting scrapping at Central Wagon Works: 4976 *Warfield Hall*, 41205, 42077, 42280, 42481, 42696, 42858, 42952, 44119, 44549, 45414, 45592 *Indore*, 45601 *British Guiana*, 45623 *Palestine*, 45657 *Tyrwhitt*, 45681 *Aboukir*, 46243 *City of Lancaster*, 61041, 61056, 61144, 90157, 90245, 90416, 90667 and 90712.

On 3 August 1965 a total of seventeen engines had congregated at Springs Branch shed for scrapping (not all necessarily at Ince) and they included: 42772, 42817, 42932, 42941, 44490, 44500, 47395, 47444, 47603, 47668, 47671, 42456, 42559, 42565, 42601, 42670 and ex-GWR pannier tank 9753. Railway enthusiast Lyndon Knott visited the scrapyard four days later and recorded the following nineteen engines still awaiting or in the process of being cut up: 3208, 4976 *Warfield Hall*, 42155, 42369, 42751, 42778, 42901, 42904, 42937, 42952, 44119, 44186, 45623 *Palestine*, 46243 *City of Lancaster*, 61056, 61144, 90245, 90426 and 90667.

Engines noted in the Central Wagon Works' scrapyard on 26 April 1966 included BR Standard 2-6-2 tanks Nos 84010, 84015 and 84028, and Black 5 No.45108.

Five

8G SUTTON OAK

Sutton Oak shed was opened by the London & North Western Railway in 1880 and was located between Sutton Oak and Peasley Cross stations on the eastern side of the railway line, on Baxters Lane. It replaced two earlier engine sheds that had been established at St Helens Junction and Clock Face by the LNWR's predecessors (the St Helens Canal & Railway Company and the Liverpool & Manchester Railway). In 1872 the LNWR converted part of the former loco works of Messrs James Cross & Co. into an engine shed but this proved unsatisfactory. So much so, that in 1879 the LNWR's loco superintendent, F.W. Webb's, report to the loco committee stated:

> ... the land for the Engine Shed for the St Helens district has now been purchased and he [Webb] recommends the erection of a shed at Peasley Cross capable of holding 40 engines; when this work is done the old building at Clock Face can be cleared away.

The engine shed converted from the works went out of use with the completion of the new Peasley Cross (later Sutton Oak) shed; and in 1889 St Helens Junction shed, which had also been disused for many years, was pulled down.

The new shed was a brick-built, ten-track, straight dead-ended building with a northlight-pattern roof and a standard LNWR ramped coaling stage supporting a water tank. Sutton Oak was predominantly a goods engine shed and standard LNWR 0-6-0s and 0-8-0s held sway for many years until the Grouping in 1923. Then ex-L&YR 0-6-0s began to supplant the LNWR examples. The shed took the code 24, and at its peak in 1910 had as many as fifty locomotives on its roster.

Sunny Sutton Oak shed in October 1961 with two of the shed's Standard 4MT 2-6-0s present and a WD 2-8-0 raising steam. The Standard 4MTs were intrinsically linked with this shed from their construction in the late 1950s until their demise in late 1967. (Eddie Bellass)

One of the Webb 2-4-2 tanks, No.6628, on Sutton Oak shed in the mid-1930s. These engines dated from the 1890s and four of this class (including this engine) were still at Sutton Oak on the last day of the LMS – 31 December 1947. They were used on some of the local passenger trains to locations such as Warrington and Earlestown. (Sutton Historic Society)

Ex-LNWR 2F (Webb) 'Coal Engine' No.8152, later renumbered as LMS 28152 and by BR as 58333, waits for its next duty at Sutton Oak shed in the late 1930s. These engines had a very long life, with the first examples turned out of Crewe in 1873. This example continued in traffic until January 1952 – or nearly seventy-five years of service! (Sutton Historic Society)

While predominantly a goods shed, Sutton Oak did have a few passenger locos on its books and from 1890 retained some Webb 2-4-2 tanks. These diminutive locos were in charge of passenger services until 1951 when the last quartet disappeared after the withdrawal of passenger trains from the St Helens branch. From around the 1950s, new Ivatt 2-6-2 tanks operated the local services to Warrington until they were displaced by diesel multiple units.

In 1920 the office accommodation at the shed was rearranged and in 1937 a 60ft-diameter turntable was installed, replacing the 42ft version originally provided. A new sand-drying plant was added in 1944 and in the 1950s the shed was re-roofed and a brick screen was installed over the front of the roof section.

Under British Railways' ownership, Sutton Oak engines wore three different shed codes over a period of nineteen years: the shed was coded 10E from 1948–55, then became 10D until 1958, then finally was grouped with the '8' district sheds, as 8G.

Coaling facilities were basic but in later years these were improved by the installation of an elevator-type conveyor belt. During the 1950s there were about 170 workers at Sutton Oak shed under a shedmaster. These included fifty-six drivers, fifty-six firemen and twenty-five cleaners.

The advent of diesel locomotives saw the end of the sheds, although an initial plan to close Sutton Oak in May 1964 was temporarily rescinded. Sutton Oak shed was closed on 19 June 1967 but the last steam loco left the shed on 27 December 1967. However, the train drivers and guards,

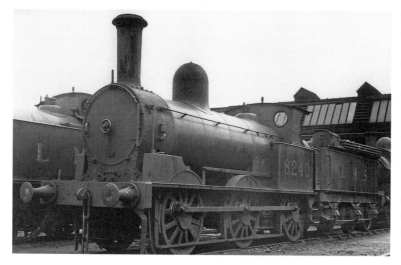

Ex-LNWR 2F No.8240 on Sutton Oak shed on 14 May 1939. Another of the ancient Webb 'Coal Engines', this example dates from June 1881 when it was turned out of Crewe Works. It lasted in service with the LMS until 30 June 1947 when it was withdrawn from Widnes shed. It was later scrapped at Crewe. (Sutton Historic Society)

who had transferred from the former Sutton Oak station in 1964, still booked on and off duty at the shed until 1970. The Sutton Oak shed building survived the end of steam and for many years was used as a supermarket by Morrisons plc until Sunday 25 June 2000, when it was finally closed and later bulldozed. A new supermarket has since been built on the former shed site.

* * *

In its heyday, Sutton Oak was surrounded by a number of avoiding lines which enabled freight trains – such as the Long Meg anhydrite trains – to travel from the west coast main line at Wigan, via Bryn and Garswood, directly to Widnes without causing congestion at the busy Pocket Nook goods yard, north of St Helens Shaw Street station (now renamed St Helens Central) and at Ravenhead.

The signal box at Broad Oak Junction controlled engine movements on and off shed, while the signal box at Sutton Oak Junction controlled access to the lines to Clock Face, Sutton Manor Colliery and Widnes. Over the years, Sutton Oak was one of the sheds in the region that was often (to their regret) neglected by railway enthusiasts, particularly with the lure of 'namers' and more prestigious engines that inhabited sheds like Edge Hill (Liverpool), Warrington Dallam and even Springs Branch (Wigan). Nevertheless, it held a fascinating mix of less glamorous but equally interesting locos of senior vintage that would see out their final years in this railway backwater.

Clarice Bedford's father, Alfred Emblem, was a driver based at Sutton Oak for many years. Alfred's father, too, had worked at the sheds as a foreman and lived in the foreman's cottage at 122 Baxters Lane, just past the shed entrance:

Over the time, names and faces became familiar. My sister and I used to enjoy visiting the sheds on a Sunday morning. There was quite a steep flight of steps down to the engines, or so it seemed, and the smell of oily rags, steam, coal, etc. was one to recall.

Names I remember [associated with the shed] include Frank Smith, Aubrey Williams, Leo McDermott, Sam Atherton (and) Harry Hughes. They were all roughly of the same age group and retired in the late 1950s or early '60s.

I understand ... there was a row of terraced houses in Manor Street, Peasley Cross, which were railway houses; they, like the foreman's cottage, have now been demolished – a Charles Archer lived there.

Memories of Sunday visits to the sheds appear to be far from uncommon. Ruth Taylor, who still lives in Sutton, has similar recollections:

One of the ex-Midland Railway's 3F 0-6-0s that inhabited smaller sheds like Sutton Oak in Lancashire in the 1940s and 1950s until more modern designs superseded them. Engines from this class, which date from the late 1880s, were all rebuilt with Belpaire fireboxes as seen on this loco, No.43763, which is fussing about in Pocket Nook sidings, St Helens, on a sunny day in 1958. This loco came from Derby shed in the period ending 25 January 1958, but had been transferred away to Gorton shed to the period ending 13 December 1958. There followed a short spell at Leicester Midland shed for five months during 1959, before it returned to Gorton in October that year. It was withdrawn from Gorton shed from 10 March 1962. (Gerald Drought)

A young admirer has a close-up look at a WD 2-8-0 resting in Sutton Oak shed, probably on a Sunday, and is no doubt in awe of the huge machine. Clarice Bedford and her sister were often taken to the sheds by their father, Alfred Emblem, when young children and would have experienced sights like this many times. (Sutton Historic Society)

Aspinall 3F 0-6-0 No.52322 is platform side at St Helens station in January 1955 when the prototype 3,300-horsepower Deltic diesel-electric comes through on a test run to Carlisle. What a contrast in motive power – the nineteenth century meets the motive power of the moment. (Gerald Drought)

My dad worked at Sutton Oak sheds, he was a goods guard and that was where he started and finished his day. I remember him taking me there as a child, I guess it was probably around 1957, and I was allowed to stand on the footplate of the engines. I still remember all the smoke from the engines.

My uncle was a signalman and worked in the box that used to be on Lancots Lane, and would have been very close to the sidings. I also remember being allowed to go in the box and watch the signals being changed. To this day I have a love of steam trains and like nothing better when on holiday to have a ride on one; what memories.

The mid-1950s was a time of considerable change on British Railways: the modernisation plan that was issued in 1955 proposed spending more than £1.24 billion in a long-term effort to eliminate steam and replace motive power with diesel and electric haulage. As part of this modernisation scheme a number of prototype diesels and electrics were introduced to assess their suitability for the demanding work expected of them. In January 1955 one of the first of these prototypes – the groundbreaking Deltic diesel-electric with an unprecedented 3,300 horsepower – ran a test train from Liverpool to Carlisle and was captured on photographic film at St Helens by Gerald Drought.

Sutton Oak had its moments of excitement, particularly on those special days when St Helens' rugby league fans travelled en masse to away matches by train – and St Helens was an influential rugby side in the 1960s. Passenger locos were loaned from other sheds to handle this boost in excursion traffic and during these times some of Stanier's finest engines could be found on 8G.

Similarly, special rugby supporters' trains from Leeds and elsewhere would arrive at Shaw Street bringing 'foreign' engines into the district and, after depositing their passengers and rolling stock in Shaw Street yard, would trundle off to Sutton Oak to replenish their tenders and take on water. Over the years, Farnley Junction-based Jubilees, among others, appeared at Sutton Oak after hauling in such special trains.

On Saturday 12 December 1959, a St Helens–Rochdale rugby league excursion was hauled by Patriot 4-6-0 No.45539 *E.C. Trench*. Upon arrival the engine turned on the Castleton triangle and spent the remainder of the afternoon in the Rochdale loop.[34]

The 18.30hrs ex-St Helens stopping train to Wigan was a regular double-headed working; at Gerard's Bridge Junction, Jubilee No.45655 *Keith* and an unidentified 2-6-4 tank are in charge, 1956. The ex-Great Central Railway bridges behind the locos have now been removed, although one or two abutments still attest to what was once there. The chimneys of Rockware Glass have also gone, as the works' site is now the St Helens Technology campus. *Keith* ended its days at Warrington Dallam shed, from where it was withdrawn in April 1965. (Gerald Drought)

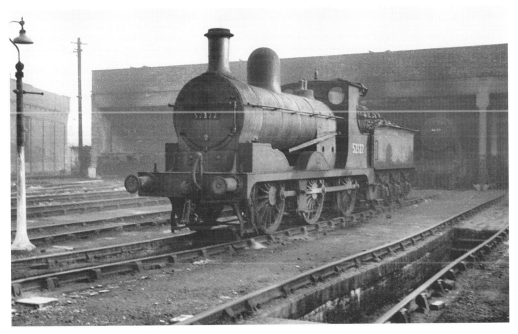

Aspinall veteran No.52322, this time on shed at Sutton Oak on 15 December 1957. This loco had a long and distinguished career, having entered service with the Lancashire & Yorkshire Railway in January 1896 and was not withdrawn until August 1960. Its final posting was Lees shed (Oldham). This loco is now preserved on the East Lancashire Railway. (Brian Swinn)

One of the Aspinall 2F 0-6-0 saddle tanks that were based at Sutton Oak in the late 1950s. These engines were originally built in the late 1870s as tender engines, by Barton Wright, but were converted to tank engines between 1891 and 1900. No.51397 was allocated to Sutton Oak from February 1957 and withdrawn in March 1959. It had spent time previously at both Speke Junction and Aintree sheds in Liverpool. (Sutton Historic Society)

Although Sutton Oak's heritage lay with the old London & North Western Railway, and in early BR days its engines were predominantly ex-LNWR or ex-LMS, many products of the 'Lanky's' Horwich Works also gravitated to St Helens. Former L&YR Aspinall 3F No.52322 (now preserved on the East Lancashire Railway), for example, was a Sutton Oak regular.

Robin Bamber visited Sutton Oak shed in June 1955. On shed he was fortunate to view thirty-two locos ranging across ten different classes.

During its lifetime, Sutton Oak's allocation was predominantly made up of freight locos, the many sidings and works (soda ash, chemicals, glass etc.) in the district meaning that shunting engines were always present. In 1950, for example, the shed's thirty-nine allocated engines included two Sentinel 0-4-0 tanks, four 3F 0-6-0s and five ex-L&YR 0-6-0 saddle tanks. Modern motive power was represented by only three Ivatt 2-6-2 tanks and four Ivatt 4 2-6-0s. Five ageing 0-8-0s worked the heavier freights but, from 1957, a pair of Standard 9Fs was drafted to the shed.

As mentioned previously, Sutton Oak did retain some passenger work on its rosters and this survived into the early 1960s. Early in BR days Webb tank engines were employed on the Shaw Street to Earlestown and Warrington passenger trains. They were replaced by new Ivatt 2-6-2 tanks from around 1950. On paper this service became dieselised in 1961 (surviving until June 1965). However, early in 1963 *The Railway Magazine* reported that push and pull trains appeared occasionally in the diesel railcar diagrams between St Helens and Warrington, which connected at Earlestown with the Trans-Pennine trains. Class 2 2-6-2 tank No.41217 is used on these turns.[35]

Another member of this class, No.41286, spent most of its life at Sutton Oak, apart from a short running-in spell at Crewe. However, it enjoyed a brief 'holiday' at Buxton in the early 1960s as recounted by railway enthusiast Mel Thorley:

In December 1961 my father gave me a rather special stocking filler – an 8G shedplate. It transpired that there were problems with the diesel railbus on the Buxton–Millers Dale

A recently ex-works 9F 2-10-0 No.92049 leaves St Helens Shaw Street station for Ravenhead sidings to pick up further wagons for a freight to Warrington Arpley sidings. This loco arrived at Warrington Dallam shed in March 1965, which would date this photograph, and was transferred to Birkenhead shed the following February. It was withdrawn from that shed when it closed in November 1967. (Gerald Drought)

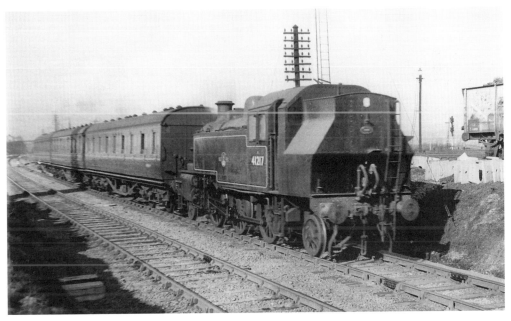

Warrington Dallam-based Ivatt 2-6-2 tank No.41217 works bunker first past Sutton Oak shed on 27 February 1963, hauling a St Helens Shaw Street–Warrington train. At this time Dallam and Sutton Oak each had two engines of this class of popular loco. No.41217 was reallocated to Southport shed from 20 June 1964 but finished its days in Carlisle, being withdrawn from Kingmoor shed in the period to 17 December 1966. (John Corkill)

[service] and rather than firing up Nos 41905 or 41906 ... push and pull fitted 41286 arrived from Sutton Oak. The problem must have been sorted out pretty quickly, as early in 1962 No.41286 was seen travelling light back to St Helens via Furness Vale.[36]

In fact, No.41286 survived as a standby engine for any failed DMUs right up to the closure of Sutton Oak in 1967. In May 1966 it again was pressed back into passenger duty when an industrial dispute at Allerton traction shed sidelined many railcars in the district and steam returned to selected services, with the tank working a number of Wigan/St Helens to Lime Street locals. This recall to passenger duties mirrored one of this engine's final regular turns on this line: a Fridays-only return trip from St Helens to Lime Street which survived until the introduction of the winter timetable in 1965.

Edge Hill fitter John Corkill spent a few months assigned to Sutton Oak from late December 1962 until March 1963 and found it an interesting if uneventful interlude away from the turmoil being experienced at his home depot:

In late December 1962, just before Christmas, I was called into the office at Edge Hill and asked would I like to go and work at Sutton Oak for a couple of months. The turns would be on regular days, Monday to Friday. This had come about because of the long-term sickness at Sutton Oak of some of the fitting staff. The shed had a lot of old hands there.

Before the New Year, 1963, I started at Sutton Oak, missing all the troubles at Edge Hill ... this was the start of the bad winter of 1962/63. The diesel situation at Edge Hill was quite dire, with steam replacing many failures, and I was missing all of this. Things were carrying on near normal at Sutton Oak, considering the bad weather, no failures, [but] late starts, yes.

Fowler 4F No.44493 blackens the sky over Sutton Oak as it gets to grips with a freight train as it passes its home shed on 27 February 1963. These hardworking six-wheelers were very much the fabric of Lancashire freight yards in the 1950s and 1960s, and could be seen working a variety of trains or shunting duties. It was withdrawn from service at Sutton Oak at the end of October 1963 and cut up at Wards, in Barrow, by the end of July 1964. (John Corkill)

The well-presented Britannia Pacific No.70010 *Owen Glendower* is shown to good effect at Ravenhead sidings, St Helens, at 8.45p.m. in July 1965. It is awaiting the assembly of the freight train it will work to Warrington. *Owen Glendower* had recently been transferred from Crewe South shed to Carlisle Kingmoor when this photograph was taken. It stayed at the latter shed until withdrawn from service on 23 September 1967, being cut up at McWilliams at Shettleston the following January – one of twenty-two 'Brits' that were disposed of there. (Gerald Drought)

> The work I was expected to do was one washout a day with booked repairs and either a 3/5 week or a 7/9 week [engine] exam. Also, I was expected to cope with the running shed repairs, so there was a lot to get on with. The washout was expected to be [completed] on finishing your turn of duty. One engine that had to have attention was the engine for the Pilkington's glass train. This was a Willesden turn and ran overnight in both directions; it usually had a Class 5 4-6-0 from 1A.

Freight-wise, rostered loco duties from Sutton Oak included shunting at Pocket Nook goods yards and at the extensive Ravenhead sidings, which were built to service the vast industrial glass-making enterprises of Pilkington and United Glass. Besides a handful of former ex-L&YR 0-6-0 saddle tanks and LMS 'Jinties', a trio of Sentinel locos was kept on standby to cover any failures in the private industrial loco fleets, maintained by local industry for use in their internal yards and sidings. In reality, the Sentinels were rarely called to step into the breach and all had departed Sutton Oak by 1958.

Locos also made trips out to Pilkington's sand quarries at Rainford on the singled former LNWR/L&YR line to Ormskirk, and could also be found working on Pilkington's other sand and soda ash traffic. Other duties for 8G's engines involved working goods trains to the yards at Widnes, Wigan, Ordsall Lane (Salford), Edge Hill and Crewe.

Railway enthusiast and photographer Brian Swinn visited Sutton Oak (10D as it was then) on Sunday 15 December 1957 and his shed log illustrates the diverse range of locos found at this facility at the weekend, including a 'foreigner', B1 from the Eastern Region:

41211	41286	41288	41289	44280	44350	44438	47166	47366	47452	47453	48654
49262	49281	49288	49304	49448	51316	61319	51441	52140	52201	52322	52366
52393	76075	76076	76077	76078	76079						

TOTAL 30

Tom O'Neill worked briefly at Sutton Oak as a fifteen-year-old engine cleaner, and demonstrates that sometimes career ambitions are shattered by unexpected circumstances.

Coming from a railway background – Tom's uncle, Tom Hartley, was an engine driver, while his grandmother worked in the shed's canteen – it was expected Tom would follow the same railway pathway.

Tom's boss at Sutton Oak was Dicky Page and one of his tasks was to go and get tea supplies from a shop near the Wheatsheaf pub: 'I had to go on a bike with about six big packets of tea for the drivers and firemen; I am only small so I could barely see over the top of the packets.'

Tom recalls being the brunt of a cruel joke by fitting staff at the shed one day: 'One thing I will never forget was helping the fitters to put a fire door [back on a loco]. Being small, they put me on the inside of the firebox and left me in there all afternoon. I was only fifteen at the time and I was not very happy.'

Later, Tom's 'world fell apart' when he failed his eyesight test and had to leave the shed and aspirations to become an engine driver. He went to work at the 'Viaduct Works' – the Earlestown Wagon Works – where he became a welder.

In the late 1950s and early 1960s the South Lancashire coalfields – bounded by St Helens and Wigan – were in full production and Sutton Oak's allocation of ex-LNWR Super D 0-8-0s was kept busy hauling heavy, unfitted coal trains from locations such as Bold, Clock Face, Haydock and Sutton Manor collieries to the Shaw Street yards for marshalling, to Springs Branch for onward destinations and to Widnes to satisfy the needs of a thriving chemical industry.

The clanking of steel, as slack couplings became taut, was a familiar sound to anyone waiting on the platform at Shaw Street and they could witness the theatrics as a heavily laden coal train began its climb up to Carr Mill Junction. Following the withdrawal of the Super Ds in the early 1960s, these duties were taken over by Austerity 2-8-0s.

The most modern steam locos to be based at Sutton Oak were the Standard Class 4 2-6-0s which arrived new at the shed in 1957. Nos 76075 to 76079 arrived after being completed at Horwich Works and were immediately put to work on a variety of freight duties. With their light axle loadings, the Standard 4s became regular visitors on the single branch line from Cowley Hill Junction to Pilkington's sandwash plant at Rainford, a line which they worked exclusively until this contract went over to road transport in 1965.

British Railways' Standard 4MT 2-6-0 No.76023 is being coaled from the mechanical elevator that replaced the old LNWR coaling stage in the 1950s onwards. Although undated, this image would have been captured between August 1960 and July 1962 while the engine was based at Sutton Oak. It finished its career at Stoke, from where it was withdrawn in October 1965, after less than thirteen years' service. (Eddie Bellass)

Edge Hill's 'Semi' No.46229 *Duchess of Hamilton* at St Helens goods yard, summer 1963. The engine, with safety valves lifting, is getting ready to work the 7p.m. St Helens–Carlisle Upperby freight. Withdrawn from service early in 1964, this was one of two engines of this class that Billy Butlin bought from BR to display at his popular holiday camps around Britain. It can now be seen on display at the National Railway Museum at York. (Gerald Drought)

On rare occasions these engines saw passenger service, working local Saturday stopping trains between Liverpool and Manchester, via Kenyon Junction and Leigh. They also banked heavy freights over the steep gradients towards Thatto Heath in the Liverpool direction and Carr Mill in the Wigan direction. Two other engines of this class arrived in 1959 – Nos 76020 and 76023 – and, after the closure of Lower Darwen shed in 1965, a further five engines (Nos 76080–76084) were drafted to Sutton Oak.

In *Modern Railways'* July 1963 issue it was reported that Stanier Pacifics from Edge Hill shed were being seen in Pocket Nook goods yard, St Helens, before hauling the 7p.m. freight to Carlisle Upperby and Glasgow: 'Last year Pacifics were seen here on rare occasions, but this is the first time Edge Hill has rostered 4-6-2s to this working instead of the usual Class 5s or 2-8-0s.'[37]

Stanier 8Fs displaced from other districts also began to arrive at Sutton Oak from 1965, and these made inroads into the shed's allocation of Austerity 2-8-0s which were either withdrawn or reallocated to the North Eastern Region.

By the summer of 1965, it was reported in *The Railway Magazine* that the appearance of Standard Class 3 2-6-0s on the North Wales coastal route was not uncommon. Regular appearances of this class, by members from Sutton Oak shed, had been noted with North Wales-bound coal trains, including No.76084.

On 25 September 1965 the Locomotive Club of Great Britain (North West branch) ran its Glazier Brakevan tour of lines in the St Helens district, hauled throughout by Sutton Oak 'Jinty' tank No.47298. With four brakevans in tow carrying camera-wielding enthusiasts, 47298 travelled from St Helens Junction to Ravenhead Junction, Marsh's Crossing, UGB's siding at Ravenhead, then back to Marsh's Crossing, to Triplex (Eccleston), Ravenhead, then from there to St Helens Shaw Street and Old Mill Lane (Rainford).

From Old Mill Lane the 'Jinty' trundled to Pocket Nook Junction, Peasley Junction, Broad Oak Junction and Marsh's siding (Fleet Lane). The brakevan train then travelled via Sutton Oak Junction to end the tour back at St Helens Junction.

The author's regrettably sole visit to Sutton Oak shed occurred on 12 April 1966 when a total of just fifteen engines were observed, but nevertheless from six different classes. These were:

41234	44815	47393	48206	48215	48326	48422	48479	48746	76071	76076	76078
76079	76083	92017									

The introduction of diesel units reduced patronage on some of the local passenger routes, and the projected closure of local coal mines all had an effect on the shed's diagrams. With the exception of 41286, the Ivatt 2-6-2 tanks were drafted away from Sutton Oak and the withdrawal of older loco types gathered pace as the depot's finale drew near.

Nevertheless, it was reported in the railway press that on 3 January 1967, Sutton Oak shed contained no less than twenty-five steam locomotives, including Black 5 4-6-0 No.45305 which was in ex-works condition and fully lined-out livery.

Brian Swinn ventured to Sutton Oak one last time before its closure to steam on Sunday 9 April 1967, when the shed still hosted twenty-five engines, although Black 8 No.48185 was withdrawn and the previously mentioned 45305 was now in store:

12072	12100	D3791	45305	48033	48121	48153	48167	48185	48193	48206	48278
48362	48614	48617	48722	48727	48746	48750	76075	76077	76079	76080	76081
76084											

Ex-Lower Darwen Standard 4MT No.76082 at Pocket Nook sidings, St Helens, in 1965. In the background can be seen a relatively rare visitor to the town: a Standard 4MT 4-6-0 from Southport shed. Photographer Gerald Drought was so appalled by the deteriorating condition of BR steam that this was the last photograph he took of any BR steam loco in service. (Gerald Drought)

A pair of Sutton Oak's ever-present Standard Class 4 Moguls, Nos 76079 and 76076. These locos could be found on a range of duties in the region, from passenger haulage, to coal freights to North Wales or simply shunting the local yards. No.76079 was saved for posterity, but not so 76076, which was cut up at T.W. Ward at Killamarsh in April 1967. (Peter Ditchfield)

Former Sutton Oak 'Jinty' tank No.(4)7298 which languished in Woodham's Barry scrapyard for several years before being rescued and restored to full working order. It is shown here taking part in a steam cavalcade in the 1980s. (Eric Clayton collection)

With the changing fortunes of local industry, workings from Sutton Oak shed gradually declined and, coupled with BR's determination to get rid of steam from less active sheds, closure to steam occurred on 19 June 1967. Surviving freight workings in the district were covered by diesels from Edge Hill and Springs Branch sheds.

After its closure to steam, Sutton Oak's Standard 4s were transferred to Springs Branch, but in reality several of the class languished in the sidings to the west of Shaw Street station until being towed away for scrap. Five engines of this class, 76075, 76077, 76079, 76080 and 76084, actually did move to Springs Branch and were still present on 3 January 1968. They appear to have seen little, if any, work before that shed also closed to steam in December 1967. Fortunately, three of this quintet (Nos 76077, 76079 and 76084) found their way to Dai Woodham's Barry scrapyard and survive in preservation. Fortunate, too, were three other ex-Sutton Oak engines – 'Jinty' tanks 47279 and 47298, and Aspinall 3F 0-6-0 No.52322. By a curious coincidence, No.76079 and 47298 both left Barry scrapyard in the same month: July 1974. Sutton Oak shed remained open to service and fuel diesel locos until 27 December 1967, and on that day two locos were on shed in the form of Black 5 No.44708 (in steam) and English Electric Type 4 diesel, D310.

Shortly after complete closure, the tracks into the shed were lifted and the remaining infrastructure (excluding the shed building) was dismantled and removed; the turntable deck was cut up for scrap on site. Sutton Oak stood abandoned for a while until a local food retailer, Whelan's, purchased the shed building and the shed yard for redevelopment. The fitting of a suspended ceiling and cladding of interior walls transformed the interior of the shed, and a car park was laid over the area previously occupied by the turntable, avoiding lines from Peasley Cross to Broad Oak. Eventually the Whelan's store was integrated into the Bradford-based Morrisons group.

The success of the Sutton Oak supermarket and expansion of the Morrisons business prompted a decision to redevelop the old shed site; Sutton Oak again closed its doors for business on Sunday 25 June 2000 pending demolition. During the early stages of demolition, removal of the false ceiling panels surprisingly revealed that the original shed lighting was still in place; some fittings still contained light bulbs, covered in smoke soot.[38]

Approval to construct a new building was received from the St Helens Council in 2001. In 2002 the Engine Shed Society's publication *Link* reported that on a 22 April inspection, 'construction of a new Morrisons superstore is well under way, with the opening scheduled for late October'.

A new Morrisons supermarket now covers the site where Sutton Oak shed once stood, but the business has not forgotten its transport past, retaining a railway theme with pictures of the old shed adorning the store's interior walls. A single line rail connection to St Helens Central remains in place as far as Baxters Lane bridge.

Six

8M SOUTHPORT AND
LORD STREET (CLC) SHED

This shed, built by the Lancashire & Yorkshire Railway and dating from 1897, was on the north-ern side of the line east of Southport Chapel Street station. The shed yard was not visible from the line. Located off Derby Road, a goods yard entrance was on the right-hand side of this road and a path led to the engine shed from this entrance.

An earlier depot had existed on this site, being built by the East Lancashire Railway around 1855. The L&YR shed was established on the site of the original ELR depot.

Southport, which was coded shed No.17 under the L&YR system, was a six-road, dead-end shed with a northlight-pattern roof. In its heyday it had an allocation of up to forty engines. Most of its roster was passenger types for working expresses to Manchester and local freights over the west Lancashire line and into the Accrington district. A few saddle tanks were retained for working the local yards and around four 0-6-0 goods engines that travelled to Salford and Preston. Rail motors also worked to Barton and Ormskirk, and a ballast train found quiet jobs for elderly drivers, of which the depot seemed always to have a good number.

About two years after the shed was opened, a tragedy occurred when an eighteen-year-old engine cleaner was killed. This account, from the county coroner's inquest into the death, was reported in the *Liverpool Mercury* on 9 December 1899:

Southport shed on 17 May 1964 with a range of engines ready for their next turn of duty (some with special reporting codes on their smokeboxes). Prominent in the foreground is Black 5 No.44950 which at the time was a Blackpool Central loco but would soon be transferred to Speke Junction. It was among the last engines to see service on British Railways, being withdrawn in August 1968. (Brian Barlow – courtesy of the Industrial Railway Society)

Yesterday afternoon Mr S. Brighouse, county coroner, held an inquest at Southport Police Court on the body of Joseph Highfield, aged 18, engine cleaner in the employ of the Lancashire and Yorkshire Company. On Wednesday night the deceased was told to rake out the ashes from an engine in the locomotive shed. On the same rails 9 feet away stood another engine; the shedman William Rimmer got on the footplate of one engine and eased it up to the other, he heard a cry and on reversing the engine found the deceased lying in the foot-way. He was taken to the Infirmary but died within a few minutes. It is presumed he was coming from under the engine to get a fresh rake and was caught between the buffers; verdict: 'Accidental death'.

In the general reorganisation of shed codes by the LMS in the mid-1930s, Southport was accorded the code 23C, coming under the control of Bank Hall shed. By 1950, it had been recoded to become 27C but still came under the district control of Liverpool's Bank Hall shed. It would keep that coding until 1963, when under a general reorganisation of shed codes and district control it was accorded 8M, and came under the control of Edge Hill. It retained its 8M code until closure in June 1966.

Ron Clough, who spent two decades at Southport Derby Road shed from 1945, never had any interest in railways as a boy, but the 'great change' took place on 11 June 1945 when on the suggestion of his cousin Bill (W.S. Johnson), he applied for a job at Southport steam locomotive depot. Bill was already employed at Derby Road as a passed cleaner.

An interview was conducted at the depot with the shedmaster, Reginald Gardner. Mr Clough said the interview was rather basic and 'well within the scope of my elementary education' of reading, writing and basic maths. The interview was followed by a medical examination conducted at Manchester Victoria station in a 'time-expired L&Y rail coach' situated on the buffers on platform 5:

> The examination was very thorough, special interest was shown in eyesight, especially colour vision. The result of the exam was sent to Southport depot by internal phone and later confirmed by letter. On returning to the depot I was told to report for duty as an engine cleaner … the following day at 8a.m. and the rate of pay [was] 36 shillings and nine pence gross per week, first week in hand.

Mr Clough said that for the first six months of his career at Southport shed he was used as a general 'dogsbody' while learning the basics of engine cleaning from the senior cleaners, not a cleaning supervisor which was practised at other sheds. Other duties involved acting as deputy fitter's mate, for which he received an extra sixpence each week in his pay packet.

Soon he met the shedmaster to pass a test that would enable him to have the title of passed cleaner and the capability of doing firing turns. The requirements of the exam included knowing the basics of firing steam locomotives and the rudiments of the workings of a steam loco, the latter being attained by voluntary attendance at Mutual Improvement Classes on Sunday mornings in the nearby weighbridge office. Instruction at these classes was provided on an unpaid basis by fitter Harry Bailey.

Having passed his exam, Mr Clough was now available to be used on local firing duties and also placed on a six-man shift of passed cleaners who were divided into six by six shifts: midnight–4a.m., 8a.m.–noon, 4p.m. and 8p.m. To qualify for a first year fireman's rate of pay, it was necessary to do 313 firing turns. This might take passed cleaners anything up to five years to attain. In Mr Clough's situation, it took him six years because he had to do National Service between 1947 and 1949. Seniority and what tasks you had done in gaining experience also had a bearing on the issuing of railway clothing, as Mr Clough explains:

> The uniform consisted only of overalls until passed for firing, then serge jackets and overalls every two years. The first overcoat issue was after attaining fifty-two firing turns.
>
> Locomen's promotion was 'dead man's shoes' throughout the system but particularly in the case of Southport and other seaside resorts. Promotion was retarded due to line promotion enabling senior men from other depots to transfer in. To illustrate just how slow

promotion was at Southport, Charles Kirk, who was born in January 1900, joined the railway in 1919 after service in the Royal Navy. He became a registered driver in June 1955 – more than thirty-five years after joining the railways. In my case, it was twenty-one years to the day, [and] then only after transfer to Lostock Hall on closure of Southport depot.

In contrast, a twenty-three-year-old passed cleaner, John Marchant, transferred to Bury shed for promotion to driver. This was the minimum age to qualify for driver registration.

Mr Clough recalls that by the end of the Second World War three mileage turns existed at Southport, providing crews with extensive travel compared to the regular duties of the shed. These were:

• The 07.00hrs Southport–Bradford–Leeds which split at Low Moor and returned on the 11.15hrs Bradford Exchange–Liverpool Exchange train, with the crew travelling home from Liverpool as passengers on a train
• The 08.55hrs Southport–York and return (228 miles); and
• The Southport crew travelling as passengers by train to Bank Hall (Liverpool) to pick up their engine, which they then took light engine to Liverpool Exchange for a 16.30hrs departure for Bradford and Leeds. This train also was split at Low Moor with the Southport men working back a 19.15hrs train for Manchester Victoria (which departed there at 21.00hrs) and arrived back at Southport at 21.57hrs (152 miles).

Other steam-hauled work from Southport shed included the 'residential expresses' to Manchester, local trains to Preston, Rochdale, Liverpool or Ormskirk, and, in summer only, trains to Blackpool and Fleetwood. There were also freights and local pick-up work from Southport to Lostock Hall (Preston), Bamfurlong (Wigan), Agecroft and Aintree.

Pete Hardy began work at Southport shed as a cleaner in February 1952. When he started, the Midland compounds that had been based there were on their way out and were being replaced by brand-new British Railways Standard 4s, Nos 75015–19. As well, Mr Hardy recalls Stanier Black 5s Nos 44728, 44729, 44989, 45228 and 45435 also being based there. He says:

All were good locos, maintained by a team of excellent fitting staff. We also had Fairburn tanks 42290–42292 and Stanier small tanks (2-6-2s) Nos 40190, 40191, 40192, 40193, 40196 and 40197, a few Lancashire and Yorkshire Railway 'A' class engines and an ex-L&YR saddle tank 51490 on which I did my very first firing turn in the coal yard.

[There were] very cramped working conditions and you had to operate the ratchet reverse lever for the driver; you were on the go all the time with plenty of traffic; I gave the driver a Capstan full strength, he lit it and put it out six times!

Mr Hardy also recalled on 'several occasions' being asked to fill the tank on engine 51490 because its regular fireman was a 'huge man of Italian extraction' who was incapable of getting on top of the saddle to put in the water bag to fill it.

Mr Hardy was also given the task of cleaning the underside of a 'Radial' tank's frames and motion only to discover when cleaned that all of the frames were painted in red and white. 'I was told by the shed foreman at the time that I'd done such a good job that in future I would be allocated the job on a regular basis, but nothing became of it, thank goodness,' he said.

He recalls there being a 'typical L&YR coal stage double ramp and very good Yorkshire hard coal' at Southport shed in the early 1950s. He continues:

When I started, Southport had lost the York jobs to Bank Hall and the two 5XP locos 45698 *Mars* and 45717 *Dauntless*. Most of the work consisted of Manchester Victoria commuter trains with some extended to Bradford Exchange, Low Moor, Rochdale, Accrington and the local Preston services. And there were, of course, the Wigan returns, [and] also a service to Liverpool Edge Hill via the [third rail] electrified line, three times daily to attach to the southbound London expresses from Lime Street. These were worked by Stanier 2-6-2 tanks as were

Southport engine No.40196 waits to depart Preston for the seaside town in May 1957. Posing beside the loco is fireman Ron Clough. This engine was one of nine allocated to Southport Derby Road shed in 1955; it was the last of its class in service when withdrawn in December 1962. (Charles Kirk)

Engines from Lancashire travelled far and wide, particularly the Jubilees that worked out of sheds like Bank Hall, Edge Hill and even Southport. Likewise, those from Yorkshire could often be found at Southport. Here, fireman Peter Hardy climbs down from the cab of Jubilee 45661 *Vernon* at Leeds Holbeck shed. The yellow stripe through the cabside of this engine dates the photograph from the period autumn 1964 to May 1965 when *Vernon* was withdrawn from this shed. (Peter Hardy collection)

the Preston services. There was also a service to Ormskirk, via Burscough Junction, that was worked by these engines.

The highlight of the day was the through train to Glasgow worked by a big-boilered 'Scot' 46121 *H.L.I.* (Highland Light Infantry) which was the regular loco for that working that departed about 8.30a.m. and was a return working for Preston men.

The Glasgow 'train' was worked into Southport with three coaches off the Preston train, by Preston men. They then worked the return back to Preston where those coaches were added to the return consist for Glasgow.

We had a few visitors from Newton Heath [shed] in the form of 5XPs (Jubilees) ... Farnley Junction 5XPs would [also] be pretty frequent visitors, including *Express*, *Vernon*, *Victory*, *Bihar and Orissa*, *Conqueror*, *Ocean*, *Cyclops*, *Seahorse*, *Irresistible*, *Prince Rupert* and *Boscawen*.

Our regular station pilot was an ex-L&YR 'Radial' 2-4-2 tank. Nothing much in the way of foreign locos came on the shed except for a Lostock Hall 'A' class in the afternoon or a Fowler 0-8-0 Austin 7.

One of Southport's small allocation of Aspinall 'Radial' 2-4-2 tank engines built by the Lancashire & Yorkshire Railway in the late 1890s, No.50746, backing a consist into Chapel Street station in the 1950s. No.50746 spent most of its BR career at Southport shed, apart from three years at Lower Darwen from September 1951 to December 1954. It was withdrawn from Southport shed in February 1961, after more than sixty-four years of service. (Michael Dawson – Step Back through Time collection)

Mr Hardy recalls Southport having two routes in from Wigan with the lines split at Bescar Lane Junction, with one line going off to the high level via Meols Cop and St Lukes, and the low level running through Blowick via St Lukes via a different platform. He said:

> I lived at Blowick and there was an extensive siding there and on a summer Saturday I used to help the steam raiser look after the locos; keep the boilers topped up and put some coal under the firebox door.
>
> There would be a variety of LNER steam in the shape of K3s from Gorton, D11s from Trafford Park and of course the Crabs.
>
> My railway career started with the spark that was trainspotting; like so many young chaps the same age, it got in the blood.
>
> Of course, there was the other shed at Southport, the two-road ex-CLC or Cheshire Lines Committee that ran along the coast to Liverpool [at Lord Street]. There was no allocation of locos to the CLC shed, engines there were from Brunswick [shed]. I never saw any staff but a D10 would sit in the shed all day long.
>
> You could go there in the daytime and see a D10 'Director' *Purdon Viccars* simmering in the shed awaiting its evening duty; if you were lucky you could also see a B17 [being] run in, ex-works from Gorton. I did see two one summer, *Harlaxton Manor* and *Clumber*, both in splendid apple green.
>
> At the same time, on the station were LNER posters telling of new build locos, namely [A2] *Owen Tudor*.
>
> I started on the railway at the same time that the CLC [shed] closed and the two CLC drivers came to Derby Road [shed].

Former Lower Ince shedman Fred Darbyshire spent time in the 1940s at Trafford Park shed and made these observations about the footplatemen at the CLC shed in Southport:

Ex-LNER locos were a regular sight in Southport into the early 1950s. Here, a visiting K3 class 2-6-0, No.61832 of Gorton shed, is in company with a J10 class 0-6-0 in July 1950. The K3 class loco survived until October 1962 when it was withdrawn after almost thirty-eight years' service. (Steamport collection)

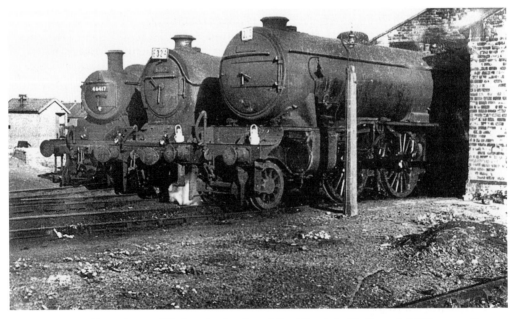

The eclectic mix of locos that could be found at Southport's Lord Street shed in the early 1950s was quite interesting, especially for such a small depot. In this September 1951 view, ex-LMS Ivatt 'Mickey Mouse' No.46417 shares the tracks with ex-LNER D11 4-4-0 No.62662 *Prince of Wales* and K3 class 2-6-0 No.61829. (Steamport collection)

Whilst talking about Manchester–Liverpool express trains [of the era] let us not forget the Southport engine crews who also worked these trains. The shed, railway lines and station in Lord Street, Southport, have long gone. Because the shed was only small, promotion was very slow, so the firemen looked as old as the drivers; this was the case when I was travelling to work at Trafford Park on day shift – I would sometimes catch a train from Irlam. [When] a Southport crew worked the slow train from Liverpool you did not know which one was the driver; the crew I was familiar with had a small chubby fireman with a dirty face always smiling as they ran into the station [with him] hanging over the side of the cab.

Their day was: get the engine ready, work a slow train to Liverpool from Southport, turn the engine, then work a slow train to Manchester Central, turn and water the engine etc. Then they'd work a 'Forty Minuter' back to Liverpool, turn their engine, then work a slow train back to Southport and then dispose the engine. Then, I suppose, my little chubby fireman could have a wash. It was said he only swept the footplate once a day; no wonder he was dirty.[39]

Ron Clough also recalls time spent at Lord Street shed which was part of the Cheshire Lines Committee (CLC) but, upon Nationalisation of the 'Big Four' railways on 1 January 1948, became part of British Railways. The shed effectively became a sub-shed of Southport Derby Road.

He says that at that time, Lord Street's complement of men was eight: four drivers and four passed firemen. Due to a reduction in the working week in July 1947, from forty-eight hours to forty-four hours, footplatemen would receive a rest day every fortnight; cover for Lord Street men on such rest days was provided by crews from Derby Road shed:

The antiquated system that existed at the CLC shed had to be seen to be believed. One man, Bill Padnock, on night turn was responsible for all shed duties, steam raising, coaling and other tasks and it was quite commonplace to see relief firemen from Derby Road carrying a can of engine oil or fire irons across town.

On one occasion passed cleaner Reg Griffiths carried a Class 4 compound loco's baffle plate on his head to replace one lost in a firebox on disposal.

One of the turns I covered departed Lord Street after 8a.m. and on arrival at Gateacre backed across on to the down platform and awaited the next train from Southport to discharge its Manchester Central-bound passengers, then continued on to Liverpool Central. My train would then proceed to Manchester Central, stopping at all stations en route, before returning to Liverpool Central all stops. Then [we would go] light engine to Brunswick shed, and travel home as passengers via the Liverpool Overhead Railway to Sandhills, where we'd transfer to a Liverpool Exchange–Southport service.

The afternoon service coupled to this loco's routing involved signing on at approximately 4.25p.m., then travelling as passengers to Brunswick depot, again via the L.O.R., take the engine left by the early turn's crew, make it ready and travel light engine to Liverpool Central for an 18.12hrs all-stations train to Lord Street, dispose of the engine and finish your shift after walking to Derby Road shed.

Mr Clough says that after Lord Street shed closed on 7 January 1952 the two senior drivers – Albert Bentham and Robert Rimmer – retired. Another, Arthur Foulks, transferred to one of the Liverpool sheds, while the fourth, Ted Shannon, transferred to Bank Hall shed. Fireman Albert Bentham (junior) took resettlement, fireman Frank Simpkins transferred to Derby Road shed, but Mr Clough is unsure of what became of the remaining two firemen.

Mr Hardy recalls that when he started at Southport shed there were three shed foremen, including Ernie Cameron who had lost an arm while hand sanding an L&YR 'A' class coming out of Brindle Heath in the 1930s:

All of the lads used to call him 'wingy'. Then there was a chap called Lambert; they used to call him 'Crackers' because at the slightest provocation he would explode and go quite crimson in the face; he was an ex-Lord Mayor of Southport and also a freemason.

Southport Lord Street was a good place to find surviving pre-Grouping types of Great Central lineage. In this June 1951 shed scene, 'Director' class 4-4-0 No.62656 *Sir Clement Royds* is prepared before taking a return excursion out of the seaside town. (Steamport collection)

Then there was a bloke who came from Doncaster; he was the best of all, you couldn't ruffle him but his name escapes me. The shedmaster was Reginald Gardner and he served his apprenticeship at Horwich. He was the only person [at the shed] to own a car – an Austin 7 Chummy. All of the top link drivers came to work on a bike!

Mr Hardy also recounts how he would get his hair cut by a boiler washer behind a stack of brick-arch bricks for the princely price of sixpence – 'not a bad little earner for him in the 1950s'. He continues:

There used to be a lot of high-jinx going on in the shed, the favourite trick was to hang a bucket of cleaning oil on the front hook and then uncouple the front vacuum pipe on the engine and stick it in the bucket. Then when some innocent went by the front of the loco the small ejector was opened up and everyone got showered with cleaning oil.

Mr Hardy points out that all L&YR engines when used as mixed traffic engines had vacuum-operated scoops for taking water from water troughs:

It was a very simple operation, just a small lever on the tender – none of the manual screwing the dip down and then not being able to get the scoop back and overfilling the tender. It was a pity that it was not generally put into practice on more modern locos.

As a general rule, the cleaners would clean three engines – a Black 5 and two Standard 4s. A white solution would be used on the engine's paintwork and a cleaning oil used on wheels and motion. Mr Hardy recalls:

There were two shifts of cleaners, six to a shift; five fitters, one steam raiser, one boiler washer, two labourers, three coal stage workers, four clerks and a foreman. It escapes me now how many loco men there would be at the shed in the early 1950s, but every driver would be matched with a fireman.

Mr Hardy didn't enjoy working with the tank engines; the Stanier Black 5s were his favourite motive power. The 'Lanky' types were 'very demanding' and needed to be fired correctly, and the injectors on the L&YR 'A' class needed to be cooled with water in summertime:

We had an extra pilot [engine] on summer Saturdays for excursion traffic and on this particular day we had a Lanky 'A' class. The driver told me to fill the box; this I did and then we got instructions from the signal box to go back on the shed.

Having duly left the loco on the coal road we retired to the mess room; ten minutes later the fire dropper came ranting and raging into the mess room and what he was going to do to my driver was nobody's business.

Freight workings for Southport men were few and far between in the 1950s and Mr Hardy can only recall one turn out of Brindle Heath (Manchester) which ran about 8p.m., roughly twenty wagons in length, with a tare weight of about 800 tons. Any non-passenger train rosters were mostly pickup workings, placing coal wagons and empties, he recalls.

Ron Clough was passed out to drive steam locomotives after ten years' service with the railways but it was an unhappy year for him because of the ASLEF's (Associated Society of Locomotive Engineers & Firemen's) seventeen-day strike: 'So futile and the monetary reward was nil in my case.'

After passing for driving, Mr Clough signed his route card to include all of the depot routes covered by steam. This was accepted practice and the management took advantage of passed firemen signing for routes they had learned while firing; the exception was where new routes occurred.

Mr Clough says the footplate staff complement at Southport shed in the 1950s was very static with seventy drivers available – thirty of which were employed on Southport–Liverpool electric services. There were also forty firemen. Passed firemen never covered electric work. As well, there were thirty-six cleaners who were employed to cover any sickness, holiday or extra firing vacancies.

The forty steam drivers at the depot were divided into six links: top link mileage and express trains – eight men; the compound link Class 2 trains – eight men; local or old men's link – six men; goods pilot – three men; shed men – three men; and No.6 link (steam/electric) to cover holidays and sickness on electric and electric work – twelve men.

On 9 August 1957 Standard 4 No.75019 ran out of control down the coal stage ramp and collided with 52123 and 41189 at the back of the shed, bringing about the withdrawal of the latter two engines.[40]

By 1958 Ron Clough was appointed deputy running shift foreman at Southport, providing cover when sickness or holidays prevented the established RSF from doing the job:

Each depot would have at least three deputies. In 1958 I was asked if I would care to be trained for the task. I was quite aware of the enormity of the job and the responsibility it carried. [This included] being in charge of a total shed staff of 200-plus men, local working regulations, extra weekend work, and the individual personalities of the loco men, not to mention the two rail union reps (Local Departmental Councillors) who often had contrary views to local practice.

As a deputy foreman it was expected of you to apply for promotional vacancies within your own department, for example smoke inspector, firing instructor or RSF. I only applied for one vacancy as firing instructor at Wigan Springs Branch shed, fully aware that my chances were nil, as a senior driver from Aintree had applied and, as expected, was appointed. It was much deserved and I knew him well, a man who had given hours of his own time to Mutual Improvement Classes at his home depot.

Mr Clough says he looks back on his supervisory lot with considerable pleasure. He made few enemies and many friends, even if the enhanced pay didn't balance the family sacrifices the job demanded.

The employing of special passenger traffic regularly brought unusual engines to Southport over the years. For example, on 14 November 1959 Royal Scot No.46116 *Irish Guardsman* of Crewe North shed arrived at Southport hauling a football excursion from Workington.

Meanwhile, Glasgow Polmadie Royal Scot No.46121 *Highland Light Infantry, City of Glasgow Regiment* was noted at Southport on 2 May 1960 working the 8.30a.m. train to Manchester, while on 20 May another 'Scot', No.46106 *Gordon Highlander* of Longsight shed, was on the lightweight 9p.m. Southport–Manchester train.

Until the mid-1960s Southport provided a direct passenger service to London via Liverpool, where the ex-Southport carriages were consolidated with a Liverpool consist. This two- or three-carriage supplement express was regularly hauled to Liverpool by a 2-6-4 tank of either Fairburn or Stanier design.

On Good Friday 1960 (15 April) an unusual pairing was observed working a Werneth (Oldham) to Southport train – 3F 0-6-0 No.43721 of Kettering shed (15B) and Crab 2-6-0 No.42871 of Newton Heath (26A). Pilot engines were always necessary on this line during the steam era because of the severe gradients between Failsworth and Oldham. However, the 3F type was particularly noteworthy for being used on passenger work, although the class had infrequently penetrated on to the line on freight workings.

Excursion visitors to Southport at Whitsun time included Willesden-based Patriot No.45547 travelling from Hazel Grove via Aintree and Burscough Junction on 5 June, while the next day York B1s 61053 and 61337 arrived with specials from Stanningley and Rothwell; on 11 June a special from Rotherham produced a Standard 9F No.92153 of Toton, at Southport, and another 92017 arrived with an excursion from Todmorden on 18 June. In the early hours of Whit Monday, Clan Pacific 72006 *Clan Mackenzie* was at Southport. It worked the 8.05a.m. to Manchester that morning and later the same day headed the 4.12p.m. ex-Manchester and 4.35p.m. ex-Liverpool combined express to Glasgow, out of Preston. Another unusual visitor to Southport on the same day was Fowler 2-6-4 tank No.42303 from Chester.[41]

During mid-July, a Bristol-based Standard Class 5, No.73068, took over a Southport diagram from the Low Moor end, making a round trip from Bradford to Southport and another to Liverpool Exchange on 19 and 20 July. Also, *Trains Illustrated* magazine recorded that Britannia class Pacifics had 'virtually disappeared' from the early morning Southport–Manchester workings in July. The 8.30a.m. train was usually worked by a Jubilee, but on 27 July one of the rare Royal Scot workings of the train occurred when 46137 *The Prince of Wales's Volunteers (South Lancashire)* of Longsight shed was used. Agecroft-based B1 No.61201 was also in charge of the 8.33a.m. Southport–Manchester stopping train on several days during July. Then on 3 August, Doncaster-based B1 No.61360 worked the 'Humber Rover' special train from Hull to Southport.

In January 1961 a pair of Ivatt 2-6-2Ts Nos 41277 and 41328 were transferred to Southport after having been in store at Burton shed (17B) since the withdrawal of the Tutbury service the previous June. The pair was to be used on station pilot duties and carriage shunting at Chapel Street station and replaced two ex-Lancashire & Yorkshire Railway 'Radial' 2-4-2Ts Nos 50746 and 50850 that carried out these duties before being put into store.

Alec Macdonald became shedmaster at Southport after a career that had begun as an apprentice at Bank Hall shed on 5 November 1946:

> I'd always been interested in railways but there was no family history of railway employment. I was the first. The workmates were good but the facilities were poor; the tools we had were often made by workers for certain jobs, such as oddly shaped spanners for removing nuts in obscure places. The main works manufactured tools for specific jobs such as removing cones from injectors.
>
> At Bank Hall there was approximately thirty to forty staff headed by a Mechanical Foreman, there was approximately six or seven apprentices.
>
> There was no sense in the 1950s that steam was on its way out – I viewed it as a job for life and that steam would continue. Into the 1960s, however, it was a different thing.

The apprentices would learn how to change gauge glasses, renew piston gland packing and change brake blocks. Fitters did the same work, in addition to changing piston rings, examining valves which distributed steam to the cylinders and checking bushes in coupling rods. Mr Macdonald recalls the most common problems were worn-out brake blocks and damaged water scoops. The heaviest and most taxing loco repairs were removing wheels on a wheel drop for attention to axle boxes which had become overheated.

Men on the footplate generally didn't like the ageing locos and preferred the newer engines; they were easier to work on due to enclosed cabs which offered better protection from the weather. The main drawbacks of servicing old locos were obtaining spare parts which had to be ordered through the main works and then waiting for delivery, which could take several weeks or even months.

Mr Macdonald says that after he finished his five-year apprenticeship in 1951 he was, fortunately, kept on at Bank Hall as a fitter, 'even though they often let people go'. Following an engine drivers' strike in 1955, he was working on nights and was asked to go and work at Liverpool's Walton on the Hill shed for a while, to 'see the engines off shed in the morning'.

Some shed staff were reluctant to grasp such opportunities and rejected these offers, but Mr Macdonald said he liked going to the 'outer sheds' to see how they operated:

> I'd had an enjoyable night [at Walton shed] and the running shed foreman there, who I got on quite well with, said I could do better if I got a transfer. I applied for the job of shedmaster at Bank Hall – I was applying for jobs all the time by now – but the senior man [who applied] got the job.

Later on, Walton's chargehand fitter was about to retire and Mr Macdonald saw there was a chance for himself. So he had a word with the chargehand fitter about the job and eventually got the position at Walton shed. Later, he went back to Bank Hall shed as assistant mechanical foreman for three months which added to his already considerable experience:

> Then in 1959 I applied for the shedmaster's post at Rhyl in North Wales and was appointed in Easter 1959; from there I deputised at Bangor until January 1960. Then I applied for a temporary vacancy at Lees (Oldham) – a lovely little place. I gained further experience there, being in charge of a breakdown train.
>
> I was there eight months and then the Southport [shedmaster's] job came up and in June 1960 I successfully applied for it. Beforehand they sent me to Bolton for a week.
>
> I was happy to take on the extra responsibilities as they came and didn't feel out of my depth due to the past experiences I'd had. Looking back to that time, staff followed instructions and worked well. I enjoyed my time there, everyone worked in harmony with one another.

At this time, Southport's allocation of locos included 2-6-4 tanks for local passenger workings and Class 5 and Class 4 4-6-0s for express passenger workings to Manchester and Leeds. The main challenge in the job was obtaining spare parts for the locos. 'As a shedmaster you were responsible for "everything", including visits to staff who had been off sick for several months, attending funerals of staff or ex-staff, overseeing and delegating [duties] to staff. I managed 300 staff and reported to the District Motive Power Superintendent [at Bank Hall].'

Mr Macdonald says conditions at Southport shed in the early 1960s were 'pretty fair', with not much having changed from the time he had spent there on loan earlier in his career. At the time there were thirty-six locos based there and four or five of those would be out of traffic at any one time.

Lots of recurring work was done on shed, to a schedule every twelve to sixteen days, when a loco was brought in for boiler washouts. There were lots of small tasks that were recurrent – such as changing boiler gauge glasses.

Mr Macdonald says that engine examinations were carried out at set mileages: for example, the No.1 exam was done between 10,000 and 12,000 miles, right through to No.6 exam carried out at 40,000 to 48,000 miles. For the heavy mileage exams, and also for any repairs that were beyond Southport's capabilities, locos were sent to Bank Hall. The most complex repairs undertaken at Southport were mainly running repairs that did not necessitate a loco being taken out of traffic.

Engines would travel maybe 100,000 miles before they went to the works for overhaul, but that was dependent on their condition. Mr Macdonald recalls:

> We had an engine, a Stanier Class 5 that went 200,000 miles before going to the works. We had one loco, 44767, the only one they built with outside Stephenson link motion. It came to Bank Hall around 1948. The foreman there appointed me to do specific jobs on it, for example it has [Timken] roller bearings axles and every time it went through a [boiler] washout, I had

to go through all of the axleboxes with special oil. It was a very strong engine and we used to use it on the Liverpool to Leeds passenger run.

In early 1962 they were transferring some engines from Bank Hall to us at Southport and I specifically asked for 44767; I was told I'd get what I was given; but in any event I did get the loco [from mid-March]. I'm very impressed that it was preserved; my only regret is that when engines were being scrapped I couldn't buy one.

By the early 1960s one of the few locations on former L&YR territory where Ivatt Class 2 tanks worked on passenger duties was at Southport, on the 'Ormskirk Motor', the name harking back to the days when this service was actually an L&YR railmotor set.

'Radial' tank No.50850 had earlier been transferred to Southport from Bolton to replace 50781 on shunting duties at Chapel Street station, after the latter sustained damage in a collision, and it became the last of its class on the books in 1961. *The Railway Magazine* reported in September 1961 that 50850 'has found regular use on pilot duties in Chapel Street station at Southport again since the commencement of the summer timetables'.[42]

During August No.50850 was seen working as additional station pilot during the annual Southport Flower Show and when it was finally withdrawn in November 1961 after sixty-two years in service, it had the distinction of being not only the last surviving ex-L&YR passenger engine, but also the last 2-4-2 in traffic on British Railways. One of the engine's final passenger workings occurred on 17 September 1960 when it hauled the Central Lancashire Railtour, covering 113 miles, most of it unaided. On 8 October 1961, the engine hauled the 12.45p.m. Southport–Ormskirk and the 1.53p.m. return trip.[43]

The summer 9.10a.m. Saturdays-only Southport–Glasgow train by 1961 was normally combined with the 9.15a.m. Liverpool Exchange–Glasgow train at Burscough Junction; however, on

The unique Stephenson link-motioned Black 5 No.44767 at Southport shed on 28 October 1961. At this stage the loco still bears the 27A Bank Hall shedplate; however, in 1962 when Bank Hall was divesting itself of some of its locos, Southport shedmaster, Alec Macdonald, requested a transfer of this engine to Southport, but was told 'he would get what he was given'. In the event his wish was respected and this excellent loco came to Southport. Withdrawn in late 1967 from Carlisle Kingmoor shed, it fortunately has been preserved. (RCTS - CHO1468)

An image rich in detail in this depiction of a derailment at St Luke's, Southport, around the summer of 1959. St Luke's was about three-quarters of a mile east of Chapel Street station, Southport, and almost adjacent to the engine shed. Depicted in this image are: bottom left hatted man facing camera, Fred Gornell; with him is chief area permanent way inspector, Billy Seed; to the right foreground, wearing a trilby hat, is loco shedmaster Reg Gardner and beside him is Harry Cork, the local permanent way supervisor; the trio sitting on the cable boxes are, from left to right: shunter Les Dobson, fireman Bob Sawyer and driver Jack Walley. Behind them, the crew on loco No.40163 are fireman John Heaton (standing) and his driver Frank Sinkins. In the background can be seen one of Southport's Standard 4MTs, No.75015, and the shed coaling stage (complete with coalman looking out of the coaling bay wondering what all the fuss is about); and nearby, one of the shed's Stanier/Fairburn 2-6-4 tanks which worked the many passenger turns to Manchester, Preston and beyond. (Mel Thorley collection)

15 and 22 July 1961 the former was a separate train of fifteen coaches. For the first of these workings Millhouses Jubilee 45654 *Hood* was sent light engine to Southport on 13 July and spent the following day on local residential expresses; on 22 July 45612 *Jamaica* was provided, once again two days in advance, returning with the Glasgow–Liverpool train on 24 July.[44]

Autumn 1961 saw several Royal Scot 4-6-0s, displaced by diesels on the Settle–Carlisle line, transferred from Leeds Holbeck to Low Moor shed. Since the engines were too wide to work the Liverpool line from Wigan Wallgate, the 'Scots' were confined to working slow trip return passenger trains between Bradford and Southport. However, by the beginning of November 1961, the 'Scots' were transferred away to Mirfield and rostered on to freight workings until their early withdrawal.[45] On 3 November, however, Britannia Pacifics Nos 70019 *Lightning* and 70023 *Venus* were at Southport when the 8.30a.m. Southport–Manchester train was powered by 70019, and the following day 70023 was in charge of the 5.40p.m. Manchester–Southport train.

Until January 1962 two daily direct express trains ran between Southport and Bradford and Leeds, via Manchester, and could be powered by anything from a Low Moor Black 5 through to the previously mentioned 'Scots'. This all ended when diesel multiple units took charge of the Calder Valley line in early 1962 and direct trains between Southport and West Riding were withdrawn.

The early 1960s also resulted in many of the experimental Black 5s congregating at Southport shed where they were employed hauling passenger trains to Manchester and Rochdale. The transferees included Caprotti valve gear-fitted engines in single- and double-chimney versions.

The early 1960s provided surprising diversity for any trainspotters congregated at Southport Chapel Street station with Standard Class 4s working expresses to Manchester, ex-LNER B1s (from Agecroft shed) hauling secondary passenger trains and Fairburn or Stanier 2-6-4 tanks in charge of Preston trains. On 8 January 1962, Clan Pacific No.72004 *Clan Macdonald* was used to head the 6.10p.m. Manchester Victoria–Southport train. While diesel multiple units were making inroads into these services, the 4.43p.m. from Manchester and the returning departure from Southport at 8.25p.m. had reverted to steam haulage. The businessman's 8.30a.m. Southport–Manchester train was still usually a Royal Scot duty, 'but Britannia Pacifics were rarely seen on this route nowadays'. While Black 5s and 2-6-4 tanks handled most of the traffic on this route, in the second half of January Edge Hill Royal Scot 46134 *The Cheshire Regiment* hauled the 5.52a.m. Preston–Southport and 8.05a.m. return and the 5.12p.m. Preston–Liverpool Exchange and the returning 7.40p.m. train.[46]

Another former railwayman who began work at Southport shed in November 1961 was Arthur Nettleton. As a schoolboy he developed an interest in local railways and began trainspotting at every opportunity. On leaving school he decided to apply for a position at Derby Road shed as an engine cleaner but was told he'd have to wait until sixteen years of age. So, a month before his sixteenth birthday, Arthur applied again and this time was accepted:

> My first day (with an 8a.m. start) was relatively easy; I was issued with regulation overalls, engineman's greasetop cap, rule book and other items I required. For the rest of the day myself and the other new cleaners were shown around the shed by one of the established cleaners. The most important place shown to us was the 'mess room' where we could brew up and have our meals during the day. We also went to the main office where we signed various documents and also met the shedmaster – Mr Alec Macdonald. Having completed first day formalities we were allowed to return home about 16.30hrs.

For some time Mr Nettleton was on regular day turns and gradually got to know the various men who worked at the shed and the foremen. Three that were contemporaneous were Harry Howard, Bill Porter and Ab Taylor. The cleaners spruced up engines in gangs of four, with the hierarchy dictating that the senior cleaner had the best job with the newest recruits having the worst tasks – the wheels and motion. At other times, Mr Nettleton would be assigned as labourer to a shed fitter or was put on pit-cleaning duties, not the most popular task. Another regular job for the cleaners was helping out on the coaling stage, refuelling locos.

By February 1962 Mr Nettleton was experienced enough to be passed out for firing duties and, along with other cleaners from around the district, he was despatched to Aintree shed to complete several weeks of firing instruction under the watchful eyes of instructor Harry Bailey:

> Harry taught us all there was to know about the intricacies of locomotive firing and having completed this instruction course I returned to Southport where I reported to Alec Macdonald. He asked me a series of questions relating to locomotives, firing and the rule book, which I answered to his satisfaction and he passed me out. So now I had the title of 'passed cleaner' or 'relief fireman'.
>
> I was beginning to think I would never get my (first) firing turn, when one afternoon shift the duty foreman informed me that the fireman on the station pilot locomotive had gone sick and I was to take his place. So, across to the station I went and found my locomotive stabled in a siding close to the signal box. I was delighted to discover that my first firing turn was to be on an Ivatt Class 2, 2-6-2 tank No.41277. I climbed aboard and made myself known to the driver, Dick Rigby. He put me in the picture about the job in hand and we continued with our duties until later in the evening when we returned to the shed where the locomotive was serviced.

In 1963 *Modern Railways* reported that for the first time in five years a Britannia Pacific had reached Southport when 70027 *Rising Star* brought in the 6.28p.m. passenger train from Preston on 18 February 1963.[47]

The following month, among engines awaiting scrapping at Horwich Works was ex-LMS Stanier 2-6-2 tank No.40196, formerly of Southport shed, which was the last member of its class in service when withdrawn in December 1962. Horwich was also overhauling engines, besides scrapping old ones. Engines running-in after overhaul at the works would often work local passenger workings, including, for example, Scottish-based Ivatt Mogul No.43133, which in April 1963 was observed working the Southport–Rochdale service after going through the works.

Southport shed could still call on 'foreigners' to work its express passenger turns to Manchester during 1963. On 6 July, for example, Bank Hall's long-time resident Jubilee No.45698 *Mars* was photographed at Bolton Trinity Street station in charge of a Southport–Manchester train.

By 1963, Southport shed retained twenty-seven locomotives on its roster board, most of them of passenger and mixed traffic design reflecting the type of work still handled by the depot. Of the allocation, three Standard 4s (Nos 75015, 75017 and 75019) had gone to Southport shed when new, in the early 1950s.

The allocation of a number of 'experimental' Black 5s – including the Stephenson link motioned 44767; Caprotti valve-geared engines such as 44742, 44743 and 44745, later joined by 44753 and double-chimney variants 44756 and 44757; plus the two later built Caprotti engines 44686 and 44687 – enabled these engines to be rostered on workings to Manchester and Rochdale.

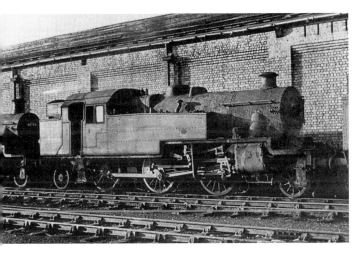

A pair of redundant Stanier 3P 2-6-2 tanks outside Southport shed, *c.*1960. In 1955 Southport had nine of these type of locos allocated, but by 1961 this had shrunk to just a trio: 40090, 40145 and 40178. They were gradually usurped by more modern machines that could handle local passenger services more effectively, such as Ivatt and Fairburn tanks. (Steamport collection)

Fairburn 2-6-4 tank No.42132 replenishes its water tanks at Southport shed on 21 March 1965 with driver Ron Clough and fireman Bob Pilkington. Southport always had a strong allocation of tank engines of either 2-6-4 or 2-6-2 wheel notation for working the many local passenger trains to Lancashire and Merseyside destinations. This example came to Southport in June 1961 from Hellifield. With the closure of Southport shed from June 1966 it was transferred to Bank Hall which promptly condemned the engine from the period ending 18 June 1966. No.42132 was cut up at Cashmore's at Great Bridge some three months later. (Ron Clough collection)

Arthur Nettleton recalls it was quite a while before his next firing turn, after the initial experience on 41277, but then regular firing turns did come his way 'and I travelled to such exotic places as Preston, Wigan, Blackpool, Colne, Accrington, Bolton, Rochdale, Manchester and Liverpool, as well as firing on engines on local freight trains'. His preference, however, was working the Southport–Preston line: 'A nice easy nineteen or so miles of mainly level track. Depending on the turn, and the locomotive, we could work either chimney or tender/bunker first.'

Another enjoyable turn he would sometimes work was taking the two-coach portion of the Southport–Euston train to Liverpool Lime Street, returning via Edge Hill. This service (where the Southport carriages were joined with the Liverpool portion for London) continued until mid-April 1966 and was regularly hauled by a Stanier or Fairburn 2-6-4 tank.

Mr Nettleton worked with many different steam drivers and passed firemen, and they were as varied as a 'box of liquorice allsorts'. However:

one driver, the late and sadly missed Joe Halsall, sticks in my mind. Joe taught me a great deal about steam locomotive practice. Alas, one day when on Southport shed I accidentally scalded Joe by putting on the locomotive injector. This resulted in Joe being off work for some time but despite this we remained firm friends, even in our later years at Steamport Railway Museum.

The relentless replacement of steam by diesel was illustrated during the summer of 1963 when excursions from Barrow to Southport over the period of 29 July to 2 August were each worked by one of Barrow shed's Metrovick Type 2 diesels.

On 15 December 1963 Walton-on-the-Hill shed in Liverpool closed and Aintree shed took over work previously handled by that shed. This created a shortage of loco crews and so various passed cleaners from the district, including Southport, were temporarily promoted to firemen to cover most of the jobs for a few months. As most of the additional jobs were freight turns, Arthur Nettleton was one of the men who got to try something a little different at 8L shed. He worked a variety of turns including working the famous 'Grid Iron' at Edge Hill and other local yards, plus trip freights to Liverpool North Dock and short trip work to destinations around the district:

After my loan period at Aintree shed I started to think about a more permanent transfer to a bigger shed with a wider variety of work [than could be experienced at Southport]. I began looking at the 'Vacancies' list and finally decided on a transfer to Edge Hill shed in June 1964 where I worked until I finished on the railways in 1968.

By early 1964, Britannia Pacifics had become regular rosters on the 08.20hrs Southport–Manchester residential train. No.70018 *Flying Dutchman* from Crewe North shed and 70041 *Sir John Moore* of Carlisle Upperby were noted hauling the train on several occasions in January and February of that year.

However, according to a correspondent to *Modern Railways* there were 'many raised eyebrows' when Fowler 2-6-4 tank No.42369 was turned out to work the 17.00hrs Manchester Victoria–Southport residential train on 20 March 1964.

In the January 1965 issue of *The Railway Magazine*, it was reported that:

the virtual closure of the former LNWR line between Manchester Victoria and Wigan North Western, and the closure of Blackpool Central, had caused an almost complete change-over on lines north-west of Manchester. From 2 November 1964, passenger trains on the former Lancashire & Yorkshire line between Manchester Victoria and Southport have been taken over by diesel multiple-unit sets with a few exceptions. The plight of the displaced steam locomotives is uncertain, but it appears that most of the 2-6-4 tank engines, so long masters of local trains and based principally at Southport and Wigan, will be scrapped.

By 1965, Southport shed was eking out an existence and only eleven engines were available on its roster, more than half of these being 2-6-4 tanks. It was also reported in the railway press that on Good Friday 1965, 'nearly all the extra Blackpool and Southport trains were hauled by Black 5 class engines from Newton Heath (9D) shed'.[48] The following month a series of tests were conducted with Brush Type 4 diesels on the Southport to Manchester line. Two of the engines used, D1813 and D1815, were allocated to Newton Heath (9D).

The conferring of nicknames to footplatemen was practised at most sheds in the steam era and Southport was no exception. Ron Clough recalls some of these names being quite cruelly applied, but the one he found the most amusing explained why one staffer became known forever after as 'Jimmy Debris':

> Jimmy was the junior member of his six-man cleaning link on an 8p.m. work allocation. Francis Lambert Spence, the shift foreman, issued cleaning work to the five senior men then told Jimmy to shift the debris from No.6 pit in the shed where the fire brigade had put out a fire in the shed roof. Jimmy departed somewhat bemused and returned to the office to ask: 'What the bloody hell's debris, Lambert?'

The annual Southport Flower Show in August 1965 brought in extra trains to the seaside town for the festival. These included Black 5s Nos 45290 and 45296, and Brush Type 4 D1806, Brush Type 2 diesel D5030 and Eastern Region Type 3 diesel D6740, all the way from Thornaby depot (51L).

From 18 April 1966 a service that provided through coaches from Southport to London Euston, via Liverpool Lime Street (where the coaches were joined with the 16.20hrs service to the capital) ceased to be steam-hauled and was replaced by diesel multiple units. In February 1966 among the engines used on this service was Southport's 42665.

The lead-up to Southport's eventual closure in June 1966 illustrated a stark period of waste. Alec Macdonald cited one example: 'We had a Caprotti Class 5 which had just come from the works

Stanier Crab No.42968 takes water from a station water tower at Southport on a fine sunny day, 18 July 1966. This engine, by now based at Springs Branch, became the last of its class to remain in service, being withdrawn on the last day of 1966. Today it is preserved in working order. (Ron Clough collection)

Fairburn 2-6-4 tank No.42233 pauses at Rainford Junction on 22 October 1966 while hauling the Liverpool University Public Transport Society's 'Wirral & Mersey' special train. The eight coach, which started at Liverpool Riverside station and ended at Liverpool Central (High Level) and took in Lancashire and Cheshire destinations, was hauled by four different locos. Apart from this engine, locos used were Crab No.42942, Edge Hill's celebrated 45015 and Britannia class No.70004 *William Shakespeare* (deputising for the advertised Jubilee class). This photograph would have been taken around 10a.m. when a brief stop was allowed for photographers on the train to capture the moment. (Michael Dawson – Step Back through Time collection)

after overhaul and it lost an oil box from one of its axles. It could have easily been replaced but they said – scrap it.'

The impending closure of Southport shed in mid-1966 was a time of great uncertainty for footplatemen working at the facility. Ron Clough recalls his feelings when hearing in May that year that it would shortly close and he was to be made redundant:

> My first reaction was one of total despair. I was the second senior man without a job, however I became aware that I was too deep into steam and rail to change. So after some soul-searching I decided to transfer to Lostock Hall, Preston, eighteen miles from home, where steam was to survive for a further twenty-six months, and so became not only a registered driver but also a part of one of the last three [main-line] steam depots in Britain.
>
> Then merging with Preston Main Line depot in 1968, a life of adventure was to follow on diesel, then electric traction, on the entire west coast main line for my final twenty-seven years.

Shedmaster Alec Macdonald was also sad about Southport's closure and the fact that there were many men 'worrying about alternative employment as they were all made redundant'.

Southport shed was officially closed on 6 June 1966 and surviving engines transferred to neighbouring depots. However, the last regular steam train out of Southport was on 11 June 1966, with Harry Langridge of Manning Road being driver on that occasion. Langridge, who at that stage had worked for the railways for twenty-five years, was driver on the train which went to Manchester and returned with empty stock. Power for this final exit was provided by Edge Hill Black 5 No.45156 *Ayrshire Yeomanry*.

* * *

It's time for a reflective moment in the cab of celebrated engine 70013 *Oliver Cromwell* at Southport in 1968. Driver Ron Clough (standing) and fireman Joe Unsworth appear to know steam's end can't be far away. (Ron Clough collection)

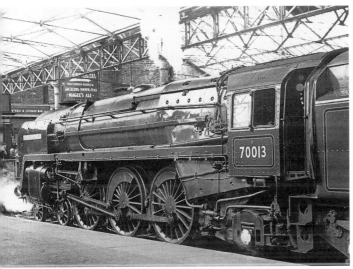

Britannia Pacific No.70013 *Oliver Cromwell* at Southport Chapel Street buffer stops after having brought in the Lancastrian No.2 railtour on 20 April 1968. This tour with a ten-coach train covered 280 miles in less than twelve hours and featured, apart from 70013, locos 45156 *Ayrshire Yeomanry* and another Black 5 No.45342. *Oliver Cromwell* hauled the section from Fleetwood via Preston to Windermere, and then the finale from Preston via Burscough Bridge to Southport, finishing at Liverpool Exchange. (John Corkill)

Ron Clough said that as a driver he always provided footplate opportunities to enthusiasts, trains-potters and inquisitive schoolboys. 'Schoolboys would often ask is it hard toil on the footplate. I always replied, "It's better than working for a living".'

With Southport's closure in June 1966, Alec Macdonald was transferred to Speke Junction shed to occupy the running shed foreman's job, deputising at times for the shedmaster, until that shed too closed in May 1968. He then moved to Birkenhead Mollington Street shed as train crew supervisor, a role he enjoyed, and then in 1980 to Liverpool's Lime Street station, again as a train crew supervisor:

In the 1980s I was suffering from a bad back – due to a slipped disk I had from 1963. The doctor said I should retire but I stuck it out as long as I could, but had to retire in 1992. I had a glorious time with the railways and went all over the country through working for the railways.

Following the end of steam on BR in 1968, Southport shed for many years experienced a revival as the headquarters of the Steamport Preservation Society. But at the end of 1997 it was decided to move its operations to Preston docks.

A general shed view of Steamport (as Southport Derby Road became) after the end of British Railways steam and preservation of steam became a burgeoning industry. A selection of industrial tanks is present on this Open Day, 25 September 1983. Keeping company with ex-British Railways diesel hydraulic Western class 52 locomotive No.1048 *Western Lady* are from front left: Hudswell Clark Works No.750 *Waleswood*; behind it is Peckett saddle tank *Whitehead* (No.1163 of 1908); and in the centre lane Peckett No.1999 of 1941 North Western Gas Board. (Steve McNicol)

For the farewell to Steamport before its closure, two weekends of farewell operations were held with locomotives from the Saddletank Trust in steam – quite fitting for a former Lancashire & Yorkshire Railway engine shed. Also adorned on the ticket are the three shed codes Southport Derby Road had allotted to it during the LMS and BR eras. (John Corkill collection)

Steamport near the end, and two ex-Lancashire & Yorkshire 'Pug' 0-4-0 saddle tanks, Nos 51231 and 51218, raise steam in familiar surroundings on 15 February 1998. No.51218 had the distinction of being the last of its class in service, not being withdrawn from BR until 1964. There is a nice touch evident here with 51218 wearing a 27C shedplate on its smokebox door (Southport), while 51231 sports a 27A (Bank Hall) plate. No.51231 appears to have its British Railways emblem affixed to the wrong tank, with the lion looking backwards compared to 51218's decal. (John Corkill)

Demolition of Southport shed began on 7 August 2000 and when the editor of the Engine Shed Society's magazine, *Link*, visited on 7 November the whole site had been levelled and cleared of debris (and with the like-named Jimmy nowhere to be found). By 2002, *Link* reported that by an 8 April site visit nothing remained of the former shed site and adjacent coal yard: 'The whole area is now occupied by the "Centre 12" retail development dominated by an Asda superstore which opened for business during March.'

In contrast, the site of the former Southport CLC shed was, by May 1997, covered by a road and, apart from the impressive frontage of Lord Street station, little evidence remains that a railway once existed in the area.

Seven

8P WIGAN 'C' (L&YR)

Wigan 'C' depot, or shed No.16 under the Lancashire & Yorkshire Railway, was situated in the angle formed by the Wigan to Liverpool and Wigan to Southport lines. The depot which people remember from the final years of British Railways' steam dated from 1905, but was preceded by three earlier depots in the area: the first, built in the 1860s, was burnt down in 1869. This was replaced soon after by a two-road shed built on the same site. Then, to meet a critical accommodation problem, a tender for around £7,000 was accepted in late 1877 for a shed to be built to house around twenty locomotives. This shed opened in 1878.

Rebuilt in the mid-1880s as an eight-lane facility, it also over time became inadequate for the large numbers of freight locomotives being shedded there. In turn, a new contract for a much larger shed was let in 1903, comprising a fourteen-road building, eighteen bays in length, a standard coaling stage and a 55ft-diameter turntable. It was completed in 1905 and the earlier eight-lane shed was abandoned. The new structure was built in the customary northlight-pattern style but was unusual in that a brick base supported a timber frame building, with the lofty roof being slated and glazed.

In its heyday immediately before the First World War, Wigan L&YR was home to more than seventy engines, a great majority of those being 0-6-0s, standard saddle tanks or 0-8-0s. However, there was sizeable local passenger traffic and up to twenty 'Radial' tanks were allocated for this work.

The surrounding land around the L&YR shed experienced a considerable amount of 'settling down' due to colliery subsidence, and, as a result, the gradients of the lines coming into the shed were constantly changing.

By 1934 Wigan 'C's allocation stood at fifty-nine engines, more than half of them being freight types. The following year the shed was recoded 23D, coming under district responsibility of Bank Hall in Liverpool. Although still showing its L&YR parentage, by the mid-1930s a few 'foreign'

A view of a largely empty Wigan L&YR shed most likely taken in the early years of the twentieth century. The falling gradient into this shed is apparent which concurs with the view of one ex-railwayman who said you had to be careful with the application of the engine's brakes in order to avoid the loco running away from you when coming on shed. (Courtesy of the Engine Shed Society)

The truncated nature of the former L&YR shed at Wigan is clearly evident in this image of redundant Stanier 2-6-2 tanks on the lanes, left exposed after the shortening of the shed. On view here, probably in the early 1960s, are Nos 40191 and 40145; the latter engine was allocated to Wigan 'C' from week ending 25 November 1961 until 2 December 1961 when it was transferred to Southport. It was withdrawn from service on 22 September 1962. No.40145 transferred to Southport from Pontypool Road in South Wales in the week ending 29 August 1959 and was withdrawn on the same day as 40191. (Brian Dobbs collection)

locos began to be drafted to the shed, including a trio of Stanier 2-6-4Ts, Nos 2405, 2409 and 2410, and two 19-inch ex-LNWR 4-6-0 goods locos.

The 2-6-4Ts increasingly displaced the 'Radials' on local work. Declining mineral traffic meant that by the end of the Second World War, the number of 0-6-0s had been halved to only thirteen, but Wigan became the last home to all three post-war surviving L&YR 0-8-0 classes, nineteen of them being withdrawn from the shed between 1948 and 1951. No.52727 was the last small-boilered Aspinall engine withdrawn in 1950; No.52831, the last saturated 6F engine, and No.52857, the last superheated 7F, were sent for scrap in February and December 1951 respectively. The last 2-4-2Ts had gone by 1953 and only a handful of L&YR locos remained out of the reduced complement of thirty-seven engines, which were mainly 2-6-4Ts and 4F 0-6-0s. Standard 78xxx 2-6-0s replaced the last of the L&YR 0-6-0s.

In later years mineral traffic in the Wigan area decreased and the importance of the shed correspondingly declined. However, the shed always retained an impressive stud of passenger tank engines which were usually well groomed and in excellent condition; these locomotives found employment on both slow and semi-fast trains in the Liverpool, Southport, Manchester and Rochdale directions.

Work in the Wigan area was concentrated as far as possible at Springs Branch, so Wigan 'C' received little in the way of improvements or modern aids. In later years it was partly demolished and a number of roads given over to wagon storage. The shed building adopted a distinctive L-shaped outline which it retained until the end.

Jack Green spent sixteen years at Wigan (ex-L&YR) shed until it closed. When he first went there, Mr Green was booked to work the No.2 passenger link. Each summer the eight 'old hand' passed firemen out of No.1 passenger link were booked to driving duties to cover holidays of the usual

An image that perfectly captures the smoky, gloomy atmosphere that often pervaded steam engine sheds in the 1950s and 1960s. This view of Wigan C taken in 1961 shows the L-shape format the shed took on after some of the roof section was demolished. As usual, a collection of mainly freight types or tank locomotives are present. (Allan Sommerfield)

Hughes-Fowler Crab 2-6-0 No.42715 photographed at Wigan 'C' shed during its second spell there in 1962. This loco was based at this shed until week ending 22 June 1963 when it was transferred to Aintree. Subsequently it saw spells allocated to Gorton, Newton Heath and Stockport Edgeley sheds, from where it was withdrawn on 26 February 1966. It was cut up at Cashmore's Great Bridge in June that year. (Brian Dobbs)

drivers. Fortunately, Mr Green was one of the 'old hands' in No.2 link who was promoted to the No.1 link.

Besides the passenger traffic, the shed also had local and mixed goods/shunting and banking jobs. Like Lower Ince, if crews had time at the end of their shift at Wigan 'C', they were expected to dispose of their engine.

Wigan 'C' was recoded 27D in 1950 and assigned the code 8P on 9 September 1963, coming under the district administration of Edge Hill shed, Liverpool. By now the shed building was becoming increasingly derelict and by 1963 it retained less than thirty engines on its roster.

For once, a sunny day at Wigan 'C' on 24 September 1961 with a fine line-up of engines. Throughout most of the late 1940s and 1950s this shed retained an allocation of around forty locos, but this had dropped to around thirty by the time this photograph was taken. On show here are a range of types, including Crab 2-6-0s, Fowler 4Fs and the inevitable tank locos for passenger workings. The shed closed on 13 April 1964. (Ken Fairey)

Ex-Lower Ince enginemen Jack Green, Bill Baxendale, Will Heppenstall and Bob Maybury transferred to Wigan 'C' shed after a short spell at Springs Branch on 12 May 1952. Mr Green became a passed fireman on 16 October 1957 and remained at Wigan 'C' shed until April 1964 when the shed closed, then transferred back to Springs Branch where he became a booked driver from 13 June 1966.

Alec Macdonald, who was shedmaster at Southport Derby Road shed from 1961 to 1966, spent a short time at Wigan 'C' in the 1950s, filling in when the shed had a staff shortage:

We used to get sent out on loan to other sheds when they were short on fitters and this happened to me for a few weeks when I went to Wigan 'C'. It was an interesting shed; it was situated on a slope and you had to be careful with locos to ensure their brakes were on or they might run away. The shed would have around half a dozen locos out of traffic under repair at any one time. Half the shed was covered and half had lost its roof.

They had ex-L&YR 0-8-0s, 'WD' 2-8-0s and ex-LMS 2-6-4 tanks there. The 0-8-0s were heavy engines and I was responsible in a way for the last one there being scrapped. I heard a funny noise when it was coming on shed one day and upon inspection it was found the crank webs had shifted. All the expense of going through the works ... it was eventually despatched to Horwich Works for scrapping, not long after.

In 1963 Wigan shed also acquired Standard 2 2-6-0 No.78002 from Machynlleth (89C) shed and one of its duties was to haul the 4.07p.m. passenger train from Wigan to Southport on 20 August. This engine was reallocated to Bank Hall later in the year.

By November *Modern Railways* was reporting that Lees (Oldham) shed was expected to close in November and that Wigan 8P and Bury 9M sheds were 'also believed to be under sentence'.

With the decline in district mineral traffic and a reduction in steam passenger-hauled trains, it was not surprising that Wigan 'C' shed was closed on 13 April 1964. The shed was demolished in 1966. The shed site now lies beneath the Miry Lane Industrial Estate.

A rare view of Wigan's turntable and possibly the location of the death of a railwayman who, according to one source, may still frequent this area in spectral form. (A.G. Ellis, courtesy of the Engine Shed Society)

Dave McGuire mentioned in the Engine Shed Society's *Link* publication that during a site visit on 8 February 2002 to the industrial estate, he was approached by an owner of one of the units. This person told him that during some excavations for a small café on the site, the turntable pit had been uncovered. It had since been filled in and no trace was evident on Dave's visit. However, the unit owner also told Dave that the site was open twenty-four hours but was locked up from early evening until the following morning, with a security guard on hand to let lorries in and out:

[One night] this guard had been making his rounds of the site in the early hours when a man on a bicycle, wearing a black coat and flat cap, had suddenly ridden past him.

Apparently, not knowing where he had come from or how he had got in as the place was locked up he turned to shout to him, only to see him disappear around about the area of the turntable. A search of the area revealed nothing, but later it was discovered that during the shed's existence, a labourer was killed by the turntable and that [presumably] what the security guard had seen was his ghost! How true this is I have no idea but, if it is, is this the first engine shed site with its own ghost?

Eight

10F WIGAN – LOWER INCE

Although it never became an '8' district engine shed, Wigan Lower Ince motive power depot deserves inclusion in this review of south Lancashire locomotive sheds, given its survival until the early years of British Railways, for its heritage as a former LNER facility in Lancashire and for its important role in keeping trains within the Wigan region operating during the busy war years and post-war period. Had Lower Ince survived a few more years, it inevitably would have been included in the '8' district grouping, as occurred with both Springs Branch and eventually Wigan 'C' sheds.

Lower Ince shed was opened on 16 October 1879 to the north of Lower Ince railway station on the western side of the line and was part of the Wigan Junction Railway. Originally built as a two-track, dead-ended shed with a gable-style slate roof, facilities included a water tank for replenishing engines based there. Sometime after 1907 (and by now part of the Great Central Railway) the shed was rebuilt as a two-track, straight-through shed. From the Grouping in 1923, as with other GCR depots it became part of the London and North Eastern Railway.

By Nationalisation on 1 January 1948, Lower Ince shed was assigned the code 13G, being in the group headed by 'A' shed, Trafford Park (Manchester), and also including sheds at Belle Vue, Heaton Mersey, Northwich, Brunswick and Walton on the Hill. In May 1950 Lower Ince was assigned the code 10F which it retained until its closure on 24 March 1952.

* * *

The late Fred Darbyshire joined the LNER in 1944 at Lower Ince shed and worked there until 1952 when, after the shed's closure by British Railways, he was transferred along with other staff to Springs Branch. Before starting work with the LNER he had worked at Irlam Steelworks from the age of fourteen but, as he neared his sixteenth birthday, a decision had to be made about acquiring a 'trade' and his fascination with locomotives, together with the fact that the war was still on, eventually influenced his family to allow him to pursue a career on the railways:

> I was going to night school ... to become a fitter ... [but] it was becoming difficult at home [and I was] missing night school for any number of reasons. ... I wanted to go to work on the railway [rather than stay at the steelworks] and as it turned out ... my mother was on my side. Three reasons: the war was not going too well and if it got worse and lasted I would have to go into the forces; in the First World War my mother lost two brothers who were killed and had a third brother wounded; and also my brother was already in the army.[49]

Late in 1943 a friend of the family, Tom Greenhall, who was a signalman in Springs Branch's No.1 signal box, got Fred an interview at Springs Branch shed with the intention of his joining the London Midland & Scottish Railway at that depot. Subsequently, Fred was called to Manchester Victoria station for a medical but failed the eyesight test because he was unable to correctly differentiate colours.

His shock at failing the test was short-lived, however, as he took matters into his own hands in early December 1943 when he took a half-day off work at the Irlam Steelworks, where he had begun in 1942, on the pretext of having to sit an exam at night school.

One of Lower Ince shed's J10 class 0-6-0s, No.65176, raises steam, probably in the early 1950s. This shed shows the typical arched entrances to the brick-built building popular in the late 1870s. (Fred Darbyshire collection)

Instead, he caught the 2.15p.m. train and got off at Lower Ince station. He took off his works' boiler suit to reveal his good clothes underneath and proceeded to the nearby engine shed.

Lower Ince engine shed sat behind the coal yard opposite the Big Rock pub, in Warrington Road, but as Fred looked around he couldn't find the way in. Panicking, he climbed over the wall by the side of the coal yard and then walked across to the cleaner's mess room where someone showed him the way to the office, which was at the front of the shed.

The office was in an old railway coach, minus its wheels and mounted upon a concrete base. Knocking on the door, Fred was greeted by Bill Ball, the boss. With him in the office was his right-hand man Jack Knowles, known as 'Peggy' because of his peg-leg. After a chat, Fred was given an application form to fill in; that done, he was told he would get a letter advising him where to go for a medical and a railway pass for the journey to Manchester. The letter duly arrived.

Fred eventually went for the test in the Great Northern Warehouse office block in Manchester, where again he submitted to an eye test:

> I remembered my last test, when I was giving a shade of colour for my answer instead of the colour of orange for red and so on; the doctor set me straight with the colours – 'you are looking for red and green, nothing else lad' – and this time there was no problem. I received a letter a few days later, with a date to start work on what would become my favourite railway company, the LNER.[50]

Reporting for work on his first day at Lower Ince (he'd cycled there from home on his 'trusty bike' dressed in ex-LMS overalls kindly donated by Tom Greenhall, with his sandwiches safely packed in an ex-army gas mask bag), Fred rode past J10 No.5170 which was parked behind the two-road shed, beside the path to the left of the shed.

He passed the fitters'/boilermakers' workshop (located at the end of the shed), then out into the open, until he came to the shed's office, with the rear of the old carriage facing towards the railway embankment which carried the old Lancashire & Yorkshire Railway main line. In there again were Bill Ball and Jack Knowles, besides two other lads he had met when attending his medical test. The pair started work on the same day as Fred. After introductions and a chat, they were taken to the mess room to meet the other cleaners and hang up their coats.

The new inductees were given the rules and regulations – what to do and what not to do around the shed – and informed who was who. Once the boss had left the mess room, the other cleaners introduced the new lads to another set of rules; later they were provided with uniforms including a cap, black coat and two sets of bib and brace-style overalls.

Fred recalled not much cleaning being done on his first day at Lower Ince shed, but before they went home the new cleaners were provided with their LNER rulebooks. The next day, one of the drivers, Bob Maybury, had the new guys in the enginemen's room to be introduced to the intricacies and what they needed to learn very quickly – for on Saturday morning of their first week they had to travel to Manchester Central to meet the footplate inspector, a Mr Adams.

Top of the list of information they needed to absorb was Rule 55 – about protecting their train and informing the signalman of where they were should a problem develop with their train. All the new boys had to learn Rule 55 'parrot fashion' and also the basics about putting coal on to a fire and water into the boiler via an injector. But because of his last job at Irlam Steelworks, and his abiding fascination with the steelworks' locomotives and through mixing with the engine crews there, Fred already had a very good grasp of the basics.

Come Saturday morning, Fred and the other two new starters were on the 08.04hrs train to Manchester Central where, at the end of the platform, they met Mr Adams together with cleaners from other sheds. Mr Adams took his charges to a waiting room, where he sat them down and delivered a chat mainly about the Rulebook and also their duties as firemen on the footplate. All were required to fill in a questionnaire and, after a cup of tea, were informed they could now be known as 'passed cleaners', effectively meaning they could be asked to go out on the footplate and act as firemen alongside a driver. Some of the older hands had taken five weeks to receive this 'test' to become passed for firing duties, but it was the luck of the draw as to when the inspector was available.

While working as a cleaner, Fred recalled that one of the important cleaners' tasks during winter was to keep the coal braziers going at the shed, at Wigan Central station and at any of the engine water columns available around the district.

In Fred Darbyshire's second week at Lower Ince he was called into the office with the other cleaners and told they would work shifts. In the 1940s the Lower Ince shifts were organised thus: on the day turn the 'old hand' cleaner would begin work at 4a.m. – he covered the early jobs; the next 'old hand' cleaner would start at 6a.m., with the remainder beginning at 8a.m. On the night turns, the 'old hand' cleaner would begin work at 1p.m., while the 'young hand' cleaner's start time was 11p.m.; the remainder started work at 5.30p.m. The structure of the start times meant that most jobs could be covered in the event of a rostered driver or fireman not turning up for duty. Passed firemen could fill in for sick drivers and passed cleaners would step up for missing firemen.

One rule, that said shed staff could only work night shifts if they were over eighteen years of age, was often conveniently overlooked during the war years. As well, extra jobs could be assigned to the shed and these could include extra trains for Haydock Park horse races, taking an engine to the

Another of Lower Ince's J10 class 0-6-0s, No.65175, departs after a halt at an unidentified station on the Wigan Central line. (Fred Darbyshire collection)

works for an overhaul, or assisting drivers from foreign sheds who required a pilot man in order to work over the local branch. So, on paper, there was always the chance of a firing turn for the new lads at the shed. The second week of Fred Darbyshire's employment at Lower Ince started with another intake of new cleaners, so Fred lost the tag of 'young hand' cleaner and with it the more unpopular shifts and duties.

Mr Darbyshire recounted some of the interesting and amusing aspects of life at this small ex-Great Central shed, shortly after his joining it, in an article in *Past Forward*, a newsletter of the Wigan Heritage Service, in its summer 2002 edition:

> The first train out in the morning was the 5.04a.m. Wigan Central, all stations to Irlam, taking the 6a.m.–2p.m. shift to the steelworks. [But] for the driver and fireman the day started much earlier ... it started at 12.01a.m. when the knocker up, Arthur Roscoe, signed on duty in the old railway carriage that was the office.
>
> Arthur could not be in two places at once ... some engine crews lived as much as three miles away from one another. As Cyril Moran [one of the 11p.m. cleaners] lived in Hardybutts, he was the knocking up expert around Scholes and Whelley.
>
> One morning Arthur asked Cyril to knock up Bill Hartford at 2.45a.m. to work the 5.04a.m. to Irlam. Bill lived in the shadows of Central station ... and was one of the older drivers who worked over his time because of the war (it was mid-1944). Cyril set off at 2.30a.m. to knock up Bill; he knocked on the door a couple of times and got a reply and headed back to the shed.
>
> But at 4a.m., night shift shed engineman, Fred Ford, came into the mess room asking who's knocked up Bill Hartford. Cyril replied, 'Me'. 'Well he's not turned up yet,' Fred replied.
>
> Fred now ... sent the 4a.m. cleaner, Frank Murphy, to give Bill Hartford's mate, a passed fireman, a lift to get the engine ready for the road; it was now 4.30a.m. and getting time for the engine to leave the shed for Wigan Central. Still no sign of Bill Hartford [so] Fred sent the engine out of the shed with Bill's mate as driver and Frank Murphy as fireman.
>
> Before long, Bill Hartford was rushing down the footpath to the shed office; once inside he demanded to know who had knocked him up as he was going to claim a day's pay because the knocker up had not waited for his reply. Fred assured him there had been a reply ... and got Cyril into the office.
>
> 'Are you sure you got a reply when you knocked me?' 'Yes,' Cyril replied. 'Are you sure it wasn't the parrot that answered?' asked Bill. Everyone was now smiling, Cyril was forgiven, and Bill went to Lower Ince station to take over his driving duties when the train returned from Irlam some time later.

Mr Darbyshire worked the 5.04a.m. to Irlam several times before Lower Ince shed closed, but he also remembered an incident involving driver Tommy Owen and Jack Clayton, who one day were in charge of the first morning train. Jack had just finished working on his fire and was leaning over the cabside when he shouted, 'I've just seen a body on the track!'

At Irlam the crew agreed to look for the body and this time both men saw the deceased man. At Culcheth station the engine driver reported their grim find. It later was found that the local man had taken his own life:

> In his pocket was an appointment for what he thought was a serious operation at Warrington Hospital, but it turned out [it would have been] only a minor one. Further investigations revealed that it was a Trafford Park crew, working the last train (bunker first) out of Wigan for the night [before], who had killed the man; the small tank engine had blood on its back end.

Working the 5.04a.m. works train from Wigan Central to Irlam brought back memories for Mr Darbyshire of the full platform over which a blue haze hung from cigarette smoke, and the 'mad scramble to get a seat' that accompanied the arrival of the train at Lower Ince. Latecomers would buy a morning newspaper from Jimmy Entwistle, the local newsagent. At Hindley station the routine was repeated with another full platform of grumpy workmen shoving and pushing, trying to find a seat on the rapidly filling train. At Irlam a quiet station suddenly came alive with the arrival of the day's first train from Wigan Central, with workers hurrying to clock on on time at the steelworks. Some were lucky that they worked at the station end of the massive works; others were not so lucky, as Mr Darbyshire noted:

> If the train was even just a couple of minutes late no amount of rushing would get them to the clock on time and they all got quartered. My first job as a fourteen-year-old was at the steelworks and I had to run every morning to clock on; not very good for the older workmen, my Dad included.
>
>   All the drivers I worked with really tried hard to keep time, both going to Irlam and the return trip back to Wigan, where a lot of men had buses to catch. If you had been on the 2p.m.–10p.m. shift then you would miss the last bus if the train was late getting into Wigan; this meant a long walk home for a very tired workman, and a mouthful [of abuse] for the engine crew the following day![51]

The return trains from Irlam were tender-first trips to Wigan, which in winter could be very cold journeys for the crew. As the train approached the canal bridge, the engine driver would not ease off on the regulator and the staff was exchanged with the signalman or signalwoman standing nervously on the small platform, holding the staff high for the exchange.

The fireman would hang on the side of the cab, holding the handrail with his left hand while catching the staff with his right – it thudded into his hand and, as Fred Darbyshire recalled, 'it hurt to catch this metal staff'. If the fireman missed this exchange, the driver would have to stop the train, inevitably making the train late when arriving at Wigan Central.

Lower Ince's coal stage was similar to many at such small depots on the LNER and other company railways, and involved large tubs being filled with coal, which the coalmen then dumped into the tenders or bunkers of engines from an elevated platform above the engine. Fred Darbyshire recalled this particular aspect of shed life:

Stanier 4MT 2-6-4 tank No.42572 heads a six-coach local train just south of Lower Ince station on 8 June 1963. As Lower Ince shed had been closed for eleven years when this picture was taken, the tank engine was based at Springs Branch shed – one of eight of this type at that shed. (John Burgess – Fred Darbyshire collection)

We had two shifts on the coal stage at Lower Ince, 7.30a.m. to 4p.m. and 5.30p.m. to 2a.m.; the reason for the two shifts was no engines came on the shed between 4p.m. and 5.30p.m. and only engines running late would come on the shed after 2a.m. The coalmen always left the tubs full for each other.

Ted Georgeson was a bit of a character. When the Big Rock pub was open, he could always be found in there having a pint. He came out when he heard the first tub on the hoist being emptied; he coaled the engine then filled the tubs then went back to the pub, and we very rarely saw him in the mess room, only when the pub was shut.

Inevitably, the best coal was saved for engines that worked passenger trains. But the best coal usually ran on to the fire bars in the engine's firebox and became solid, which was bad because it reduced air circulation within the fire; the engine then did not steam well. A quick remedy for crews was to run the 'straight dart' fire tool through the fire while the engine was working, though Fred Darbyshire said this made the fire worse in the long run:

When the passenger engine came on the shed you knew it would be a bad fire to clean; you would have to put the straight dart through the fire and break up the solid clinker to a suitable size so you could get it out through the firehole door. The clinker shovel or 'paddle' would get very hot, so you used a rag in each hand or got burned. Sometimes the shovel would turn over at the end, so whilst red hot you would hold it on a flat surface and hammer it flat. You would clean one side of the fire at a time; spade coal on the clean side then spade the fire from the dirty side across. This kept the fire alive and well, [and] you used a bent dart for the clinker under the door to push it forward then spade it out of the firebox and throw it on to the side of

A truly evocative image of a Stanier 2-6-4 tank in full cry, with the low sun picking out every detail on the train and trackside. No.42647 is seen at Hindley South hauling a class C parcels and mixed goods train in the early 1960s. This engine was transferred to Wigan 'C' shed to the period week ending 26 October 1963, and then to Springs Branch upon the former shed's closure in April 1964. It had a further lease of life when it was reallocated to Birkenhead shed in week ending 23 July 1966. It was finally withdrawn by BR on 13 May 1967 after more than twenty-eight years' service and scrapped at Cashmore's Newport in October. (John Burgess)

the ash pit, where it stayed hot. You needed to be careful when moving ashes; they stayed hot underneath for a long time.

The war years brought with them constant fear of enemy bombings, although places such as Wigan were probably secondary to the Luftwaffe's priority targets of major ports like Liverpool and cities like Manchester. However, Fred Darbyshire recalled one comical incident on shed during the war years which demonstrated an engineman's resolve to protect the company's assets:

Fred Horrocks was on duty as shed engineman [and] we are all in the mess room on the 5.30p.m. shift, playing cards … when Fred burst in: 'A say! A say! Red alert, air-raid warning over the phone, German bombers are coming … the German bombers are coming.'

'Good,' said Cyril [Moran]. 'I hope they drop a bomb on yon J10 on't blocks.' Fred went out, got his mate, took another engine up to the blocks at the back of the shed and dragged the engine Cyril had spoken about down into the shed. When he came back into the mess room he said: 'They won't bomb it there … they can't see it.'[52]

Fred Darbyshire recalled 'umpteen tricks played with the fog signals', the detonators that would be placed on the rails to protect an engine if it broke down and visibility was poor for any following trains. Each engine had a supply in the cab so were easy to obtain, but if you played tricks with 'fogs' it meant trouble if you were caught.

He recalled someone at the shed managing to get hold of a dud bomb case, around 10in long, to the end of which was fastened a fog signal. One of the lads climbed up one of the lamp poles in the shed during an evening shift and dropped this improvised 'bomb' on to a brick at the bottom of the pole. The resultant explosion caused the evening shift's shed engineman to come rushing out of his office, thinking the Germans had dropped a bomb on the shed!

Later in 1944, after several cleaners were transferred to Trafford Park shed, Mr Darbyshire finally got his long-awaited firing turn. However, it came out of the blue with no indication on the daily roster. He had booked on for the 5.30p.m. shift when shed engineman, Fred Ford, informed him to go with driver Walter Molyneux and prepare J10 class No.5836 ready for the road. They were to take the loco to Gorton Works for overhaul:

It was already getting dark and Walter was going round with the oil can; he watched me fill the front oil cups and sight feed lubricator on the footplate with thick black oil, stressing the need for care; he showed me how to set the lubricators and checked the tools and fire irons. I tightened the smokebox door, filled up the tender with water, spread the fire and put a round [of coal] on and we were ready for the off, but not before a cuppa in the mess room with the rest of the lads.

After the brew we walked to our loco and Walter asked … are you ready Fred? Yes was my answer (even though I had my doubts), I was on cloud nine. Through Lower Ince station, over the moss between the flashes where I used to swim as a schoolboy … under the Whelley line bridge through Hindley and Platt Bridge station … a shake of the head, this can't be true, it's not happening to me, am I dreaming?

'Put some coal on Fred,' Walter says, waking me from my 'dream', more familiar sights as we pass through another station. A trolley bus going over the station, St Peters church and Hindley and Abram Grammar School in the distance, the dirt rooks behind Leyland park, then under the LNWR bridge, the flash on the right after the bridge, the three craters left by the German bombers earlier, in the distance Bickershaw and Abram station, the level crossing gate is open for us, the signal is in our favour.[53]

At Irlam, memories began to flood back because it didn't seem all that long ago that Fred had been working at the steelworks. Later, they reached Gorton shed and works and it was now dark. While Walter dealt with the 'red tape' of despatching their loco, Fred had a quick look around the shed – which he described as a veritable 'Aladdin's cave full of strange-looking engines'. Walter returned to inform him that if they hurried to the 'Lighthouse' (an elevated control cabin for the entire shed), they could get a lift to Manchester London Road station. This they did, climbing aboard the cab of a 'big black ramshackled engine' that was to work a mail train from London Road. Fred recalled all its mechanical joints were knocking, with steam blowing everywhere from leaking joints. Eventually reaching the station, the loco backed on to its load for the evening. As they left the footplate and went to the front of the engine, Fred was astonished when he saw the nameplate: it was none other than A1 Pacific, *Flying Scotsman*:

> It was after midnight now and we walked across Manchester to Exchange station where we caught the 1.20a.m. paper train, getting off at Wigan North Western station and then walked back to the shed. The lads back at the shed could not believe that I had seen and ridden on the footplate of *Flying Scotsman*.[54]

Mr Darbyshire 'returned back to earth' the following day. Despite being still excited by the previous day's events, there was routine work to be done around the shed as a passed cleaner. After a spell at Trafford Park shed from 1944 to 1946, Mr Darbyshire returned to Lower Ince and found that things had changed considerably during his absence.

Drivers who had worked past their retirement days because of the war had all retired by the time he returned: Harry Christie, Charlie Cordon, Fred Horrocks, Bill Harford and Jimmy Atherton. The latter, whose nickname was 'Gannon', was involved in a bad accident while out walking through Rylance sidings and Whitley crossing and had to have a leg amputated.

1948 Allocation at Lower Ince Shed:

65128	65151	65159	65162	65170	65173	65175	65176	65189	65196	65199	65203
65208											

The rates of pay for railwaymen in the early 1950s are interesting to note and they illustrate that rates of pay didn't increase dramatically despite many years of service in a certain category. The following weekly wage rates were provided by ex-driver John Green from an official British Railways' document:

Cleaner and passed cleaner age 16yrs	£2 5s 0d
Cleaner and passed cleaner age 19yrs	£4 19s 0d
First year booked fireman	£5 3s 0d
Sixth year booked fireman	£5 17s 0d
First year booked driver	£6 4s 0d
Sixth year booked driver	£6 18s 0d

When a passed cleaner had amassed 313 firing turns (that is, 365 days in a year, less fifty-two Sundays) he would receive a fireman's rate of pay, irrespective of whether he was firing or cleaning engines. In later years this threshold was reduced to 258 firing turns. In practical terms, however, Fred Darbyshire said it took him well over twelve months to accrue the necessary 313 firing turns and much longer to become a booked fireman.

Rostered Sunday work was mainly passenger trains, according to Fred Darbyshire; the 'unwritten rule' being that spare men got the work: passed firemen did the driving with passed cleaners doing the firing. This was classed as overtime and was paid at time and a third.

He recalled an interesting situation in the early 1950s with an ex-GN tank engine, which was sent to Lower Ince as a replacement for one of their J10s:

> It's Monday ... and we're on the 5.30p.m. shift, I could not believe my eyes, an 'old friend' stood on the pit outside the office: GN tank engine No.4511 which I had often fired when on the Cornbrook pilot. What was it doing at Lower Ince? The shed engineman said it had come from Trafford Park as replacement for a sick J10.

Stanier 4MT 2-6-4 tank No.42426 works bunker first on a five-coach local train out of Hindley South, probably sometime between early 1962 and late 1964 – the period when it was based at Springs Branch shed and would be available for such duty. This engine travelled far and wide during its thirty years of service. By 1948 it was an Edge Hill engine, then it spent time at Chester and in North Wales. By the early 1960s it was in Scotland, based at Parkhead and Kipps sheds before moving to Carlisle Upperby ahead of its Wigan transfer. Its final shed was Bolton, from where it was condemned in December 1965. (John Burgess – Fred Darbyshire collection)

No.4511 was being used on the evening Risley job with Driver Jack McCann and passed fireman Len Bickerdyke. They'd had problems with 4511 not steaming and were late into Wigan Central; all hell broke loose in the office. Jack was threatening not to go off shed again with 4511, while Len was sweating cobs in disposing the engine. We had to listen to the story all over again, later in the mess room.

On Wednesday I sign on duty as the old hand and the shed engineman tells me I'm going with Jack McCann on the Risley job. Once more 4511 was our engine and Jack was telling me all about what had gone on, on Monday and Tuesday; we had some good coal on board for a change. We get to Risley, back up on our train of five coaches and wait for the workers to finish work.

Now, our turn to leave comes; we get right of way and the look on Jack's face was one of panic. But with a nice thin fire with water in the top nut, the engine blowing off steam in delight at having an old mate working on the footplate, Jack was nursing the engine along until I went across to him and told him to give the engine its head. It's all right Jack, I said, they steam better if you work them hard. I told him I'd worked on this engine before.

We are now flying across Glazebrook Moss, the longest stretch between stations; we are in before time at Wigan Central. Well done, was Jack's remark. There was very little fire to clean on the shed. On Thursday and Friday, Len had no problems in firing 4511. But I was a bit surprised Len had been having trouble earlier with the engine as he'd transferred to Lower Ince from the east coast and should have worked on this engine type before.[55]

By early 1952 rumours of the impending closure of Lower Ince shed had begun to increase; then, in early March 1952, a fateful memo was circulated to staff and the rumours became fact:

Date: 5th of March 1952

From: J. Briggs Supt, Springs Branch.   *To:* Footplate staff, Lower Ince.
Subject: Proposed closure of Wigan [Lower Ince] Motive power depot.

In accordance with the terms of clause 21 of the Footplate staff promotion, transfer and redundancy scheme – arrangements have to be made by the sectional council for the placing of the redundant staff.

Consideration will be given to transferring you to an existing vacancy at another depot in your own grade and to this connection you will see from the vacancy list now posted at which depots there are vacancies for drivers and firemen at the present time.

Work for 19 sets of men will be transferred to Springs Branch.

Will you please therefore complete the attached form and return it to me as quickly as possible.

The completion of this form will in no way affect your position in so far as clause 16A of the promotion, transfer and redundancy arrangement for footplate staff is concerned.

Signed: J. Briggs

Immediately before the shed closed, a meeting of footplatemen was organised at the New Inn pub, across the road from the engine shed. Fred Darbyshire recalled that Bob Maybury proposed that the branch secretary of the union should write a letter to the 'powers that be' about the shed closure, but his brother, Harry, had piped up: 'I think the branch secretary should say nowt. They will shut the shed whatever is said, let's all go get drunk.'

Then, later in the month further confirmation came that the end was nigh, with this memo from the district 'A' shed, Springs Branch, with the below copy addressed to passed cleaners:

Date: 18th March 1952   Ref: XA/LDC4

To: Passed cleaner R. Fox   *From:* Springs Branch.
Subject: Closing of Wigan [Lower Ince] M.P.D.

In connection with the above, please note you will be transferred to Springs Branch motive power depot from Monday next, 24th March 1952.

Mr Darbyshire remembered being booked alongside driver Harry Maybury during the last week of work at Lower Ince shed, working the late goods to Dewsnap via Guide Bridge, which had an 11p.m. booking-on time at Lower Ince shed.

An image of Lower Ince shed reputedly on its last day. Engines are either out on workings or have already been transferred to Springs Branch. An air of desolation hangs over the area, despite some lingering rolling stock. (Jim Peden collection)

The Dewsnap jobs started at Wigan goods and picked up at Westleigh and Lowton, then right away to Dewsnap. Mr Darbyshire said that as his engine got on the main line at Guide Bridge, he noticed for the first time all the work going on with electrification of the main line: 'A lot had changed since I had last worked over this section of line from Trafford Park; we now had overhead gantries etc. to contend with.' At Dewsnap, the crew uncoupled their engine, then ran around the triangle to turn it, ready for the return trip.

Mr Darbyshire and Driver Maybury had to leave their engine, a J10, at Springs Branch after their final trip – and a sight Mr Darbyshire thought he'd never see came to pass: a J10 parked alongside a Super D. He recalled that being the last time he ever worked on a J10:

We checked the work roster before walking back to Lower Ince shed to book off duty and say our sad farewell to the old shed that had brought us many happy times. I was made a booked fireman in the Control link with Driver Billy Williams, and my first turn was 1p.m. on the following Monday afternoon.[56]

Mr Darbyshire said that if a J10 broke down at Springs Branch it was replaced by either an ex-LMS Class 4 tank or a Super D; the latter, he noted, had nothing super about them, other than being superheated: 'they were not popular with me or my mates,' he noted ruefully.

Another Lower Ince fireman, Jack Green, recalled firing for Bob McSorley on the very last day of Lower Ince's operation as a shed. The crew took a J10 to Springs Branch shed, checked the work roster for the following week, then walked back to Lower Ince to book off duty. On Monday morning Jack was on duty at Springs Branch at 12.35a.m., booked with Driver Railton in a goods link; they worked a goods train to Crewe with a Black 5, returning home as passengers.[57]

Stanier 4MT 2-6-4 tank No.42465 heads a through mineral or empty wagon train through Wigan Central in the early 1960s. These engines were very much part of the Wigan landscape in the 1950s and early 1960s, and most versatile. This example was a long-standing resident of Springs Branch shed, only spending a brief two months at Chester Midland shed in 1956. It was withdrawn from service in February 1965 after more than twenty-eight years' service with the LMS and BR. (Fred Darbyshire collection)

Lower Ince shed as it stood in 1953. The yards are empty and the coaler lies idle. No more would J10 0-6-0s ply their trade from this Lancashire outpost of the former London & North Eastern Railway. (Industrial Railway Society)

Yet another Lower Ince man, Bill Baxendale, remembered his last day at Lower Ince as being booked with driver Tommy Farrell on a Saturday, with two trips to Manchester Central with a J10: 1.45p.m. Wigan to Manchester; 3.33p.m. Manchester to Wigan; followed by the 5.05p.m. Wigan to Manchester and return 7.12p.m. Manchester to Wigan. After this they ran light engine to Springs Branch where they checked the work roster for the following Monday, before walking back to book off at Lower Ince. Bill became a booked fireman in the branch's shunt link.

Fred Darbyshire said the last fireman to be passed for driving at Lower Ince shed before its closure was Bob Parkinson. He had been the shed engineman's mate when Fred had begun his railway career at the shed. Unfortunately, another fireman, Ted Hughes, who was the same age as Parkinson but a 'younger hand' because of birthdays, should have been passed for driving with Bob on the same day. For some reason, Ted was unable to go for the test and the shed closed before another could be arranged. At Springs Branch shed, Ted was no longer an 'old hand' and next up for a driver's test. Instead, he had to wait another three years before taking his test.

* * *

A snippet in *Trains Illustrated* for September 1960 said that Lower Ince depot at Wigan, which was closed 'over six [sic] years ago', was being used for the breaking up of withdrawn engines.

In 2011, the Engine Shed Society's *Link* publication recorded that a visit to the former shed's location on 5 April revealed the old shed site was occupied by a modern housing estate that extended almost to the current railway embankment.

The former shed entrance was in Railway Street which was on the left of Warrington Road, immediately after the railway overbridge that carries the still-in-use Bolton to Wigan Wallgate line and almost opposite the now derelict 'Rocket' public house.[58]

Nine

ORMSKIRK

Although outside the general brief of this book, which covers the remaining '8' district steam engine sheds not in *Shed Side on Merseyside* during the British Railways era, mention should also be made in passing of the small, four-lane engine shed that existed at Ormskirk until the mid-1930s.

Ormskirk was situated to the north of the existing station, on the eastern side of the main line in the fork of the Preston and Rainford Junction lines. The Lancashire & Yorkshire Railway, which opened the shed on 5 December 1894, coded it 29, and in LMS days it received the code 23G. The shed was closed on 29 September 1935.

The shed's allocation in 1929/30 included three railmotors, six 0-6-0s and one 2-4-2 tank. The railmotors were used on the local services to Rainford Junction (the 'Skelm Jazzer') and from Ormskirk to Town Green. Passenger engines based at this shed were also used on some Southport locals. The 0-6-0s found employment on general freight and coal traffic duties on the Rainford Junction branch; however, all of the collieries on this branch had closed by the late 1930s, so this may well have had some bearing on the shed's closure. After the closure, the passenger engines were transferred to nearby Aintree shed.

Regarding the 'Skelm Jazzer', former Aintree engineman Bill Tomlinson recalled that at one of the halts on the line, crews would drop off a few choice lumps of coal at one of the farmhouses and in return get half a dozen eggs. 'All a bit naughty but they all did it,' he recalled.

A fine broadside view of the four-lane Ormskirk engine shed (ex-Lancashire & Yorkshire Railway), possibly shortly after closure in September 1935. (Courtesy of the Engine Shed Society)

A view of Ormskirk engine shed. To the right can be seen the coaling stage with overhead water tank. Responsibility for providing motive power to the area was transferred to Aintree shed following Ormskirk's closure. (Courtesy of the Engine Shed Society)

Eric Mason, in his book *The Lancashire & Yorkshire Railway in the 20th Century*, noted that Ormskirk 'found local passenger work for three or four of Wright's bogie tanks and goods work for a 0-6-0 tender engine, usually one of Wright's 4ft 6in type'.

The April 1930 edition of the *Railway Observer* gave the shed's allocation at that time as: Railmotors Nos 10601, 10604 and 10613; 2-4-2T No.10676; and 0-6-0s 12052, 12085, 12184, 12288, 12390 and 12417 = ten locos. In April 1934 the same publication listed Ormskirk's allocation as being: coal tanks Nos 7624, 7635 and 7696; Railmotor No.10600; 2-4-2T No.10673; and 0-6-0s Nos 12288 and 12390. Both of these 0-6-0s were still based at Ormskirk on its last day; 12288 was transferred to Wigan (L&YR), while 12390 was reallocated to Aintree shed.

The site of the shed was, in 1993, part of a rather bumpy football pitch, according to the Engine Shed Society's *Link* magazine!

SHED TRACK PLANS

8B WARRINGTON (DALLAM) Motive Power Depot

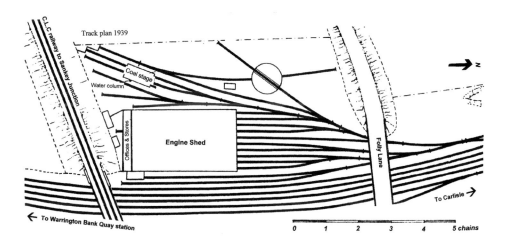

WARRINGTON (ARPLEY) Sub-shed of Warrington Dallam

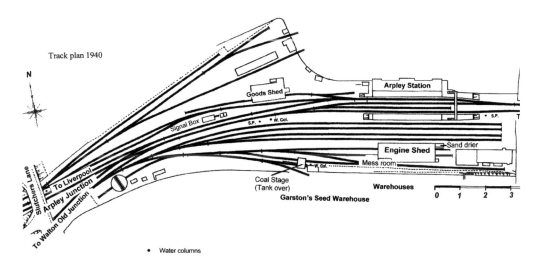

8D WIDNES Motive Power Depot
Track plan 1957

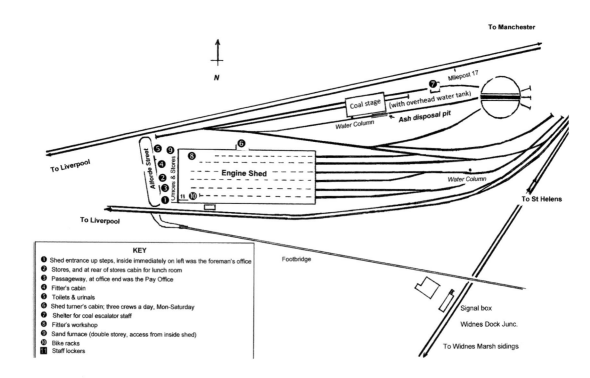

To Manchester

Milepost 17

Coal stage (with overhead water tank)

Water Column
Ash disposal pit

To Liverpool

Alforde Street

Offices & Stores

Engine Shed

Water Column

To St Helens

To Liverpool

KEY
❶ Shed entrance up steps, inside immediately on left was the foreman's office
❷ Stores, and at rear of stores cabin for lunch room
❸ Passageway, at office end was the Pay Office
❹ Fitter's cabin
❺ Toilets & urinals
❻ Shed turner's cabin; three crews a day, Mon-Saturday
❼ Shelter for coal escalator staff
❽ Fitter's workshop
❾ Sand furnace (double storey, access from inside shed)
❿ Bike racks
⓫ Staff lockers

Footbridge

Signal box
Widnes Dock Junc.

To Widnes Marsh sidings

8F SPRINGS BRANCH Motive Power Depot

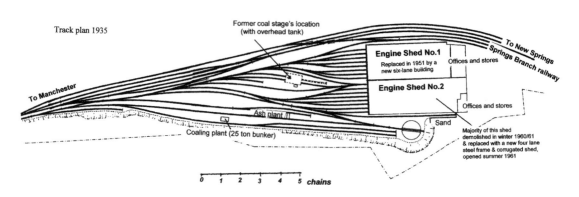

Track plan 1935

Former coal stage's location
(with overhead tank)

To New Springs
Springs Branch railway

Engine Shed No.1
Replaced in 1951 by a
new six-lane building

Offices and stores

Engine Shed No.2

To Manchester

Offices and stores

Ash plant

Sand

Coaling plant (25 ton bunker)

Majority of this shed
demolished in winter 1960/61
& replaced with a new four lane
steel frame & corrugated shed,
opened summer 1961

0 1 2 3 4 5 chains

8E NORTHWICH Motive Power Depot

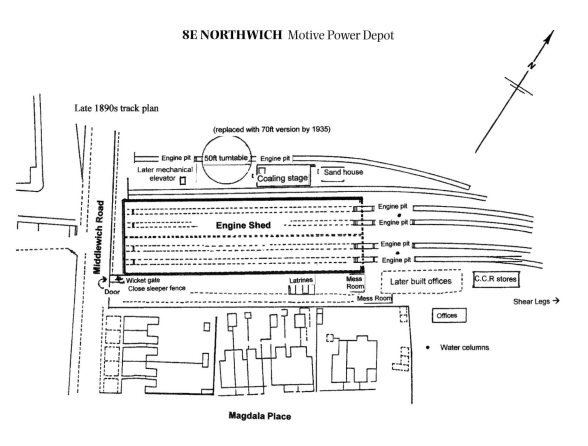

Late 1890s track plan

(replaced with 70ft version by 1935)

Engine pit | 50ft turntable | Engine pit
Later mechanical elevator
Coaling stage | Sand house

Middlewich Road

Engine Shed

Engine pit
Engine pit
Engine pit
Engine pit

Wicket gate
Door
Close sleeper fence

Latrines

Mess Room

Later built offices

C.C.R stores

Mess Room

Shear Legs →

Offices

• Water columns

Magdala Place

8G SUTTON OAK Motive Power Depot
Track plan 1957

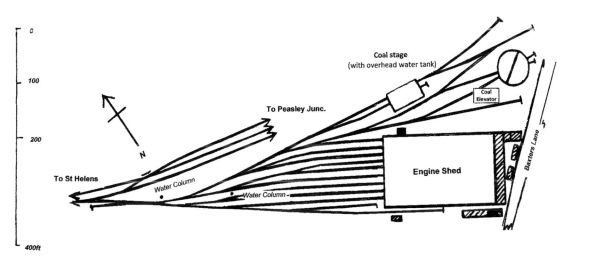

0

100

200

400ft

Coal stage
(with overhead water tank)

Coal Elevator

To Peasley Junc.

N

Baxters Lane

Engine Shed

To St Helens

Water Column

Water Column →

8M SOUTHPORT DERBY ROAD Motive Power Depot

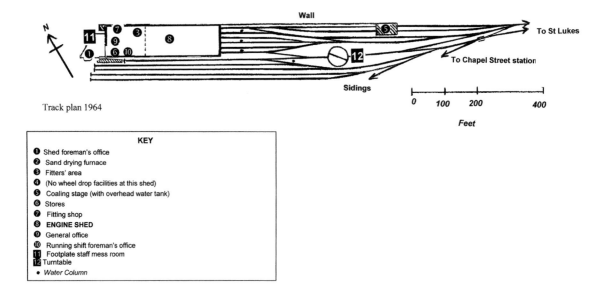

Track plan 1964

```
KEY
❶  Shed foreman's office
❷  Sand drying furnace
❸  Fitters' area
❹  (No wheel drop facilities at this shed)
❺  Coaling stage (with overhead water tank)
❻  Stores
❼  Fitting shop
❽  ENGINE SHED
❾  General office
❿  Running shift foreman's office
11  Footplate staff mess room
12 Turntable
•  Water Column
```

10F LOWER INCE Motive Power Depot

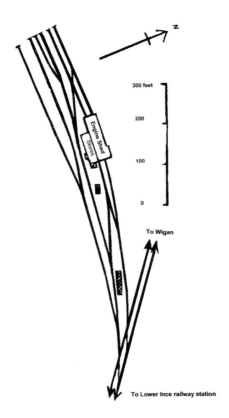

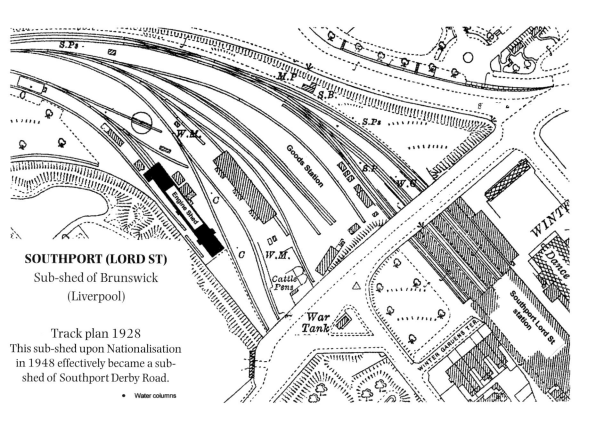

SOUTHPORT (LORD ST)
Sub-shed of Brunswick
(Liverpool)

Track plan 1928
This sub-shed upon Nationalisation in 1948 effectively became a sub-shed of Southport Derby Road.

• Water columns

8P WIGAN 'C' (ex-L&Y Railway) Motive Power Depot

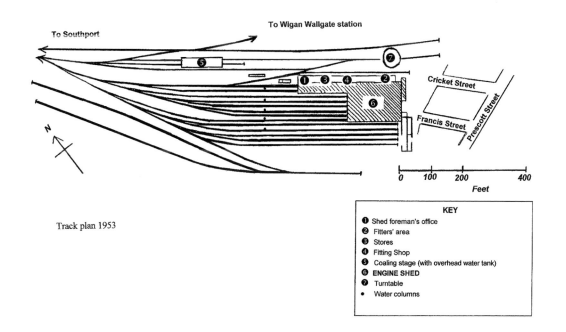

To Southport

To Wigan Wallgate station

Cricket Street

Francis Street

Prescott Street

N

0   100   200   400
Feet

Track plan 1953

KEY
❶ Shed foreman's office
❷ Fitters' area
❸ Stores
❹ Fitting Shop
❺ Coaling stage (with overhead water tank)
❻ **ENGINE SHED**
❼ Turntable
• Water columns

STEAM LOCOMOTIVE ALLOCATIONS FOR SOUTH LANCASHIRE AND CHESHIRE 1947–1968

The eight engine sheds (and sub-sheds) of South Lancashire and Cheshire were, in the 1950s and 1960s, the vibrant hubs for maintaining and fuelling hundreds of locomotives (both steam and diesel). They were also the crew signing-on points during the twenty years from Nationalisation to the closure to steam at Northwich motive power depot in 1968. Tremendous changes were wrought during those two decades, reflected in the declining numbers and variety of motive power based at these depots and the type of work undertaken at each facility. The following tables chart this progression through engine allocations from the last day of the 'Big Four' private railway companies on 31 December 1947, until the closure of the last of this group of sheds on 4 March 1968.

A note on numbers: In the 1947 allocations, BR equivalent numbers can be seen by adding 40000 to the listed LMS numbers or 60000 to the LNER numbers of engines, the latter based at Northwich and Lower Ince sheds. The exception to this rule is engines with 2XXXX numbers which were completely renumbered by British Railways (if not withdrawn beforehand) into the 5XXXX series.

* Signifies named locomotives which are listed below:

45516 *The Bedfordshire & Hertfordshire Regiment*	46128 *The Lovat Scouts*
45521 *Rhyl*	46168 *The Girl Guide*
45524 *Blackpool*	62650 *Prince Henry*
45546 *Fleetwood*	62652 *Edwin A. Beazley*
45563 *Australia*	62653 *Sir Edward Fraser*
45583 *Assam*	62655 *The Earl of Kerry*
45590 *Travancore*	62658 *Prince George*
45633 *Aden*	62661 *Gerard Powys Dewhurst*
45638 *Zanzibar*	62664 *Princess Mary*
45655 *Keith*	62665 *Mons*
45671 *Prince Rupert*	62669 *Ypres*

Date or Year	Warrington (Dallam, Arpley# or Central)	Widnes (including Tanhouse Lane#)	Northwich	Springs Branch	Sutton Oak	Southport (Derby Road or Lord Street#)	Wigan 'C'	Lower Ince
31 Dec. 1947	80, 81, 84, 207, 2583, 2606, 3207, 3283, 3314, 3357, 3389, 3398, 3615, 3657, 4897, 5001, 5026, 5032, 5035, 5095, 5109, 5149, 5196, 5252, 5321, 6603, 6663, 6688, 6710, 6718, 6906, 6920, 6924, 7268, 7352, 7376, 7387, 7591, 7652, 7654, 7657, 7794, 8944, 9008, 9075, 9085, 9136, 9178, 9247, 9302, 9338, 9411, 12100, 12118, 12140, 12175, 12250, 12330 (58)	527, 8907, 8939, 9020, 9038, 9058, 9067, 9071, 9073, 9074, 9079, 9170, 28095, 28107, 28221, 28239, 28253, 28262, 28428, 28457, 28507, 28527, 28585, 28598 (24)	2650, 2652, 2655, 4367, 5131, 5134, 5138, 5139, 5140, 5142, 5146, 5147, 5155, 5156, 5158, 5165, 5166, 5171, 5187, 5190, 5191, 5202, 5205, 9052, 9062, 9262, 9293, 9335, 9349 (29)	397, 561, 2303, 2379, 2455, 2456, 2465, 2539, 2563, 2572, 2588, 4892, 5019, 5030, 5141, 5413, 5425, 5449, 7703, 7885, 7888, 7896, 8824, 8834, 8930, 9014, 9023, 9024, 9026, 9029, 9030, 9043, 9053, 9090, 9124, 9125, 9129, 9134, 9141, 9149, 9159, 9176, 9192, 9197, 9207, 9221, 9257, 9306, 9310, 9311, 9422, 9424, 12021, 12022, 12023, 12024, 12032, 12045, 12053, 12063, 12064, 12172, 12208, 12269, 28403, 28417, 28450, 28589, 28592 (69)	4125, 4358, 4473, 6628, 6637, 6676, 6692, 7180, 7183, 7184, 7393, 7453, 7692, 7752, 7765, 8918, 8954, 9152, 9303, 9312, 9317, 11204, 11316, 11319, 11471, 11491, 11495, 12091, 12126, 12177, 12280, 12349, 12366, 12393, 12397, 12449, 12453, 28509, 28549, 28583 (40)	1085, 1193, 1196, 2291 2292, 2293, 2294, 4056, 4062, 4471, 4474, 4887, 4926, 4989, 5061, 5200, 5334, 5415, 5435, 10678, 10687, 10696, 10728, 10743, 10746, 10752, 10778, 10849, 10865, 11490, 12161, 12197, 12256, 12271, 12272, 12381, 12400, 12523 (38)	678, 679, 680, 2362, 2381, 2472, 2537, 2554, 2557, 2569, 2592, 2614, 2631, 2632, 2640, 2641, 2642, 10692, 10757, 10844, 10887, 12093, 12152, 12169, 12189, 12290, 12312, 12360, 12413, 12588, 12598, 12602, 12727, 12806, 12827, 12828, 12834, 12837, 12839 (39)	5128, 5151, 5159, 5162, 5170, 5173, 5175, 5176, 5189, 5196, 5199, 5203, 5208 (13)
1950	40042, 40180#, 40397#, 40464#, 40522#, 40529#, 40583#, 40679#, 40683#, 40926#, 41162#, 41166#	40125, 46421, 46422, 46423, 46424, 48462, 48554, 48558, 48708, 48753, 48764, 48771	48045, 48046, 48135, 48258, 48613, 48667	42266, 42442, 42453, 42454, 42456, 42465, 42539, 42563, 42572, 42610, 45019, 45235	40080, 40084, 40108, 43026, 43027, 43028, 43029, 44379, 46628, 46643, 46658, 46727	40190, 40191, 40192, 40194, 40195, 40196, 40197, 40198, 41102, 42291, 42292, 42293	40199, 40580, 40587, 40678, 40684, 41101, 42297, 42299, 42537, 42554, 42557, 42569	65128, 65159, 65162, 65164, 65170, 65173

Date or Year	Warrington (Dallam, Arpley# or Central)	Widnes (including Tanhouse Lane#)	Northwich	Springs Branch	Sutton Oak	Southport (Derby Road or Lord Street#)	Wigan 'C'	Lower Ince
	41173#, 42606,	48772, 49020,	48697,	45313, 45413,	47180, 47181,	42294, 44728,	42592, 42614,	65175,
	42607, 42949#,	49073, 49079,	48706,	45425, 45449,	47393, 47444,	44729, 44737,	42631, 42632,	65176,
	43237, 43282,	49116, 49343,	48717,	47877, 47881,	47451, 47453,	44887, 44926,	42640, 42641,	65189,
	43283, 43329,	58373, 58383,	48718,	47884, 47896,	49205, 49262,	44989, 45061,	42642, 42644,	65196,
	43389, 43398,	58393, 58413,	48756,	48895, 48930,	49312, 49377,	45200, 45334,	49568, 49585,	65199,
	43615, 43618,	58415, 58430,	62650*,	49018, 49023,	49389, 51316,	45415, 45435,	49587, 49610,	65203
	43657, 44897,	68547#	62652*,	49024, 49030,	51319, 51397,	51490, 52161,	51474, 52169,	(12)
	45001, 45032,	(27)	62655*,	49050, 49082,	51471, 51491,	52162, 52183,	52197, 52288,	
	45035, 45072,		65131,	49090, 49092,	52177, 52280,	52278, 52582,	52360, 52379,	(Shed closed
	45109, 45149,		65134,	49129, 49160,	52349, 52366,	65130#, 65133#,	52390, 52413,	from March
	45196, 45252,		65138,	49228, 49264,	52393, 52397,	65177#, 65180#,	52450, 52549,	1952)
	45255, 45305,		65139,	49268, 49306,	52449, 58394,	65192#, 69265#,	52727, 52822,	
	45321, 45328,		65140,	49310, 49331,	58410, 58900	69298#, 69344#,	52831, 52870,	
	45354, 45370,		65147,	49341, 49352,	(38)	69356#	52906, 52910,	
	45521*, 46608,		65151,	49378, 49381,		(39)	52916, 52945	
	46701, 47268,		65156,	49394, 52045,			(42)	
	47352, 47376,		65158,	52051, 52053,				
	47387, 47591,		65165,	52098, 52107,				
	47603, 47652,		65166,	52250, 58398				
	47654, 47657,		65169,	(50)				
	48366, 48436,		65171,					
	48466, 48664,		65187,					
	48689, 49008,		65190,					
	49149, 49247,		65191,					
	50697, 50703,		65202,					
	50705, 52088,		65205,					
	52598, 52608,		65208,					
	65126#, 65136#,		69052,					
	65142#, 65149#,		69062,					
	65153#, 65155#,		69262,					
	65163#, 65172#,		69293,					
	65182# 69254#,		69335					
	65258# 69272#,		(38)					
	69288# 69339#,							
	69342# (83)							

1955	40143, 40202, 41210, 41211, 41212, 42606, 42607, 43237, 43282, 43314, 43329, 43398, 43615, 43618, 43633, 43657, 43787, 44237, 44356, 44384, 45032, 45035, 45196, 45255, 45271, 45328, 45354, 45495, 47268, 47352, 47362, 47376, 47387, 47591, 47603, 47652, 47654, 47657, 48142, 48188, 48247, 48348, 48349, 48491, 48520, 48673, 48714, 48715, 49008, 49093, 49119, 49249, 50643, 50644, 50705, 52225, 52432 (57)	40134, 40138, 40201, 46420, 46421, 46422, 46423, 46424, 47630, 48017, 48462, 48554, 48558, 48720, 48753, 48771, 49073, 49079, 49081, 49116, 49126, 49343, 49416, 58427, 65138, 65198 (26)	43538, 43651, 44155, 44341, 44456, 48045, 48046, 48155, 48254, 48340, 48426, 48521, 48555, 48605, 48613, 48667, 48697, 48711, 48717, 48742, 49304, 49405, 49435, 62653*, 62658*, 62661*, 62664*, 62665*, 62669*, 65131, 65134, 65139, 65158, 65165, 65169, 65202, 69255 (37)	42454, 42456, 42462, 42465, 42539, 42572, 42610, 42663, 45026, 45135, 45313, 45314, 45408, 45425, 45449, 45454, 46428, 46432, 46434, 46448, 48895, 49007, 49023, 49025, 49129, 49144, 49154, 49155, 49160, 49203, 49228, 49268, 49306, 49311, 49315, 49322, 49342, 49352, 49376, 49381, 49385, 49393, 49401, 49402, 49408, 49436 (46)	41286, 41288, 41289, 43025, 43035, 44280, 44358, 44438, 47181, 47288, 47298, 47293, 47366, 47393, 47452, 47453, 49239, 49281, 49288, 49318, 51204, 51316, 51319, 51441, 51491, 52125, 52177, 52196, 52338, 52397, 52429, 52453 (32)	40190, 40191, 40192, 40194, 40195, 40196, 40197, 40198, 40199, 41186, 41187, 42291, 42292, 42293, 42537, 44728, 44729, 44887, 44989, 45061, 45077, 50712, 50721, 50746, 50781, 52161, 52183, 52582, 75015, 75016, 75017, 75018, 75019, 84014 (34)	40680, 42179, 42180, 42362, 42381, 42472, 42473, 42554, 42557, 42569, 42592, 42614, 42631, 42632, 42640, 42641, 42642, 43952, 44105, 44220, 44221, 44225, 44240, 44464, 44544, 51474, 52095, 52275, 52289, 52387, 52413, 52437, 90121, 90570, 90584, 90599, 90671 (37)
1961	41210, 41211, 41213, 41288, 43240, 43257, 43295, 43410, 43514, 43615, 43657, 44061, 44063, 44237.	40007, 40134, 40143, 41217, 41221, 41230, 41237, 41244, 47349, 47490, 47597, 47616, 48139, 48206.	42340, 42359, 42369, 42393, 44155, 44341, 44456, 48017, 48039, 48045, 48135, 48155, 48254, 48340.	42235, 42303, 42317, 42465, 42471, 42564, 42572, 42607, 44069, 44076, 44121, 44125, 44280, 44303, 44445, 45017, 45019, 45026, 45057, 45092, 45108.	41212, 41286, 41324, 44075, 44086, 44117, 44192, 44266, 44300, 44305, 44315, 44350, 44358, 44497.	40090, 40145, 40178, 41277, 41328, 42063, 42290, 42292, 42293, 42435, 42451, 42537, 42551, 42645.	42179, 42180, 42473, 42475, 42554, 42555, 42557, 42569, 42592, 42614, 42621, 42624, 42631.

Date or Year	Warrington (Dallam. Arpley# or Central)	Widnes (including Tanhouse Lane#)	Northwich	Springs Branch	Sutton Oak	Southport (Derby Road or Lord Street#)	Wigan 'C'	Lower Ince
	44356, 44384, 45516*, 45524*, 45544, 45546*, 45549, 44827, 44986, 45035, 45050, 45256, 45271, 45321, 45328, 45343, 45354, 45380, 45381, 45495, 47268, 47362, 47406, 47591, 47654, 47657, 47669, 48094, 48188, 48268, 48373, 48520, 48715, 48746, 49137 (49)	48296, 48308, 48326, 48425, 48709, 78034, 78035, 78039, 90242, 90423, (24)	48426, 48462, 48511, 48521, 48631, 48683, 48711, 48764, 78038, 78055, 78057 (25)	45109, 45135, 45314, 45347, 45372, 45373, 45388, 45408, 45425, 45431, 45449, 46428, 46448, 46470, 47270, 47392, 47444, 47671, 48915, 48942, 49007, 49008, 49020, 49023, 49025, 49049, 49077, 49122, 49125, 49130, 49142, 49144, 49164, 49191, 49267, 49344, 49408, 49422, 49438, 49447, 49451, 90173, 90257, 90317, 90509, 90667, 90686 (68)	44596, 47293, 47298, 47366, 47376, 47393, 47452, 47453, 49288, 76020, 76023, 76075, 76076, 76077, 76078, 76079, 90170, 90178, 90212, 90464. 90702 (35)	42662, 44056, 44887, 44989, 45061, 45105, 45218, 45228, 50850, 75015, 75016, 75017, 75018, 75019 (28)	42632, 42640, 42641, 42642. 42731, 42734. 42821, 42864, 43952, 44221. 44222, 44240, 44464, 44486, 44544, 78060. 78061, 78062. 78063, 78064 (33)	
1963	41211, 41217, 44063, 44219, 44232, 44237, 44239, 44356, 44384, 44494, 44522, 44589, 45018, 45035, 45150, 45271, 45321, 45328, 45343, 45354, 45381, 45414, 45495, 45583*, 45638*, 45655*, 45671*, 47362, 47654, 47657, 48106, 48268, 48715	46423, 46424, 47616, 47656, 48045, 48129, 48139, 48296, 48308, 48536, 48709 (11) (Shed closed 13 April 1964)	44155, 44456, 48017, 48039, 48118, 48135, 48155, 48166, 48254, 48340, 48426, 48462, 48511, 48521, 48631, 48683, 48716, 48727, 48740, 48764, 78019, 78038, 78057 (23)	42235, 42327, 42426, 42462, 42465, 42572, 42607, 42664, 42751, 42777, 42894, 44041, 44069, 44076, 44121, 44246, 44280, 44301, 44303, 44444, 44492, 44514, 45017, 45019, 45024, 45026, 45055, 45057, 45070, 45073, 45108, 45109, 45135, 45140, 45188, 45278, 45281, 45314, 45347, 45372, 45373, 45380, 45388, 45408, 45425, 45431, 45449, 45521*, 46128*, 46168*, 47314.	41212, 41286, 44075, 44086, 44117, 44127, 44192, 44266, 44300, 44350, 44493, 44596, 47298, 47393, 47452, 47453, 47490, 47668, 76076, 76077, 76078, 76079, 90170, 90178, 90212, 90464. 90566, 90606. 90702 (29)	44742, 44743, 44745, 44767, 44809, 44816, 45017, 45055, 45083, 45109, 45135, 45337, 45375, 75015, 75017, 75019, 84012 (17)	42135, 42180, 42297, 42494, 42554, 42555, 42557, 42569, 42589, 42631, 42634, 42644, 42680, 42731, 42734, 42794. 44222, 44240, 44486, 44544. 78027, 78057, 78061, 78062. 78064 (25) (Shed closed 13 April 1964)	

1965	47444, 47493, 47517, 47603, 47671, 90140, 90148, 90157, 90173, 90257, 90261, 90268, 90317, 90423, 90440, 90493, 90509, 90667	42061, 42078, 42132, 42645, 42662, 42675, 44686, 44687, 44757, 44809, 45055 (11)	41286, 44075, 44086, 44350, 47298, 47367, 47377, 47393, 47453, 47668, 48053, 48326, 48479, 48623, 48647, 48727, 76076, 76077, 76078, 76079, 76080, 76081, 76082, 76083, 76084, 90178, 90212, 90390, 90702 (29)	42174, 42235, 42295, 42462, 42587, 42647, 42948, 42953, 42954, 42959, 42960, 42961, 42963, 42968, 42977, 44490, 44500, 44779, 44823, 44918, 45019, 45024, 45070, 45108, 45140, 45221, 45278, 45281, 45296, 45314, 45372, 45375, 45385, 45408, 45425, 45431, 45449, 46402, 46419, 46447, 46484, 46486, 46487, 46517, 47314, 47444, 47493, 47603, 47671, 48114, 48125, 48187, 48261, 48275, 48278, 48379, 48494, 48675, 90183 (59)	48118, 48135, 48155, 48221, 48462, 48615, 48631, 48639, 48640, 48683, 48735, 48764, 77011, 77014 (14)	44115, 44181, 44294, 44349, 44522, 44658, 44730, 44731, 44819, 44930, 44935, 45041, 45078, 45109, 45129, 45238, 45256, 45303, 45436, 45563*, 45590*, 45633*, 92048, 92049, 92053, 92055, 92058, 92059, 92070, 92078, 92086, 92116, 92119, 92124, 92126, 92156, 92160, 92163 (38)
May 1966		42078, 42132, 42233, 42665, 44809 (5) (Shed closed 6 June 1966)	41234, 41286, 47279, 47289, 47298, 47377, 47393, 47603, 47668, 47671, 48033, 48121, 48149, 48167, 48193, 48206, 48215, 48251, 48326, 48362,	42102, 42235, 42954, 42963, 42968, 42462, 42577, 42587, 42611, 42647, 44678, 44679, 44842, 44873, 44962, 45019, 45024, 45091, 45128, 45140, 45278, 45281, 45296, 45305, 45321, 45372, 45385, 45395, 45408, 45425,	46405, 46414, 46487, 48057, 48100, 48118, 48151, 48155, 48334, 48408, 48462, 48631, 48639, 48640, 48643, 48683, 48735 (17)	44658, 44730, 44779, 44819, 44920, 44930, 44934, 44963, 45041, 45070, 45109, 45133, 45221, 45232, 45238, 45256, 45303, 45312, 45323, 45375,

Date or Year	Warrington (Dallam. Arpley# or Central)	Widnes (including Tanhouse Lane#)	Northwich	Springs Branch	Sutton Oak	Southport (Derby Road or Lord Street#)	Wigan 'C'	Lower Ince
	45436, 92055, 92058, 92078, 92116, 92119, 92124, 92126, 92132, 92156, 92218, 92224, 92227 (33)			45431, 45449, 46432, 46447, 46517, 47314, 47444, 47603, 47671, 48114, 48125, 48187, 48221, 48261, 48275, 48278, 48319, 48338, 48379, 48494, 48675, 48715, 48764 (53)	48422, 48479, 48614, 48623, 48647, 48722, 48727, 48750, 76051, 76075, 76076, 76077, 76079, 76080, 76081, 76082, 76083, 76084 (38)			
May 1967	44658, 44819, 44920, 44934, 45041, 45133, 45221, 45256, 45303, 45312, 45323, 45375, 92055, 92058, 92119, 92126, 92132, 92156, 92224 (19) (Shed closed from 2 October 1967)		48036, 48063, 48100, 48151, 48212, 48271, 48272, 48304, 48334, 48347, 48408, 48421, 48631, 48632, 48639, 48643, 48681, 48683, 48699, 48735 (20)	44678, 44679, 44711, 44732, 44842, 44873, 44962, 45048, 45198, 45267, 45278, 45281, 45282, 45296, 45305, 45321, 45331, 45350, 45395, 45425, 45431, 45449, 48117, 48125, 48132, 48261, 48275, 48278, 48319, 48325, 48338, 48410, 48675, 48678, 48715, 48724, 48752, 48764 (38) (Shed closed 4 December 1967)	48153, 48167, 48192, 48193, 48206, 48362, 48614, 48617, 48722, 48727, 48750, 76075, 76077, 76079, 76080, 76081, 76084 (17) (Shed closed from 19 June 1967)			
Feb 1968			48036, 48063, 48212, 48272, 48304, 48340, 48617, 48632, 48722, 48727 (10) (Shed closed from 4 March 1968)					

STEAM LOCOMOTIVES THAT SURVIVED INTO PRESERVATION

Of the hundreds of locomotives that were based at the steam locomotive sheds of South Lancashire and Cheshire during the two decades to 1968, it is hardly surprising that a few survived the end of steam and became preserved locos. Fortunately, a number of engines became visionary acquisitions before the preservation movement really took off in the 1970s and 1980s, and were purchased directly from British Railways upon withdrawal.

Equally fortunate was the sale of a sizeable number of engines from the North West to Woodham's scrap merchants in Barry, South Wales. Although Woodham's bought several hundred ex-BR locomotives from 1959 onwards for scrapping, during the mid-1960s the firm focused on scrapping the old rolling stock that was also purchased, creating a 'stay of execution' for 213 of the nearly 300 condemned engines it had bought. Of the following locomotives, fourteen were purchased from Woodham's from 1972 through to 1987 – with BR Standard Class 4, No.76077 (rescued in May 1987), spending almost twice as long in the South Wales scrapyard than it did in service with British Railways! Regrettably, another loco from this class, No.76080, spent four years in the scrapyard before it was scrapped – one of only two British Railways' Standard Class locos broken up at Barry after the end of steam.

Due to the fluid nature of the preservation scene in Britain, the locations listed below of various locomotives should be taken only as a guide. Operational engines frequently move between various preserved railways as 'guest' motive power from time to time, or are loaned out to other operators for specific trains or operating seasons.

42968
Ex-LMS Stanier Crab 5MT 2-6-0 built at Crewe Works in 1934. It was allocated to Springs Branch shed from May 1964 until May 1965, when it was transferred to Gorton, and then Heaton Mersey the following month. The loco returned to Springs Branch in January 1966 from where it was withdrawn in December that year. Arriving at Woodham's at Barry in June 1967, the loco was eventually rescued for preservation in December 1973. It is now in operational condition and is usually based at the Severn Valley Railway.

44767
Ex-LMS Black 5 built in 1947 at Crewe Works and featuring Stephenson valve gear that made it unique to its class. Allocated to Bank Hall shed by September 1950 and reallocated to Southport from March 1962, it was transferred to Carlisle Kingmoor from December 1964 and withdrawn from there three years later. This loco was preserved from 1968. In preservation it was given the name *George Stephenson*. In 2012 it is back in service and is usually based at the North Yorkshire Moors Railway.

45305
Ex-LMS Black 5 4-6-0 built by Armstrong Whitworth & Co. in 1937. Allocated to Springs Branch from August 1965, it was transferred to Speke Junction in December 1967 and eventually finished

its days at Lostock Hall (Preston) shed. Withdrawn by BR in August 1968, the loco was preserved. From 21–28 April 2012 it featured prominently on a nine-day charter train, Great Britain V (GB V), with No. 70013 *Oliver Cromwell*. In preservation, the loco carries the name *Alderman A.E. Draper*.

45337

Ex-LMS Black 5 4-6-0 built in 1937 by Armstrong Whitworth & Co. It was allocated to Southport shed from August 1963 until transferred to Carlisle Kingmoor in November 1964. The loco was withdrawn from service in late January–early February 1965 and despatched to Woodham's at Barry (arriving January 1966), from where it was saved for preservation in May 1984. In 2012 it was operational and based at the East Lancashire Railway.

46115 *Scots Guardsman*

Ex-LMS Royal Scot class 7P 4-6-0 built by the North British Locomotive Co. Ltd in the late 1920s. This loco was allocated to Springs Branch shed from May to July 1964, after which it was transferred to Carlisle Kingmoor shed. It was withdrawn from Kingmoor at the end of December 1965 (being the last of its class in service). The loco was subsequently preserved and has now been returned to main-line operational condition and is usually based at the Birmingham Railway Museum, Tyseley.

46428

British Railways-built (based on LMS class) 2MT 2-6-0, constructed at Crewe Works in 1948. This engine was transferred to Springs Branch in March 1951; it then went to Lower Ince shed in May 1951, before returning to Springs Branch in April 1952. Transferred to Rhyl shed in North Wales in May 1954, it returned to Springs Branch in September that year. The loco stayed at Springs Branch until February 1962 when it was transferred to Bourneville shed in the Midlands. Its final allocation was to Crewe South shed from October 1966 until it was withdrawn the following month. Despatched to Woodham's at Barry (arriving in September 1967), it was rescued from there in October 1979. This engine is at the East Lancashire Railway where there are plans to restore it.

46447

British Railways-built 2MT 2-6-0 constructed at Crewe Works in 1950; allocated to Springs Branch from December 1959, it was transferred to Llandudno Junction in June 1960. After spells at other sheds it was reallocated to Springs Branch in May 1964, from where it was withdrawn from service in December 1966. Despatched to Woodham's at Barry (arriving June 1967), it was rescued in June 1972. It is currently under restoration and located at the Buckinghamshire Railway, near Aylesbury.

Ivatt 2MT 2-6-0 No.46447 photographed at Springs Branch shed in the mid-1960s (the engine was shedded to Springs Branch from May 1964 through to its withdrawal in December 1966). It arrived at Woodham's at Barry in June 1967 and was rescued from there in 1972. Currently it is under restoration at the Buckinghamshire Railway. (RCTS - Ward 371)

47279

Ex-LMS 'Jinty' 0-6-0T built at Vulcan Foundry Ltd in 1925. It was transferred to Sutton Oak shed in November 1966, but withdrawn from service by British Railways the following month. This loco was despatched to Woodham's at Barry (arriving June 1967), and was rescued from there in August 1979. In operational condition, it is usually based at the Keighley & Worth Valley Railway.

47298

Ex-LMS 'Jinty' 0-6-0T built in 1924 by the Hunslet Engine Co. It was allocated to Sutton Oak shed from August 1954 until its withdrawal by British Railways in December 1966. It was despatched to Woodham's at Barry (arriving June 1967) from where it was rescued in July 1974. It is currently (2012) in operational condition and is usually based at the Llangollen Railway in Denbighshire, Wales.

47406

Ex-LMS 'Jinty' 0-6-0T built in 1926 at Vulcan Foundry Ltd; allocated to Warrington Dallam from March 1960 until August 1962 when reallocated to Workington. Eventually it was withdrawn from Edge Hill shed, Liverpool, in December 1966 and sent to Woodham's at Barry (arriving June 1967) from where it was rescued in June 1983. Now restored to operational condition and, in 2012, based at the Great Central Railway.

47493

Ex-LMS 'Jinty' 0-6-0T built in 1927 at Vulcan Foundry Ltd. It was allocated to Springs Branch in July 1962 until September 1965 when it was transferred to Edge Hill. Withdrawn from that shed in December 1966 it was despatched to Woodham's at Barry from where it was rescued in November 1972; it was first steamed in January 1976. It is currently in operational condition and based at the Spa Valley Railway at Tunbridge Wells, Kent.

48151

Ex-LMS Stanier 8F 2-8-0 which entered service in September 1942. From 1948 onwards it was based at Grangemouth, Canklow, Staveley (Barrow Hill) before being transferred to Edge Hill shed, Liverpool, in April 1964. It was then reallocated to Northwich in the week ending 12 March 1966 from which shed it was withdrawn in January 1968. Despatched to Woodham's at Barry, South Wales (among the last seven locos to arrive in September 1968), it was rescued from there in November 1975. It has now been restored to main-line operational condition. It is usually based at the Great Central Railway or the West Coast Railway Company at Carnforth.

48305

Ex-LMS Stanier 8F which entered service in November 1943. It was variously based at Wellingborough, Northampton and Crewe South from 1948–65 until transferred to Northwich in the period week ending 24 July 1965. Less than two months later it was transferred to Speke Junction shed from where it was withdrawn in January 1968. Despatched to Woodham's at Barry (arriving there in September), it was rescued in November 1985 and is currently (2012) in operational condition; usually it is based at the Great Central Railway.

52322

Ex-Lancashire and Yorkshire Railway Class 27 0-6-0 built at Horwich Works in 1896. It carried the number 1300 with the L&YR and during LMS days was numbered 12322. The loco was allocated to Springs Branch shed from August 1952 and then transferred to Sutton Oak in June 1956 until January 1958, when it moved to Newton Heath. It was purchased privately upon withdrawal in August 1960. This locomotive is now (2012) at the Ribble Steam Railway.

76077

British Railways Standard 4MT 2-6-0, built at Horwich Works in 1956. It was allocated new to Sutton Oak shed in December 1956 and remained allocated to that depot until its closure in June

Returning from a season working tourist trains on the Cambrian coast in Wales, Standard 4MT 2-6-0 No.76079 approaches Old Alder Lane bridge, Winwick, near Warrington, en route to its home at the East Lancashire Railway, on 1 July 2005. (Eddie Bellass)

1967, when it was transferred (at least on paper) to Springs Branch. Among the last seven arrivals at Woodham's scrapyard, Barry, in September 1968 (along with engines including 48151, 48305, 76079 and 76084), it was eventually rescued from the scrapyard in May 1987. In early 2012 the loco was awaiting restoration at the Gloucestershire Warwickshire Railway at Toddington.

76079
British Railways Standard 4MT 2-6-0, built at Horwich Works in 1957. It was allocated new to Sutton Oak shed from February in that year. It remained allocated to this shed until its closure in June 1967, and then was transferred (at least on paper) to Springs Branch shed. Withdrawn from service in December 1967, it was despatched to Woodham's at Barry from where it was eventually rescued in July 1974. It is now in operational condition and usually based at the North Yorkshire Moors Railway.

76084
British Railways Standard 4MT 2-6-0, built at Horwich Works in 1957. It was allocated to Sutton Oak from March 1965 to June 1967 when it was transferred (at least on paper) to Springs Branch. Withdrawn from that shed in December 1967 it was despatched to Woodham's at Barry (arriving in September 1968) from where it was rescued in January 1983. It is currently (2012) under restoration at Ian Storey Engineering, at Hepscott.

78019
British Railways 2MT 2-6-0 was built at Darlington Works and entered traffic in March 1954. It was allocated to Springs Branch shed from week ending 30 April 1960 until transferred to Northwich from week ending 10 June 1961. From week ending 25 May 1963 this loco was reallocated to Willesden. It was withdrawn from service from Crewe South in November 1966. Despatched to Woodham's at Barry, it was rescued for preservation, leaving in March 1973. It is now usually based at the Great Central Railway at Loughborough in operational condition.

And one that might have been saved ...

76080
British Railways Standard 4MT 2-6-0, built at Horwich Works, entered service in February 1957. This loco was allocated to Sutton Oak shed from week ending 13 March 1965, remaining there until June 1967 when it was reallocated (at least on paper) to Springs Branch. Withdrawn in December that year, it was later despatched to Woodham's at Barry. When a shortage of rolling stock necessitated a resumption of cutting up steam locomotives, regrettably 76080 was cut up, in April 1972.

Appendix 4

SHED LOGS

The following shed logs provide an insight into the diversity of locomotives that could be found at the steam depots of south Lancashire and Cheshire during an era spanning the late 1940s until the end of steam within the region. All logs are from the author unless otherwise indicated.

Warrington Dallam

Sunday 27 November 1960
40173, 41324, 42859, 42962, 43189, 43257, 43282, 43295, 43387, 43410, 43615, 44061, 44384, 44538, 44800, 44832, 45072, 45254, 45524 *Blackpool*, 45549, 45305, 45429, 45410, 45688 *Polyphemus*, 47268, 47352, 47387, 47406, 47657, 47669, 48106, 48294, 48308, 48421, 48519, 52225, 73038
Total: 37 ~ Engine Shed Society

8 August 1964
44349, 44522, 44589, 44711, 44766, 45097, 45200, 45238, 45633 *Aden*, 45652 *Hawke*, 45730 *Ocean*, 47416, 48094, 48108, 48139, 48318, 48558
Total: 17 ~ Lyndon Knott

5 June 1965
42819, 44181, 44522, 44815, 44964, 45020, 45254, 45279, 45347, 45437, 45531 *Sir Frederick Harrison*, 45565 *Victoria*, 45583 *Assam*, 45653 *Barham*, 45655 *Keith*, 48390, 48549, 48712, 48763, 70010 *Owen Glendower*, 92009, 92058, 92105, 92119, 92126
Total: 25

26 June 1965
44294, 44349, 44712, 44731, 45274, 45296, 45303, 45307, 45563 *Australia*, 47493, 48625, 92009, 92078, 92116, 92119, 92124, 92156, 92160
Total: 18

July 1966
44730, 44779, 44819, 44855, 44863, 44930, 44935, 44963, 45070, 45129, 45220, 45232, 45256, 45278, 45303, 45316, 45375, 45393, 48054, 48506, 70030 *William Wordsworth*, 73137, 92020, 92026, 92055, 92116, 92119, 92124, 92126
Total: 29 ~ John Frisby

23 October 1966
44658, 44690, 44730, 44934, 44963, 45041, 45070, 45129, 45221, 48433, 48466, 92095, 92116, 92119, 92124, 92132, 92133, 92156, 92224, 92227
Total: 20

10 December 1967
44934, 45256, 45323, 48053, 92050, 92156
Total: 6 ~ Lyndon Knott

Warrington Central

6 March 1966
45269, 48344, 48356
Total: 3 ~ Lyndon Knott

16 July 1967
44665, 44851
Total: 2 ~ Lyndon Knott

Widnes

16 September 1961
40134, 40143, 41227, 41244, 47490, 48308, 48711, 78035, 90367, 90423
Total: 10 ~ Lyndon Knott

3 March 1963
42754, 44428, 47349, 47616, 78035, 78039, 90140, 90147, 90157, 90242, 90532
Total: 11 ~ Lyndon Knott

Northwich

3 March 1963
42760, 42945, 44110, 44155, 44456, 45039, 48017, 48039, 48046, 48118, 48135, 48155, 48166, 48295, 48389, 48426, 48521, 48605, 48631, 48683, 48693, 48709, 48740, 48764, 78038, 78057, 90457, 90716
Total: 28 ~ Lyndon Knott

1 May 1965
45059, 46487, 48118, 48135, 48262, 48354, 48373, 48458, 48462, 48615, 48631, 48683, 48717, 48774, 77011, 77014
Total: 16 ~ Lyndon Knott

8 May 1966
46405, 46414, 46487, 46517, 48012, 48018, 48100, 48151, 48249, 48334, 48408, 48462, 48631, 48639, 48693, 48709, 48717, 48735, 92107, 92166
Total: 20 ~ John Frisby

July 1966
44836, 45323, 46405, 46414, 46487, 46517, 48057, 48100, 48178, 48334, 48408, 48462, 48527, 48545, 48546, 48640, 48683, 48717, 48735, 92024
Total: 20 ~ John Frisby

18 February 1968
48036, 48100, 48151, 48267, 48304, 48334, 48340, 48363, 48365, 48408, 48421, 48631, 48632, 48639, 48722, 48727, 48735, 48750, 92088
Total: 19 ~ Lyndon Knott

Springs Branch

Sunday 11 April 1948
207 (Warrington Dallam), 561, 2303, 2348, 2455, 2456, 2465, 2539, 2561 (Patricroft), 2563, 2572, 2588, 4892, 5019, 5030, 5091 (Preston), 5129, 5141, 5184, 5235, 5252 (Warrington Dallam), 5424 (Patricroft), 5425, 5428 (Patricroft), 6225 *Duchess of Gloucester* (Camden), 7737 (Plodder Lane), 7885, 7896, 8824, 8834, 8930, 8934 (Carnforth), 8944 (Warrington Dallam), 8962, 9014, 9024, 9030, 9053, 9055 (Stourton), 9090, 9124, 9129, 9134, 9141, 9149, 9159, 9176, 9192, 9207, 9306, 9331, 9341, 9370 (Crewe South), 9422, 28403, 28417, 28450, 28592, 52022, 52045, 52053, 52063, 12140, 12250
Total: 64 ~ Engine Shed Society

8 August 1964
4976 *Warfield Hall*, 41205, 42456, 42481, 42517, 42554, 42555, 42560, 42569, 42709, 42751, 42820, 42858 42878, 42959, 42963, 44119, 44121, 44216, 44246, 44266, 44464, 44490, 44753, 44772, 45069, 45094, 45228, 45254, 45296, 45372, 45449, 45642 *Boscawen*, 46419, 46447, 46486, 47228, 47314, 47395, 47444, 47493, 47603, 48280, 48500, 70028 *Royal Star*, 73139, 75019, 75039, 75041, 75058, 90157, 90257, 90283, 90147, 90317, 90369, 90399, 90423, 90552, 90561, 90585, 90667, 90669, 92080
Total: 66 ~ Lyndon Knott

October 1965
42102, 42174, 42235, 42462, 42484, 42577, 42587, 42611, 42647, 42953, 42954, 42959, 42963, 44490, 44500, 44696, 44772, 44823, 44873, 44903, 44906, 45015, 45019, 45024, 45039, 45091, 45108, 45128, 45140, 45236, 45238, 45278, 45281, 45296, 45305, 45314, 45321, 45372, 45385, 45425, 45431, 45449, 46419, 46447, 46517, 47314, 47447, 47603, 47671, 48017, 48114, 48125, 48187, 48221, 48275, 48278, 48422, 48675, 48764, 70004 *William Shakespeare*, 75064, 76076, 76083, 92079, 92102, 92110
Total: 66 ~ John Frisby

July 1966
42102, 42233, 42235, 42462, 42577, 42587, 42647, 42954, 42963, 42968, 44667, 44732, 44809, 44844, 44962, 45019, 45024, 45091, 45128, 45140, 45223, 45297, 45372, 45408, 45425, 45431, 45481, 46432, 46447, 46515, 47314, 47603, 47671, 48050, 48082, 48114, 48125, 48187, 48221, 48275, 48278, 48319, 48338, 48379, 48494, 48623, 48675, 48764, 70006 *Robert Burns*, 70046 *Anzac*, 73130, 75043, 76076, 92017, 92134, 92233
Total: 56 ~ John Frisby

31 December 1966
42954, 42968, 45019, 45024, 45203, 45321, 45372, 46432, 46515, 46517, 48082, 48114, 48187, 48614, 48699, 48709, 76077, 92095
Total: 18

8 April 1967
42577, 42954, 42968, 44678, 44710, 44737, 44842, 44858, 45015, 45048, 45198, 45267, 45278, 45282, 45296, 45312, 45321, 45368, 45372, 45395, 45408, 45431, 46432, 46515, 48114, 48165, 48187, 48212, 48221, 48261, 48319, 48325, 48338, 48379, 48410, 48421, 48494, 48675, 48678, 48715, 48764, 73045, 76051, 92023, 92073, 92109, 92224
Total: 48

5 September 1967
44658, 44732, 44776, 44831, 44985, 45116, 45198, 45276, 45278, 45282, 45296, 45331,

45350, 45431, 46432, 46515, 48082, 48206, 48275, 48261, 48304, 48319, 48395, 48665, 48676, 48724, 48765, 76075, 76077, 76081, 92058, 92118, 92152
Total: 33

10 December 1967
44658, 44678, 44679, 44682, 44776, 44819, 44831, 44873, 44920, 45048, 45187, 45198, 45267, 45281, 45331, 45368, 45431, 48056, 48125, 48153, 48206, 48340, 48675, 48676, 48724, 70021 *Morning Star*, 76075, 76077, 76079, 76080, 76084, 92125, 92212
Total: 33 ~ Lyndon Knott

23 June 1968
48752
Total: 1 ~ Lyndon Knott

Sutton Oak

October 1965
41234, 41286, 44075, 47298, 47377, 47393, 48290, 48326, 48479, 48626, 48647, 76077, 76078, 76079, 76080, 76081, 76082, 92015
Total: 18 ~ John Frisby

12 April 1966
41234, 44815, 47393, 48206, 48215, 48326, 48422, 48479, 48746, 76071, 76076, 76078, 76079, 76083, 92017
Total: 15

July 1966
41234, 41286, 45305, 45436, 47298, 47377, 47668, 48033, 48206, 48215, 48326, 48652, 48746, 76077, 76078, 76079, 76080, 76081, 76082, 76083, 76084
Total: 21 ~ John Frisby

19 August 1967
45386, 45388, 48121, 48153, 48276, 48362, 48617, 48676, 48746, 76051, 76080
Total: 11 ~ Lyndon Knott

Southport

16 September 1961
40113, 40194, 40196, 40199, 42132, 42292, 42293, 42435, 42634, 42637, 42645, 42662, 42706, 44689, 44728, 44989, 45105, 45195, 45218, 45228, 45246, 50850, 73163, 75015
Total: 24 ~ Lyndon Knott

7 March 1965
42061, 42078, 42132, 42251, 42645, 42662, 42675, 44687, 45055
Total: 9 ~ Lyndon Knott

Wigan 'C'

16 September 1961
40145, 40191, 40195, 40197, 40198, 41206, 42297, 42299, 42471, 42475, 42554, 42557, 42614, 42624, 42640, 42644, 42696, 42731, 42734, 42794, 43952, 44221, 44240, 44486, 45435, 48915, 48942, 49007, 49023, 49191, 78061, 78063, 78064
Total: 33 ~ Lyndon Knott

<u>11 May 1963</u>
42135, 42494, 42644, 42731, 42821, 44222, 44240, 44544, 45316, 46439, 78057, 78061, 78062, 78064
Total: 14 ~ Lyndon Knott

Central Wagon Works (Ince) scrapyard

<u>7 March 1965</u>
4976 *Warfield Hall*, 41205, 42077, 42280, 42696, 42858, 42952, 42956, 44119, 44186, 44549, 45623 *Palestine*, 45681 *Aboukir*, 46243 *City of Lancaster*, 47549, 61041, 61056, 61144, 90157, 90173, 90182, 90219, 90245, 90416, 90552, 90667
Total: 26 ~ Lyndon Knott

Of the 305 steam engines disposed of at Central Wagon Works, a total of twenty-two ex-Great Western Railway locos and twenty-nine ex-LNER locos were scrapped. Many of these engines were stored in sidings at Springs Branch shed loco pending their final movement to the scrapyard. Among those at Springs Branch by the mid-1960s included ex-GWR pannier tank 9753 and '2251' class 0-6-0, No. 3208.

SOUTHPORT MOTIVE POWER DEPOT ENGINEMEN 1945–1966

The following list of footplatemen has been compiled from the recollections of former driver Ron Clough. Some of the drivers working from Southport shed worked only on electric trains and are differentiated from steam loco drivers with the prefix E/Dvr. Other abbreviations used are: Fm – Fireman; PC – Passed Cleaner (able to fire when required); and P/Fm – Passed Fireman (able to drive when required).

PC James Abbott
Dvr John Abraham
Fm Christopher Ackers
PC Brian Adams
PC Frank Adamson
E/Dvr Thomas Ainscough
E/Dvr William Ainsworth
Dvr Arthur Almond
PC Richard Alty
Dvr Anthony Ambrose
PC Jack Ashcroft
Dvr R. Aspinwall

Dvr Henry Ting Bailey
E/Dvr John Ball
Dvr Henry Ball
PC John Ball
PC John Banister
PC William Banister
E/Dvr William Barton
Dvr William Baxter
PC Joseph Bibby
E/Dvr Gordon Binks
PC Victor Binks
PC Alexander Blackburn
PC John Blomley
Dvr Clifford Bold
P/Fm Patrick Brannon
PC David Brookfield
E/Dvr George Brown
PC Irvine Bullen
Dvr Albert Edward Buck

PC Brian Buck
PC Richard Buck
P/Fm Laurence Henry Burnley
Dvr Thomas Burnley
E/Dvr Frederick Burrell

Dvr Thomas Cadwell
PC Henry Caven
PC Clifford Chapman
PC Robert Chatterton
PC Keith Cheetham
PC Alexander Chorley
PC Robert Clark
Fm Joseph Clarkson
P/Fm Ronald Clough
Fm John Coates
E/Dvr Thomas Coates
PC John Colclough
P/Fm Michael Conway
PC Frank Cook
PC Michael Cooksey
Dvr Charles Crabtree
PC Martin Crimp
P/Fm Laurence Critchley
Dvr Richard Cropper

Dvr Henry Dandy
PC Ivor Davies
PC Robert Dawson
PC Peter Defty
PC William Defty
PC Robert Dent

PC Thomas Dent
Dvr Edward Doherty
Fm Vincent Durkin

Dvr John Eccles
PC Ronald Edmondson
Dvr John Henry Edwards
E/Dvr William Edwards
Dvr Richard Edwards
E/Dvr James Egan
PC John Elliot
PC Duncan Emsley
P/Fm James Etchells

PC David Fairhurst
PC Thomas Farrington
PC Thomas Fazakerley
PC Darryl Ford
E/Dvr Daniel Forshaw
PC John Forshaw
Fm Mark Forrest
E/Dvr Luke Foster
Dvr William Foster
Dvr James France

Dvr Jack Gerrard
PC William Gibson
PC David Gow
E/Dvr Leslie Gregory
E/Dvr Arthur Green
PC Edward Green
Dvr Kenneth Greenwood
PC Reginald Griffiths
PC Barry Guy

Dvr John Hale
PC Brian Hall
Dvr John Hector Hall
Dvr Nicholas Hall
PC Alan Halliwell
PC Brian Halsall
PC David Halsall
E/Dvr Edwin Halsall
PC Jack Halsall
E/Dvr John Halsall
Dvr Joseph Halsall
Dvr Robert Halsall
P/Fm R.V. Halsall
PC William Halsall
E/Dvr James Douglas Halton
E/Dvr Ernest Hamer
P/Fm Eric Hampson

E/Dvr Henry Hankin
Fm James Hardicker
E/Dvr John Hardicker
DC Thomas Harding
PC Peter Hardy
PC Barry Hargreaves
PC George Hargreaves
PC Robert Hargreaves
P/Fm Stanley Hargreaves
Dvr H. Hart
Dvr Frederick Hawkins
E/Dvr James Hawkins
P/Fm John Heaton
Dvr Henry Hesketh
Dvr Richard Hesketh
Dvr James Highfield
Dvr Terence Hill
PC Reginald Joseph Hogg
Dvr Albert Holland
E/Dvr Henry Houghton
P/Fm Leonard Houghton
E/Dvr Thomas Houghton
PC Anthony Howard
PC Henry Howard
PC Kenneth Howard
PC Leslie Howard
P/Fm Richard Howard
PC Robert Howard
Dvr William Howard
PC Robert Hoyle
PC Alan Hughes
PC David Hughes
Dvr Hugh Hughes
PC Joseph Hughes
PC William Hughes
E/Dvr George Hulme
Fm Albert Hulme
E/Dvr Benjamin Hunter snr
PC Benjamin Hunter jnr
PC John Hunter
E/Dvr Leonard Hunter
Dvr Ronald Hurst
P/Fm Donald Huyton

Dvr Albert Iddon
PC John Irish

P/Fm Arthur Jackson
PC Norman Jackson
Dvr Richard Jackson
E/Dvr Horace James
PC Brian Johanneson

E/Dvr George Johnson
P/Fm Jack Johnson
PC Joseph Johnson
PC Raymond Johnson
Dvr Thomas Johnson
Fm William Sweetman Johnson
PC Joseph Jones
Dvr Wilfred Jones
PC Kenneth Jopson

E/Dvr George Keen
PC Peter Keen
E/Dvr Henry Kelly
E/Dvr William Kendall
Dvr Charles Kenrick
E/Dvr Patrick Kerrigan
E/Dvr Charlie Kirk

PC Richard Langley
PC George Langridge
P/Fm Henry Langridge
PC William Langridge
Fm Harold Spiby Lee
E/Dvr Joseph Lee
Dvr Walter Lee
Fm George Leigh
Dvr Percy Lewis
Dvr Harold Leyland
E/Dvr Fred Little
E/Dvr James Little
PC A. Lloyd
Dvr Arthur Lloyd
P/Fm Harry Lloyd
Fm Robert Lloyd
PC Tony Lloyd
E/Dvr Wilfred Lloyd
PC Frank Lunt

PC Dennis Mahoney
PC John Marchant
PC Peter Marsden
E/Dvr Leonard Marshall
PC Randolph Clark Marsh
Dvr Arthur Mawdsley
PC Brian Mawdsley
Dvr Samuel Mawdsley
E/Dvr Thomas Mawdsley
E/Dvr William Mawdsley
Dvr Henry Mawson
Dvr James Mawson
Dvr Robert McConlough
PC Frank McDowell

PC Paul McGuinness
PC David McClelland
PC Daniel McNally
PC Kenneth Meadows
Dvr Henry Mercer
Dvr John Mercer (1)
Dvr John Mercer (2)
Dvr Henry Mercer
P/Fm Wilfred Mercer
PC Barry Merone
Dvr Robert Miller
E/Dvr William Minshull
E/Dvr James Monk
Dvr Arthur Moorcroft
PC Clifford Moore
PC Frank Moore
Dvr John E. Moore
E/Dvr Joseph Moore
PC Kenneth Morgan
Dvr James Edward Morris
Dvr T. Morris
E/Dvr Ernest Moss
E/Dvr James Arthur Moss
Dvr John Murray
PC Brian Myers

PC Arthur Nettleton
PC Keith Newton
PC James Nightingale

E/Dvr Thomas Peet
Dvr Henry Pendleton
E/Dvr William Picton
Dvr James Pilkington
P/Fm Robert Pilkington
E/Dvr Leonard Pinch
P/Fm George Pirie
P/Fm Gordon Pirie
PC Leslie Pittam
PC Norman Pittam
PC Richard Pittam
E/Dvr William Porter
Dvr Ernest Powell
PC John Powell
Dvr K. Pye

Dvr Joseph Rainford
E/Dvr William Rainford
PC Harold Reeves
PC James Richards
Fm Leslie Rigby
Dvr Richard Rigby

Dvr William Rigby
PC Brian Riley
PC Eric Rimmer
PC James Rimmer
P/Fm John Faulkner Rimmer
E/Dvr Norman Paul Rimmer
P/Fm Owen Rimmer
P/Fm Peter Rimmer
E/Dvr Robert Rimmer (1) (*Black Bob*)
E/Dvr Robert Rimmer (2) (*Quiet Bob*)
PC William Rimmer
PC Brian Robertshaw
PC Robert Robertson
P/Fm Thomas Rooke
PC Michael Rooney
E/Dvr Richard Rotherham
Dvr Charles Rowlands
Dvr Leslie Rowlands
PC Edward Ruscoe

PC John Sargeant
PC Alan Saunders
P/Fm R. Sawyer
PC Joseph Schofield
Dvr Henry Seddon
E/Dvr Thomas Seddon
E/Dvr William Seddon
PC Frederick Service
PC Gerald Shaw
PC Richard Shepherd
Dvr George Shillington
P/Fm Stanley Shore
Dvr Frank Simpkins
E/Dvr John Smith
PC Neil Smith
P/Fm William Smith
E/Dvr Thomas Snape
E/Dvr John Spooner
Dvr Thomas Spooner
E/Dvr Horace Stead
PC Sydney Stott
Dvr Henry Sumner
PC Kenneth Sutton
Dvr Robert Sutton

Dvr Albert Taylor
PC Derek Taylor
P/Fm James Edward Taylor
E/Dvr John Taylor
Dvr Albert Thistleton
PC Alexander Thomas
PC Terence Tinsley
PC Kenneth Turner

PC Geoffrey Vickers

PC Edward Walker
PC Ronald Wall
PC Alexander Walmsley
E/Dvr John Walters
PC Brian Ware
Dvr Frank Wareing
E/Dvr John Wareing
P/Fm Arthur Watkinson
PC David Watts
Dvr George Whalley
Dvr Jack Whalley
E/Dvr William Whalley
PC Gerard Whewell
PC Peter Whiting
PC George Whyte
P/Fm Kenneth Wilcox
E/Dvr James Williamson
E/Dvr Thomas Williamson
Dvr James Winrow
PC Walter Winter
PC James Wood
P/Fm John J. Wood
PC Albert Woodbridge
E/Dvr Eric Woosey
P/Fm Alan Wright
E/Dvr Benjamin Wright
Dvr Ernest Wright
E/Dvr William Wright
E/Dvr Frederick Wynne snr
Dvr Frederick Wynne jnr

Southport Shed Personnel in its Heyday (1940s)

Ex-driver Joe Halsall recalled that in its heyday, Southport shed boasted some forty-four steam engine drivers, thirty-one electric train drivers and thirty steam/electric drivers, passed cleaners and cleaners. Mr Halsall said that drivers at Southport shed worked one of seven links:

No.1   Top Link (Steam)
No.2   Compound Link
No.3   Goods Link
No.4   Steam/Electric Link
No.5   (Wessy) or Old Man's Link
No.6   Shedman's Link
No.7   Goods Pilot Link

As well, the shed employed a Motive Power Superintendent, six office staff, four running shift fore-men, three storekeepers, a leading fitter, six fitters and six fitters' labourers, three washout men, two tube sweepers, two boilermakers, two steam raisers, three fire droppers, four coalmen, three shed labourers, two water softener plant workers, two outdoor machinery workers, plus other minor workers.

Some of the key people filling the above roles were, according to Mr Halsall:

M.P.D. Superintendent	Reggie Gardner
Office staff	Reggie Price, Ted Wilson, Harry Gerard and Vera Coldrick
Running Shift Foreman	Lambert Spence, Chas Harrison, Ernie Cameron and Harry Howard
Storekeepers	Pat Abram, Bill Todd and Wilf Watkinson
Fitters	Harry Litherland (leading fitter), Harry Hidderley, Eddie Wignall, Frank Bowman, Harry Bailey, Geo Hare and Roy Ashall
Fitters' labourers	Jim Winrow, Laurence Tartt, Geo Lowe, Harold Greenwood, Dennis Grover and Tom Bond
Washer-outs	Bill Mathewman and Bill Dyson
Tube sweepers	Ben Green and Norman Bishop
Boilermakers	Bill Ashton and Bill Johnson
Steam raisers	Harry Pye, Peter Barton and Bill Drummond
Fire droppers	Dick Bracy, Hughie Rimmer and Arthur Niblett
Coalmen	Alf St Leger, Mick Trees, Dick Aughton and Tom Coates
Shed labourers	Jim Aughton, Bill Edmondson and 'Spud' Hughes
Water softener plant staff	Bill Smith and Bill Mawdesley
Outdoor machinery staff	Lawson Aindow and Bill Marshall

STAN MORRIS'S FIRING LOG 1928–1932 AT LOWER INCE AND ALTRINCHAM SHEDS

The following information was obtained from a draft manuscript for Fred Darbyshire's self-published book, *A Footplateman Remembers*, and was intended as an appendix for that book. The author is indebted to Fred's wife, Mrs Bessie Darbyshire, and daughter Kathryn Boyd for access to this material.

Stan Morris had his first firing turn on 13 August 1928 when he was at Altrincham shed. However, as is evident, the firing opportunities were irregular, such was the availability of other experienced staff and rostered turns, and he transferred back to Lower Ince shed, Wigan, in February 1929. Aged twenty-three and having spent five years as a cleaner, Stan had amassed just 187 firing turns and only added a further 100 before his last firing duty in 1932.

Stan was made redundant by the London & North Eastern Railway on 21 January 1933 at a time when the Depression had led to the retrenchment of many experienced railwaymen, as it did in other occupations. Fortunately some good came out of redundancy. After leaving the railways, Stan and his wife established 'a small chain of confectioner's shops' in the Irlam district. Mr Darbyshire said Stan told him at one stage they employed up to thirty people.

Date	Locomotive No.	Driver	Time
13 August 1928	5597	A. Bennett	12.20p.m.
18 August 1928	Shed	W. Critchley	6.00p.m.
20 August 1928	5597	G. Glover	5.07a.m.
26 August 1928	5593	J. Priestley	12.25p.m.
27 August 1928	5591	G. Glover	4.50a.m.
7 September 1928	5597	J. Kettle	5.40a.m.
8 September 1928	5581	J. Kettle	2.50p.m.
11 September 1928	5117	H. Thomas	1.40p.m.
14 September 1928	5597	A. Barnett	2.30p.m.
15 September 1928	5597	A. Barnett	1.45p.m.
19 September 1928	5028	C. Kirke	8.00a.m.
20 September 1928	5028	C. Dean	7.15a.m.
8 October 1928	5592	H. Thomas	4.20a.m.
17 October 1928	Instruction van (loco duties)		7.00a.m.
22 October 1928	5834	C. Kirke	1.00p.m.
23 October 1928	5597	H. Thomas	12.20p.m.
25 October 1928	5597	J. Kettle	12.20p.m.
5 November 1928	5028	C. Dean	3.10p.m.
4 December 1928	5028	J. Kettle	2.50p.m.
19 December 1928	5590	J. Kettle	3.55p.m.

Date	Locomotive No.	Driver	Time
28 December 1928	5597	A. Bennett/	
	relieved by	H. Thomas	4.45p.m.
29 December 1928	5489	As above	2.45p.m. then light engine
			to Stockport 5.45p.m.
December 1928	5597	Barnett	
4 January 1929	5597	A. Barnett	12.20p.m.
5 January 1929	5597	A. Barnett	1p.m. to 6p.m.
8 January 1929	5846	C. Kirke	12.15p.m.
19 January 1929	5597	J. Kettle	10.20a.m. to 2.45p.m.
20 February 1929	5421		
Note: Stan Morris transferred back to Lower Ince shed		J. Shringler	5.20a.m.
23 April 1929	5833	J. Foy	5.35a.m.
17 May 1929	5833	J. Foy	5.35a.m.
5 June 1929	5830	E. Dennerly	5.35a.m.
13 June 1929	6428	J. Shringler	5.25a.m.
14 June 1929	6421	J. Shringler	5.25a.m.
28 June 1929	5497	J. Hardman	4.30a.m.
29 June 1929	5830	J. Hardman	4.30a.m.
2–5 July 1929	5830	E. Dennerly	12.45a.m.
6 July 1929	6428	W. Hickson	2.45a.m.
8 July 1929	6421	W. Wright	2.15p.m.
9 & 10 July 1929	5826	A. Holland	4.40p.m.
17 July 1929	5497	W. Hickson	4.15a.m.
18 July 1929	5826	W. Hilton	5.35a.m.
19 July 1929	5497	W. Hickson	4.15a.m.
20 July 1929	6421	J. Shringler	5.25a.m.
26 July 1929	5586	W. Hilton	4.00p.m.
27 July 1929	6421	R. McSorley	5.50p.m.
2 August 1929	5830	E. Dennerly	5.35a.m.
20 August 1929	5830	J. Shringler	5.25a.m.
21 August 1929	5833	J. Shringler	5.25a.m.
22 August 1929	5833	J. Forster	5.35a.m.
23 August 1929	5876	F. Horrocks	11.55a.m.
24 August 1929	5826	W. Hickson	8.15a.m.
27 August 1929	5833	H. Maybury	4.15a.m.
28 August 1929	5810	F. Barker	4.15a.m.
29 August 1929	5833	J. Shringler	5.25a.m.
30 August 1929	5810	F. Barker	4.15a.m.
31 August 1929	5812	H. Maybury	4.30a.m.
7 September	5786	H. Collins	8.55a.m.
26 September 1929	5826	J. Little	5.35a.m.
27 September 1929	5786	J. Little	5.35a.m.
7 October 1929	(As shed engineman's mate)	J. Smith	Midnight
12 October 1929	5812	W. Wright	1.00a.m.
29 November	5797	A. Foy	12.45a.m.
18 December	5786	J. Forster	4.40p.m.
19 December	5843	W. Hickson	1.45p.m.
31 December	5812	J. Sephton	2.00a.m.
3 January 1930	5810	C. Cordon	6.50a.m.
21 January 1930	5812	C. Cordon	8.50p.m.
23 January 1930	5786	C. Cordon	8.50p.m.
25 January 1930	5812	J. Forster	5.35p.m.

Date	Locomotive No.	Driver	Time
3 February 1930	(Loco relief)	J. Atherton	1.50p.m.
4 February 1930	5830	E. Dennerly	5.45p.m.
5 February 1930	5835	H. Maybury	2.15p.m.
6 & 7 February	(Loco relief)	R. McSorley	2.00p.m.
8 February 1930	5842	J. Forster	5.35a.m.
11 February 1930	5591	W. Hickson	6.50a.m.
12 & 13 February	5810/5836*	C. Cordon	6.50a.m.
14 February 1930	5836	J. Atherton	6.25p.m.
18 February 1930	5836	H. Livesey	3.10p.m.
19 & 20 February	5812/5833	J. Hardman	2.15p.m.
21 February 1930	5836/5845	J. Sephton	2.30p.m.
22 February 1930	5813	J. Foy	4.05p.m.
23 February 1930	5845	F. Barker	9p.m./11.50p.m.
25 February 1930	5833	J. Sephton	2.00p.m.
27 & 28 February	5810/5830	W. Hickson	8.45a.m.
4 March 1930	5830	J. Atherton	8.50p.m.
5 March 1930	5842	P. McSorley	8.50p.m.
6 March 1930	5797	H. Collins	2.15p.m.
7 March 1930	5812	H. Livesey	9.35a.m.
11 March 1930	5836	F. Horrocks	6.25a.m.
12, 13 & 14 March	5810/5830/5836	C. Cordon	6.25a.m.
17 & 18 March	5830/5833	W. Hickson	10.30a.m./9.35a.m.
19 & 20 March	5812	C. Cordon	9.55a.m.
8 April 1930	5842	S. Pearson	12.40p.m.
9 April 1930	5810	A. Holland	5.35a.m.
11 April 1930	5823	R. Maybury	1.15p.m.
31 [sic] April 1930	5797	H. Maybury	8.50p.m.
1 May 1930	5842	H. Livesey	2.15p.m.
4 May 1930	5836	W. Hickson	4.45a.m.
6 May 1930	5842	R. Maybury	8.30a.m./1.45p.m.
8 May 1930	5812	W. Hickson	1.15p.m.
22, 23 & 24 May	5787/5836/5823	H. Collins	11.25a.m./7.15a.m.
27 May 1930	5812	W. Hickson	2.15p.m.
28 & 29 May 1930	5797/5812	J. Little	8.50p.m.
3 & 4 June 1930	5797	J. Atherton	11.25a.m.
5 June 1930	5836	H. Collins	6.25a.m.
17, 18 & 19 June	5845/5810/5845	W. Hickson	6.50a.m.
24 & 25 June 1930	5812/58 [sic]	E. Dennerley	9.55a.m.
26 June 1930	5833	A. Foy	11.20p.m.
27 June 1930	5830	E. Dennerley	9.55p.m.
28 June 1930	5830	H. Maybury	5.20p.m.
3 July 1930	5842	H. Collins	6.50a.m.
4 July 1930	5830	H. Maybury	5.15a.m.
8 July 1930	5810	A. Foy	9.55p.m.
9, 10 & 11 July	5826/5830/5830	C. Cordon	8.50p.m.
15 July 1930	5812	W. Wright	6.50a.m.
16 July 1930	5845	R. Maybury	7.45a.m.
21 July 1930	5812	H. Maybury	8.50p.m.
22–25 July 1930	5842/5845/5845/5797	J. Hardman	8.50p.m. for three days then 2.15p.m.
26 July 1930	5813	R. McSorley	4.20p.m.
28 July 1930	(Shed relief)	R. Maybury	1.00p.m.

Date	Locomotive No.	Driver	Time
29 July 1930	5845	W. Wright	6.50a.m.
30–31 July 1930	5835	R. Maybury	11.25a.m.
1 August 1930	5830	R. Maybury	6.50a.m.
2 August 1930	5830	J. Shingler	3.55a.m.
12–15 August	5833 for three days then 5810	J. Forster	6.25a.m.
17 August 1930	5836	F. Barker	10.45p.m.
19 August 1930	5812	J. Atherton	8.50p.m.
20 August 1930	5836	H. Livesey	2.45p.m.
21 August 1930	(Shed relief)	R. Maybury	1.20p.m.
22 August 1930	5845	R. McSorley	11.55a.m.
23 August 1930	5810	R. Maybury	7.30a.m.
26 August 1930	(Shed relief)	C. Cordon	2.00p.m.
8 September	5845	F. Horrocks	12.40p.m.
9–11 September	5823/5810/5823	J. Little	6.25a.m.
12 September	5810	W. Wright	5.35a.m.
16–17 September	5812	J. Atherton	8.50p.m.
18 September	5842	J. Atherton	2.15p.m.
19 September	5833	F. Horrocks	2.30p.m.
20 September	5845	E. Dennerley	5.35p.m.
24 September	5797	J. Shingler	4.45a.m.
25 September	5835	F. Horrocks	9.20a.m.
30 September	5833	H. Christy	9.55p.m.
1 & 2 October	5836	H. Christy	9.55p.m.
3 October 1930	5823	F. Horrocks	3.10p.m.
7 October 1930	5836	F. Horrocks	9.15a.m.
8 October 1930	5845	F. Horrocks	9.15a.m.
9 October 1930	5845	F. Horrocks	9.15a.m.
10 October 1930	5845	F. Horrocks	8.15a.m.
11 October 1930	5797	W. Wright	4.00a.m.
12 October (Sun)	5836	J. Little	4.00a.m.
26 October (Sun)	5833	F. Barker	6.25p.m.
14 December	5833	W. Wright	7.45a.m.
24 January 1931	5823	H. Christy	9.55p.m.
7 February 1931	5797	W. Hickson	7.00p.m.
15 February (Sun)	5074	J. Atherton	7.55a.m.
26 April 1931	5845	J. Hardman	7.30a.m.
28 April 1931	5835	A. Holland	12.15a.m.
2 May 1931	5823	G. Gregory	5.25p.m.
15 May 1931	5786	H. Maybury	7.20a.m.
30 May 1931	5826	J. Yarwood	12.40a.m.
14 June (Sun)	5812	J. Hardman	9.00p.m.
30 June 1931	5833	R. McSorley	9.00p.m.
1 July 1931	5812	R. McSorley	9.00p.m.
2 July 1931	5833	R. McSorley	9.00p.m.
3 July 1931	5897	R. McSorley	9.00p.m.
6 July 1931	5810	J. Forster	9.55a.m.
7–10 July 1931	5797	R. Maybury	9.55a.m.
15 July 1931	5830	C. Cordon	6.15p.m.
21 July 1931	5833	H. Maybury	9.00a.m.
22 July 1931	5845	H. Collins	12.40p.m.
23 July 1931	5835	H. Maybury	9.00a.m.
24 July 1931	5237	H. Maybury	11.15a.m.

Date	Locomotive No.	Driver	Time
28–30 July 1931	5845	R. McSorley	9.00a.m.
31 July 1931	5845	R. McSorley	9.00a.m.
11 August 1931	5826	J. Yarwood	12.15a.m.
12 August 1931	5812	G. Hurley	9.55p.m.
13 August 1931	5813	A. Holland	4.40p.m.
14 August	5797	R. McSorley	2.15p.m.
16 August (Sun)	5812	W. Wright	7.30a.m.
18 August 1931	5836	W. Wright	9.40a.m.
19 August 1931	5812	J. Atherton	6.15a.m.
20 August 1931	5836	J. Atherton	6.15a.m.
21 August 1931	5842	H. Christy	4.25a.m.
22 August 1931	5830	G. Hurley	3.15a.m.
25 & 26 August	5830	J. Hardman	12.40p.m.
27 & 28 August	5830/5833	W. Hickson	12.40p.m.
1–4 September	5823	W. Wright	12.40p.m.
6 September	5812	H. Maybury	7.30a.m.
7 September	7381	W. Hickson	10.55a.m.
8–11 September	5836	R. McSorley	9.40a.m.
16 September	5833	W. Harford	4.25a.m.
17 September	5810	R. Maybury	9.40a.m.
21 September	5318	C. Cordon	9.40a.m.
22–25 September	5830/5810/5830/5812	E. Dennerley	4.15a.m.
9 October 1931	5830	E. Dennerley	3.15a.m.
26 October 1931	5845	J. Little	12.15p.m.
3 December 1931	5812	J. Hardman	10.00a.m.
4 December 1931	5845	W. Wright	9.40a.m.
5 December 1931	5845	H. Collins	8.15a.m.
14 December	5823	H. Christy	9.40p.m.
21 December	5835	G. Gregory	11.40p.m.
24 December	5812	J. Atherton	8.50p.m.
31 December	(Shed relief)	R. Maybury	10.00a.m.
8 January 1932	5818	A. Foy	11.40p.m.
15 January 1932	5800	R. Maybury	10.00a.m.
22 January 1932	5818	A. Foy	9.20p.m.
24 January 1932	5842	J. Little	7.30a.m.
27 January 1932	5823	J. Forster	10.55a.m.
28 January 1932	5818	R. Maybury	10.05a.m.
2 February 1932	5836	E. Dennerley	11.40p.m.
3 February 1932	5845	J. Atherton	8.50p.m.
11 February 1932	5830	R. McSorley	9.45a.m.
13/15 February	5815	H. Collins	9.40a.m./8.50a.m.
21 February 1932	5800	W. Hickson	8.55p.m.
5 March 1932	5527	H. Livesey	8.50p.m.
23 & 24 March	5845/5800	R. McSorley	7.30a.m.
13 May 1932	5835	F. Horrocks	11.55a.m.
14 May 1932	(Shed relief)	J. Hardman	7.30p.m.
20 May 1932	5818	A. Foy	11.40p.m.
22 May 1932	5835	F. Barker	10.00a.m.
1 June 1932	5835	W. Wright	1.35p.m.
20 June 1932	5527	H. Livesey	5.50p.m.
24 June 1932	5836	J. Hardman	3.45p.m.
25 June 1932	5527	C. Cordon	4.35p.m.

Date	Locomotive No.	Driver	Time
26 June 1932	5830	R. Maybury	8.55p.m.
10 & 11 August	5812	H. Maybury	6.30a.m.
14 August 1932	5815	R. McSorley	7.30a.m.
? September	(Shed relief)	H. Bradshaw	6.00a.m.
18 September	?	R. Maybury	8.55p.m.

* Fred Darbyshire noted that J10 0-6-0 No.5836 was the engine he worked on in his first firing turn in the early 1940s.

On 23 February 2004 a letter received from Neil Cain informed Fred Darbyshire that Stan Morris had passed away the previous day.

A Note on the Numbers

During the era when Stan Morris worked at Altrincham and Lower Ince sheds the LNER had its original numbering system, which was quite different to the logic that came out of the 1946 renumbering, and led to a much easier translation of ex-LNER numbers into British Railways' counterparts by (with some exceptions) generally adding 60000 to the former LNER number – e.g. B1 class No.1012 became BR No.61012.

In the late 1920s and early 1930s, engines with numbers in the general range of 5001 to 6153, and then 6164 to 6411 and even beyond, were former Great Central Railway engines, but could be drawn from quite different classes, though their numbers appeared in the same range. For example, engines often appearing in Stan Morris's firing log, such as 5074, 5812 and 5797, were all from the same class J10 0-6-0s (becoming 65172, 65148 and 65138 in BR stock). But sandwiched in between were locos such as 5591 (an ex-GCR O4 class 2-8-0; later BR 63616) and 5527, an N5 0-6-2 tank engine that became BR's No.69261 from 1948.

It merely illustrates the legacy of diverse locomotive types and a confusion of former numbers that British Railways was presented with upon its formation in 1948.

End Notes

1. Smith, Colin, 'Shed News from the Past', *Link – the Journal of the Engine Shed Society*, autumn 1994, p.46.
2. *The Railway Magazine*, July 1964, p.600.
3. Paul Wright, Disused Stations site record, Over & Wharton, found at www.disused-stations.org. uk/o/over_and_wharton/index.shtml.
4. *Ibid.*
5. The former LNWR's Earlestown Wagon Works were situated at Newtown Junction where the line north from Warrington met the Liverpool to Manchester line. In 1853 the company had leased a factory (the Viaduct Foundry) and soon after named the area Earlestown in honour of the senior director of the LNWR, Hardman Earle. The LNWR board authorised the outright purchase of the factory in 1860. Originally, the works provided additional facilities for the manufacture of wagons for the rapidly expanding railway. But eventually, rationalisations at Crewe, Wolverton and Saltley resulted in the manufacture of all LNWR wagons being concentrated at Earlestown. The works became part of the London Midland & Scottish Railway in 1923 and British Railways in 1948. After a long and distinguished life, the works was closed in 1964. (Information sourced from the London & North Western Railway Society's 'Wagons of the LNWR' web pages.)
6. Bull, Stephen, 'Sights of Sites', in *Link*, Issue No.59, winter 2001.
7. 'Widnes area freight developments', *Modern Railways*, August 1964, p.96.
8. *Link*, No.62, autumn 2002, p.43.
9. Sommerfield, Allan, *Northwich – a Retrospective Review*, in *Link*, Issue No.16, spring 1991, p.8.
10. Darbyshire, F., *A Footplateman Remembers – the staff and workings at Lower Ince shed*, self-published, 2005, pp.44–5.
11. Coates, Chris, *The Wigan Sheds – volume 1, Springs Branch*, Steam Image, Cheadle Hulme, 2010, p.126.
12. 'Motive Power Miscellany', in *Modern Railways*, April 1962, p.279.
13. *Modern Railways*, October 1963, p.275.
14. Winding, P.F., *Modern Railways*, November 1964, p.343.
15. Hawkins, C., Hooper, J. & Reeve, G., *British Railways Engine Sheds – London Midland Matters*, Irwell Press, Pinner, 1989, p.11.
16. Darbyshire, F., *A Footplateman Remembers*, p.96.
17. *Ibid.*, p.93.
18. *Ibid.*, p.94.
19. *Ibid.*, p.96.
20. *Ibid.*, p.97.
21. *Ibid.*
22. *Ibid.*, p.99, from conversations with Eric Clayton.
23. *Ibid.*, pp.98–99.
24. Coates, Chris, *The Wigan Sheds – volume 1, Springs Branch*, p.153.
25. *Ibid.*, p.61.
26. *Ibid.*
27. *The Railway Magazine*, April 1963, p.293.
28. *Modern Railways*, July 1964, p.66.

29. Coates, Chris, *The Wigan Sheds – volume 1, Springs Branch*, p.161.

30. Bartlett, Bob, 'The Last Five Hundred', in *Link*, summer 1992.

31. Coates, Chris, *The Wigan Sheds – volume 1, Springs Branch*, p.61.

32. Melling, Charles Henry, transcript of his recollections (WMS 26), held in the Museum of Wigan Life, Wigan Leisure & Culture Trust.

33. In fact, Bolton's ex-L&YR 'Radial' tank No.50850 was specially turned out on 2 January 1960 to work the last regular passenger trains on the Blackburn–Chorley–Wigan branch (*Trains Illustrated*, March 1960, p.182).

34. *Trains Illustrated*, February 1960, pp.115–16.

35. *The Railway Magazine*, March 1963, p.219.

36. *Link*, Vol.23, Issue No.89, summer 2009, p.40.

37. *Modern Railways*, July 1963, p.62.

38. Dobbs, Brian, 'The Cauliflowers are on Road Four', in *Link*, Issue No.80, spring 2007.

39. Darbyshire, F., *A Footplateman Remembers*.

40. Smith, Colin (comp), 'Shed News from the Past', in *Link*, Issue No. 25, summer 1993, p.28.

41. *Trains Illustrated*, August 1960, p.502.

42. *The Railway Magazine*, September 1961, p.664.

43. 'Motive Power Miscellany', *Modern Railways*, January 1962, p.59.

44. *Trains Illustrated*, September 1961, p.566.

45. Greenwood, R.S., *London Midland Steam on the ex-L&YR*, D. Bradford Barton Ltd, Truro, 1975, p.13.

46. 'Motive Power Miscellany', in *Modern Railways*, March 1962, p.205.

47. *Modern Railways*, May 1963, p.352.

48. *The Railway Magazine*, June 1965, p.366.

49. Darbyshire, F., *A Footplateman Remembers*.

50. *Ibid.*, p.14.

51. Darbyshire, F., 'Another Great Day on the Great Central', in *Past Forward*, No.31, newsletter of the Wigan Heritage Service, summer 2002.

52. Darbyshire, F., *A Footplateman Remembers*, p.85.

53. *Ibid.*, p.29.

54. *Ibid.*, p.30.

55. *Ibid.*, p.88.

56. *Ibid.*, p.89.

57. *Ibid.*

58. 'Sights of Sites', in *Link*, Vol. 25, Issue No.97, summer 2011.

Further Reading

Books

Beavor, E.S., *Steam Motive Power Depots*, Ian Allan, 1983

Bolger, P., *An Illustrated History of the Cheshire Lines Committee*, Heyday Publishing, 1984

Bolger, P., *BR Steam Motive Power Depots*, Ian Allan, 1983

Coates, Chris, *The Wigan Sheds – volume one, Springs Branch*, Steam Image, Cheadle Hulme, 2010

Darbyshire, Fred, *A Footplateman Remembers – the staff and workings at Lower Ince shed*, self-published, 2005

Greenwood, R.S., *London Midland Steam on the ex-L&YR*, Truro: D. Bradford Barton Ltd, 1975

Griffiths, R.P., *The Cheshire Lines Railway*, Oakwood Press, 1947

Hawkins, C. & Reeve, G., *LMS Engine Sheds: Their History and Development, vol. 3 – the Lancashire & Yorkshire Railway*, Wild Swan Publications, 1982

Hawkins C., Hooper, J. & Reeve, G., *British Railways Engine Sheds – London Midland Matters*, Pinner: Irwell Press, 1989

Hitches, Mike, *Cheshire Railways in Old Photographs*, Sutton Publishing, 1994

Mason, Eric, *The Lancashire & Yorkshire Railway in the 20th Century*, Ian Allan, 1975

Simmons, Jack (ed.), *The Oxford Companion to British Railway History*, Oxford University Press, 1997

Articles/Oral Histories

Darbyshire, Fred, 'Another Great Day on the Great Central', *Past Forward*, No.31, newsletter of the Wigan Heritage Service, summer 2002

Dobbs, Brian, 'The Cauliflowers are on Road Four – an affectionate look at Sutton Oak Shed, 1948–2001', in *Link*, Engine Shed Society, Nos 79 & 80, winter 2006 and spring 2007

Dowd, Steve, 'Earlestown Wagon Works: the Viaduct Foundry', in *The Railway Magazine*, August 1953 (see http://newton-le-willows.com)

Melling, Charles Henry, recollections from his railway career (WMS 26), held in the Museum of Wigan Life, Wigan Leisure & Culture Trust

Smith, Colin, 'Shed News from the Past', in *Link*, Engine Shed Society, autumn 1994

Sommerfield, Allan, 'Northwich – a retrospective', in *Link*, Engine Shed Society, spring 1991

Winding, P.F., 'Block freight workings into the Northwich area', *Modern Railways*, November 1964

Websites

BR locomotive database: www.brdatabase.info/sites.php?page=depots&subpage=snap&id=533

Disused stations – closed railway stations in the UK: www.disused-stations.org.uk

Earlestown Wagon Works, on the LNWR Society's website: www.lnwrs.org.uk/Wagons/EarlWorks.php

Locomotive scrapyards: www.railuk.info/steam/scrap_search.php

Preserved locomotives database: www.heritage-railways.com/locosdb/locosdb.php

Sutton Beauty & Heritage: www.suttonbeauty.org.uk

Also consulted in compiling this book were various volumes of railway periodicals, including *Trains Illustrated*, *Railway World*, *The Railway Magazine*, *Steam World*, *Steam Railway*, Ian Allan's *ABC Combined Volumes* (various editions) and issues of the Engine Shed Society's *Link* journal.

Index

Visit our website and discover thousands of other History Press books.

www.thehistorypress.co.uk

The
History
Press